Date Due

BRODART   Cat. No. 23 233   Printed in U.S.A.

MASTERS OF
POLITICAL THOUGHT

VOLUME ONE · *Plato to Machiavelli*

MASTERS OF POLITICAL THOUGHT

Under the Editorship of
EDWARD McCHESNEY SAIT

✳

VOLUME ONE : *Plato to Machiavelli*
MICHAEL B. FOSTER
CHRIST CHURCH, OXFORD

VOLUME TWO : *Machiavelli to Bentham*
W. T. JONES
POMONA COLLEGE, CALIFORNIA

Under the Editorship of
W. T. JONES

✳

VOLUME THREE : *Hegel to Dewey*
LANE W. LANCASTER
UNIVERSITY OF NEBRASKA

MASTERS OF

POLITICAL THOUGHT

VOLUME ONE · *Plato to Machiavelli*

BY Michael B. Foster, M.A. (*Oxon.*),

PH.D. (*Kiel*), LATE TUTOR OF CHRIST

CHURCH AND LECTURER IN PHILOSOPHY,

OXFORD UNIVERSITY

Essay Index in Reprint

Core Collection Books, inc.
GREAT NECK, NEW YORK

International Standard Book Number
0-8486-3005-X

Library of Congress Catalog Number
77-092519

PRINTED IN THE UNITED STATES OF AMERICA

Editor's Introduction

Masters of Political Thought marks a departure from current practice. For undergraduates the medium of instruction in political theory has too often been the comprehensive and encyclopedic textbook. The writers are catalogued and their doctrines summarized, sometimes upon the basis of other and more specialized summaries and not upon the basis of the original works. While the textbook may be indispensable for certain purposes, anything like exclusive dependence upon it inculcates superficiality.

The conventional textbook is more appropriate to some branches of Politics than to others. I believe, for example, that its use is necessary or at any rate desirable in the first approach to American government or to international relations, among other courses. Political theory, however, stands apart. It is peculiar in being tied, in the closest fashion, to the personality and genius of the individual thinker, and even to his literary form and his mode of argument. An epitome of Plato's *Republic* or of Hobbes' *Leviathan* can be little more adequate than a paraphrase of *Paradise Lost*. Two centuries ago a wise man warned us against treating books like members of the nobility; that is, against learning their titles and bragging afterwards of acquaintance with them. One cannot become acquainted with the *Republic* by reading what another man thought about it.

Ideally the original works should displace the textbook. There would be more intellectual profit in reading eight or ten such works than in committing to memory a tabulation that brought within its encyclopedic sweep all the political philosophers from Plato to Dewey. But the ideal must give way to the practicable. The undergraduate course, according to firmly established tradition in America, presents a systematic survey of the whole range of theory. Is there, then, no way of escape from the textbook method? Some measure of relief has been afforded by the supplementary use of the sourcebook or book of readings, an anthology or golden treasury of extracts, which establishes a precious contact with the original sources, awakens in persons of discernment a desire to make that contact still more intimate, and so deserves our gratitude. But the sourcebook, aside from the brevity and the arbitrary selection of quoted passages, does not meet all our needs. It does not, in scattered comment and interpretation, shed light upon obscurities as they arise, or emphasize points that otherwise might receive scant attention, or show the significance of environment in accounting for some vagary of doctrine. It does not weave together the various extracts and present the writer's doctrine as a whole — at least in its major aspects.

The textbook supplemented by the sourcebook is better than the textbook alone. But another possibility suggests itself and is embodied in the *Masters of Political Thought*. It brings us a stage nearer to familiarity with the most conspicuous theorists. It assigns to the textbook the purely subordinate rôle of filling interstices wherever teacher or student may wish to do so. That is the plan that has been adopted here. The plan calls for concentration upon a few great masters from Plato to the present and recourse to numerous and lengthy quotations, quotations that have been chosen judiciously and then elucidated and woven together by unobtrusive comment. Aquinas or Montesquieu speaks for himself, in his own words. Comment, instead of supplanting the original and disguising its flavor, is designed to clarify and interpret. Whoever reads the first volume of the *Masters of Political Thought* will find that he has had before him, not Foster on Plato — although Dr. Foster ranks among the two or three greatest living authorities on Plato — but Plato himself, with interpretative notes by Foster.

Concentration, though an essential feature of the plan, involves some difficulty. There are degrees of concentration. Shall the list of philosophers be confined to a few men of undisputed pre-eminence in the field of theory? Or shall we listen favorably to the claims of Dante and Marsiglio of Padua, Harrington and Paine, John Stuart Mill (along with Bentham) and Lenin (along with Marx)? Where shall the line be drawn between the great and the near-great? Opinion will differ as particular claims are advanced. This much is clear. The list would grow portentously in length and defeat the whole object of the plan unless each claim were subjected to rigid scrutiny. In designing the

Masters of Political Thought a high standard of selection has been applied, the integrity of the plan protected. Teacher or student may feel that some philosopher who has been left out deserves a place among the masters. In such a case he can, as I have already pointed out, fill the vacuum partially by turning to one of the textbooks in the library. But surely he will wish to have more than a formal bowing acquaintance with an authentic master and so will seek intimate friendship by reading the master's own works.

Politics, like many other branches of learning, has been subdivided for the purposes of specialization. An expert in international law may know very little about political parties or public administration; and, carrying subdivision still farther, an expert in theory may be reluctant to speak as an authority in matters that lie outside his chosen and limited field, which may embrace only one or two centuries. This will explain why *Masters of Political Thought* appears in three small volumes, each by a different author.

Each volume consists of extracts — which tend to preponderate — and interpretative comment. Extracts are distinguished from comment, not by any change in the size of the type, but by (1) indentation and (2) the appearance of a type ornament at the beginning of the quotation, and also at the beginning of each full page of quotation.

EDWARD McCHESNEY SAIT

Acknowledgments

THE EXTRACTS PRINTED in this volume are derived from the following translations:

Plato, translation by B. Jowett, 3d edition, Oxford, 1892; quoted by permission of the Jowett Copyright Trustees and of the Clarendon Press.

Aristotle, Politics, translation by B. Jowett, revised by W. D. Ross, Oxford, 1921; quoted by permission of the Jowett Copyright Trustees and of the Oxford University Press.

Aristotle, Nicomachean Ethics, translation by W. D. Ross, Oxford, 1925; quoted by permission of the Jowett Copyright Trustees and of the Oxford University Press.

Cicero, translation by C. W. Keyes, Loeb Classical Library, 1928; quoted by permission of the Trustees of the Loeb Classical Library.

Augustine, translation by John Healey, 1610.

Aquinas, I have made my own translation for the occasion.

Machiavelli, Discourses, translation by C. E. Detmold, Boston, 1882.

Machiavelli, The Prince, translation by N. H. Thomson, 3d edition, Oxford, 1913; quoted by permission of the Clarendon Press.

I have altered the translations in some places where I thought I could improve them; but the alterations have not been considerable except in Plato's *Republic*.

I have used the utmost freedom in adopting ideas from other writers, but of debts of this kind I have not made acknowledgments.

I desire to express my gratitude to the Trustees and Publishers mentioned above, who have granted me permission to use their copyrights.

M. B. F.

Contents

MASTERS OF
POLITICAL THOUGHT

VOLUME ONE · *Plato to Machiavelli*

"ALMOST EVERYTHING that sets us above savages has
come to us from the shores of the Mediterranean."

Dr. Samuel Johnson

PUBLISHER'S NOTE

THE PROPORTION of text and quoted material has made necessary a special type arrangement. The author's comments and the quotations from the masters of political thought are in the same size type and have the same leading. Quoted passages are indented slightly from the left and are further marked by a type ornament at the beginning of the passage and at the head of each full page of quotation.

CHAPTER ONE
Introductory

WHAT is attempted in the following volume is to present to the reader a series of actual excerpts from the writings of the greatest political theorists of the past; selected and arranged so as to show the mutual coherence of various parts of an author's thought and his historical relation to his predecessors or successors; and accompanied by introductory notes and intervening comments designed to assist the understanding of the meaning and importance of the doctrine quoted. The book does not purport to be a history of political theory, with quotations interspersed to illustrate the history. It is rather a collection of texts, to which I have endeavored to supply a commentary. I have tried rather to render the work of Aristotle, Augustine, and the rest accessible to the student, than to write a book about them; and the main object of this work will have been achieved if it serves not as a substitute for a further study of the actual works of these authors, but as an incentive to undertake it.

Nor does the commentary make any pretension of being exhaustive. Very often after a long passage has been quoted, a single point only has been selected for comment; and sometimes this point has been selected not because it was the most important, but because it was one on which I had something to say. I have not tried to cover all the ground, and shall have done my part if the reader is stimulated, by the samples which I have offered, to complete a commentary of his own.

The selection has been confined to a few authors, for reasons not only of space, or of limitations of my own knowledge (though either of these reasons would have been sufficient), but because it is part of the plan of the book to concentrate attention upon the most important works. A knowledge of Plato's *Republic*, of Aristotle's *Politics*, of parts of Augustine's *City of God*, belongs to a general education. The works of lesser writers, or the lesser works of these writers, are doubtless worth reading; but a man who is not a specialist may ignore them without any sense of shame.

If the commentary is secondary to the text, still more so must be any introductory remarks which I make here. In commending the writings which follow to the reader's attention, I will indeed stake my credit on the assertion that the study of them will correct the judgment and enlighten the understanding upon matters in which it is important to be enlightened and correct. But if a proof of this assertion is demanded, there is no proof except that of asking the inquirer to make the experiment. The introducer may suggest lines of reasoning, he may try to convey certain lights which he has himself derived from the study, but in doing this he must be tentative and not dogmatic, and in the last resort he must say to the reader, "Go and read for yourself, and try whether this is confirmed by your experience." In this respect his position is like that of the critic of a work of art. However useful the critic's remarks may be in preparing an approach to the work, they can never dispense the reader from the necessity of studying the work itself, nor deprive him of the right, on the basis of this study, of turning critic himself and standing in judgment on the reasonings by which he was led to it in the first place.

What, then, is the advantage which we may hope to derive from a study of the political writers of the past? A view prevalent in earlier ages would have provided a simple answer to this question. A work of politics, it would have been said, is the handbook of an art, the art of governing. Just as a man of superior knowledge or skill in the art of carpentry may compile a work in which his knowledge is made available to those who aspire to be good carpenters, so a man of superior wisdom in the art of politics may set down his knowledge in a book for the instruction of those whose business it is to found, govern, or preserve states. If this is what political theory is, there is no difficulty in determining what advantage may be expected from the study of great political works. They will be consulted for purposes of instruction by those who have to govern states.

Some of the greatest political writers [1] have believed themselves to be offering such a system of practical instruction, and many students

[1] I have refrained from ascribing the theory to any political philosopher by name, because there is none who presents it in quite the naked simplicity in which I have stated it. In order to attribute it to X, I should have needed to add such and such qualifications, or to Y, such and such others, and should thus have been engaged in a task too large to be undertaken in an introduction. But the reader will find different forms of this theory underlying the works of Plato, Aristotle, Machiavelli, and indeed of most political philosophers until comparatively recent times.

of their works in the past have undoubtedly sought, and may have found, in their pages that practical guidance which they have professed to offer. But this is certainly not the advantage which a modern reader can be promised from a study of their works. This entire conception of politics as an art and of the political philosopher as the teacher of it rests upon assumptions which it is impossible to accept. If it were correct, the writers of political theory would need to be themselves past masters in the art of governing, and statesmen would need to apprentice themselves to them in order to learn their job. But we find that this is not so. Few political philosophers have themselves exhibited any mastery of the art of governing, and few successful statesmen have owed their success to the study of political writings.

The reason why politics cannot be an art is that the historical situation in which the politician has to act is always unique. An art presupposes a material which does not vary. There can be an art of carpentry, because the natures of oak, deal, and the other woods in which the carpenter works remain constant in essentials. Of course it is true that every carpenter who sets out to make an oak table is in a situation in some respects different from that of every other carpenter who has done the same. But the differences are accidental, not essential; they may affect his application of the principles of his craft, but they will not modify the principles themselves. On the other hand, situations in which the statesman has to act — and by the statesman I mean not only the professional politician, but every citizen who has a share in the government of his country — these situations are unique in a more thoroughgoing sense. They are not to be covered by a single, unchanging set of principles, requiring only to be differently applied. And if the would-be statesman were to succeed in eliciting a system from the works of a previous writer, it would inevitably be a system applicable only to an age already past.

I do not think that I need elaborate this point at length, for I do not think that any reader of this book, whatever benefit he may expect to derive from it, will expect this benefit. He will not expect the works which follow to provide the same kind of instruction for the political student as his medical textbooks provide for the medical student. If he did, he would certainly confine his attention to the most up-to-date, and would no more think of learning his art from Aristotle than the medical student thinks of learning his from the pages of Galen.

If political theory is not a body of science for the instruction of statesmen, what is it? There is a doctrine, the "dialectical materialism" of Karl Marx, which gives a fundamentally different account of its nature. According to this doctrine, political theory is not prior, but posterior, to political fact. Men acting politically are not guided in their actions by a knowledge of political principles, in the way in which a doctor is guided in his actions by a knowledge of medical science. On the contrary, the political actions of men are performed irrationally. Laws are not passed or repealed, nor constitutions evolved, modified, or destroyed, in obedience to a theory. There will, indeed, always be a theory, since man is a theory-making animal; but the theory is always something invented afterward, to fit the facts; it is not the reason which directed their production. It is rather like the "rationalizations" which psychologists speak of, when a man who has performed an action from irrational, perhaps unconscious, motives seeks to justify to himself what he has done by ascribing it to a rational purpose. In such a case, the reasoning seems to be the motive which has produced the act, but in reality the act has given birth to the reasoning. According to the Marxian doctrine, political theories are "rationalizations" of a similar kind, being secondary and subsequent to the political facts which they pretend to justify.

Although political actions are, according to Marx, irrational, they are not uncaused. They are themselves the product of something more fundamental still, namely, of economic forces. It is a necessity of his condition upon earth that man must produce to supply his wants. Throughout history men have struggled with one another to control the means of production. When one body of men succeeds in acquiring this control to the exclusion of the remainder, a distinction of economic classes is introduced; there is the dominant class, which controls the means of production, and the class which labors under the control of the former. This fundamental economic relation is then, as it were, clothed in a system of legal and political relations. The powers of the master-class are transmuted into rights, and economic dominance into political supremacy. But the legal and constitutional system is always determined by the economic relationship, never vice versa. Any change in the economic relationship, any shift in the preponderance of economic power, is followed by, and reflected in, a political change, whether by way of reform or by way of revolution;

so that economic change is the original spring of the movement of history. Political theory, finally, being itself dependent upon political fact, is thus the reflection of a reflection. As it conforms to each constitutional change or political revolution, the succession of theories which make up the history of political philosophy is only one of the remoter effects of the succession of economic changes.

The Marxist theory thus completely reverses the relation of priority between political theory and political fact which was implied in the theory which I began by mentioning; and it is clear that a very different estimate of the value of studying political theory will follow, according as we adopt one or the other of these two conflicting views of its nature. According to the former of them, it will be almost the most important study which a man can undertake, and an indispensable qualification for all who claim a share in the direction of public affairs. According to the latter, since theory can in no case determine how a man will act, the study of it has no importance, and only an academic interest.

I will not conceal my own opinion that, while the former doctrine errs by rating the value of this study too high, the latter errs by rating it too low.[1]

If we were to press the Marxist with the following question: "According to you, a change in the balance of economic power is the ultimate cause, upon which depend all the other changes of human history — of political history, of the history of thought, of religion and the rest. What then causes the changes in the balance of economic power?" — if the Marxist were pressed with this question, I believe he would be forced to expose a weakness of his theory at a vital point. Marx himself gives different answers in different places. Sometimes (and most often) he says that each succeeding system of economic relationships is generated by a dialectical necessity from the contradictions inherent in the preceding one. In other places he says that the changes are brought about by changes in the technique of production. The former alternative explains nothing, and to adopt it is simply to take refuge in mystery. A latent contradiction in a state of affairs

---

[1] I do not, of course, intend to suggest that these are the only two views that have been held about the nature of political theory. I have selected them simply in order to illustrate certain points by contrasting them.

can lead to the alteration of that state of affairs and its replacement by another, upon one condition only: namely, that it is recognized as a contradiction by an intelligent being, and acts as a stimulus to him to remove it. But to affirm, as Marx does, that a contradiction, as though it were some kind of physical force, possesses a motive power in its own right, and without such passage through an intelligence — this is to use words to cloak an absence of thought. The second alternative is indeed an explanation, but it leads to consequences which a Marxist cannot uphold. Changes in the technique of production have been caused by successive developments of natural science. If it is these which cause the changes of economic relationship, upon which in turn all other historical changes depend, then the ultimate cause of these changes is not economic; the ultimate cause is that upon which economic change itself depends, namely, the progress of natural science. This is a very odd result. Natural science is a theoretical activity. All other theoretical activities of man, the developments of religion, philosophy, and art, are declared by Marx to be consequences of his economic system. It now appears that the activity of natural science is excepted from this doctrine. It is so far from being merely a consequence, that it is the cause of all alterations of the economic system itself. Even if we are content to accept this oddity, and to place natural science, without any reason, in a position so different from that of man's other theoretical activities we shall still be occupying a position very different from that which Marx purports to maintain. To say that the progress of natural science is the ultimate cause of historical change is a different thing from saying that the ultimate cause of historical change is economic; and if anyone wishes to maintain this doctrine, he must find another name for it than dialectical materialism.

This is not to say that Marx is not right in many of the points on which he is in conflict with the other view which I have described. I believe that he is right in denying to theory the magisterial authority which that view ascribes to it.[1] That it is possible by reasoning to determine what end the state should fulfill, and to deduce in detail the means by which it can fulfill it best — that it is the task of political theory to conduct such reasoning, and the duty of political practice to

---

[1] I do not, of course, mean that this denial is peculiar to Marx, nor that he was the first to make it. If we were concerned here to determine questions of authorship, the merit of originality in this respect would have to be attributed rather to Marx's teacher, Hegel

be guided by it — this notion is readily intelligible, straightforward, and congenial to common sense.[1] We should be prone enough to accept it if the evidence permitted us to do so. But the evidence does not permit it. If it were so, the various political theories which occur at different epochs in the history of philosophy would be related to one another as various, more or less successful, attempts to solve an identical problem, and the solutions would agree with one another so far as they were successful in attaining to the truth. No doubt, since all human efforts are imperfectly successful, there would in fact be individual variations among the theories, and the local and historical conditions in which the different authors had grown up would be reflected in these points of variation. But their theories would be thus historically conditioned only in so far as they failed to reach the truth, not in so far as they attained it. I will illustrate this by an analogy. Suppose a class of students to whom the task is set of solving a mathematical problem. In proportion as they are successful, their solutions will agree with one another; individual variations will occur only in so far as mistakes creep in. The mistakes will be conditioned by the psychological idiosyncrasy of the individual concerned. If A goes wrong in this way, and B in that, these deviations will have their causes in the different mental histories and previous environments of A and B respectively. But in so far as the solutions are correct, they are no longer conditioned by the individual characters and circumstances of their authors. If X arrives at the true answer, he does so because this answer is the truth, and because he has perceived it to be so. His answer will be identical with those of Y and Z, in so far as theirs are correct, irrespective of his and their individual peculiarities of mental history and environment.

But it is necessary to confess that the great political theories which have appeared in the course of history are not related to one another in the way in which the attempts of students to solve an identical problem are related to one another. Each of them is individual (as a work of art is), not merely in respect of the accidents of its presentation, certainly not merely in respect of its failures and defects, but through and through. Certainly the several theories contain truth (as a work

---

[1] It may be suggested that it is congenial to common sense because it is a Greek notion, and because what we call common sense is deeply impregnated by Greek ways of thought.

of art does not), but not in the way in which truth is contained in a mathematical theorem. It is not possible by discarding the individual peculiarities of each theory as due to accident or error to expose an identical core of truth in which they all agree; for, if everything individual were discarded from them, there would be nothing left. Nor is the succession of theories, as they follow one another, like a succession of attempts to solve a single problem. Certainly the succession is not haphazard, and it is possible to follow it as an intelligible development; but it is not a progress in which each succeeding stage eliminates some of the errors of its predecessor and thus approximates more nearly to the attainment of an identical goal.

Nor is it true, finally, that these political theories are historically conditioned only in respect of what is accidental or erroneous in them, and that in respect of what is essential they escape into a realm of timeless truth. On the contrary, the historical element penetrates to the very essence of the theory. It is sometimes said that every great thinker transcends the limitations of his own age, and there is a sense in which this is true. But it is not true if it is meant that the great thinker passes into a kind of undenominational realm of eternal truths. The greater an author is, the more accurately does he represent the essential spirit of his own age. Plato himself, the great exponent of the view which I am criticizing, does not become denationalized in proportion to his greatness; on the contrary, he is most Greek where he is greatest.

This is only to say that the theory which an age produces is an expression of the spirit of that age in the same sense in which its art, its political and social institutions, its religion are expressions of it. (The other view presupposes a fundamental cleavage between thought, as the work of reason, and the other mental activities.) Since they are all expressions, in different media, of the same spirit, it will be possible to trace connections and correspondences between them, at once intimate and subtle. It will be possible to say that not one of them could have been essentially different from what it was without the whole complex being different too; for example, that the political theory of Plato and Aristotle could have arisen only in a social system based upon slavery (and based not upon slavery in general, but upon the unique form of slavery which was characteristic of Greece). This is true; but it is no less true to say that the Greek institution of slavery could have arisen only in a people of the Greek character, that is to say, in a people imbued with those moral and political convictions which become explicit in the works of Plato and Aristotle.

So much, I think, must be accepted. Marx, as we have seen, is not content with the assertion of such reciprocal interdependence, but takes a further step (in which indeed the essence of his system consists). Out of the complex of interrelated factors which compose a civilization, he selects one factor, the economic, and asserts this alone to be the cause of which all the others are effects. This assertion appears to me to be arbitrary, dogmatic, and false.

But if what I have said of political theory is admitted to be true, the question presents itself with hardly diminished force: What is the use of studying the political theories of the past? If each is tied so closely to the conditions of the age from which it sprang, how can it be relevant to the conditions of our own?

First it may be answered that this very discrepancy is part of their value. Only by help of the contrast with other civilizations can we become aware that the principles upon which our own is founded are peculiar and unique. Philosophy consists in attaining to a conscious realization of what we have previously taken for granted; it is a reflection upon the presuppositions of our own thought and action, including, of course, our political action. But it is hardly possible to be aware that such presuppositions exist, let alone to become conscious of their nature, until we become acquainted with men in whose thought and action they are lacking.

The Greeks, who knew no history of any civilization except their own, were vividly aware of the contrast between themselves and uncivilized men; all who were not Greeks they termed "barbarians." This contrast gave them occasion to reflect upon the distinctive principles of their own thought and action. But because for them the distinction between Greek and non-Greek coincided with that between civilized and uncivilized, they inevitably identified the principles of their own thought with those of civilized (or, as they would have said, "rational") humanity as such.

The knowledge of history enables (or forces) us to take a different point of view from this, for it brings us acquaintance with the thoughts of men who differ from ourselves not in being uncivilized or less civilized, but in being differently civilized. We are thus made conscious that our own civilization is a unique form of civilization, and not to be identified with civilization in general. No doubt this truth may be recognized by those who have made no special study of the history of thought. Indeed the recognition is implicit in the usage, now growing common, by which men are becoming accustomed to use the designation "Western" or "Modern" or "Christian" Civilization, in place of "civilization" simply. This adoption of a proper name in place of a general term implies in itself a recognition of the fact that the civilization thus designated is peculiar and unique. But a study of past theories is necessary for the understanding of all that is implicit in the recognition; it enables us to see the present with something of the same objective vision with which we look upon the past.

But this is not the main value of the study. The works of which this book and its companion volumes contain selections, ranging from Plato to the present time, are not simply foreign. They represent stages of a single tradition of thought, at the end of which we stand. They are products of civilizations which are not alien to our own, but are the sources of our own. When we study the works of these writers, we are studying ideas which have been assimilated into our own ways of thinking, however much they may have been altered in the process.

Modern civilization is a product of history, in a sense in which other civilizations have not been so. We may be inclined to charge the Greek thinkers with a defect of historical sense, because they did not seek in the past for the sources of their own civilization; and it is true that they were lacking in the curiosity to investigate their own antecedents. But it is also true that they were under the less obligation to do so, in that Greek civilization had not its sources in the past. This is not to deny that the Greeks built on foundations which were there before them, and made use of what was ready to their hand. But what they derived from the past was their materials, rather than their inspiration. The peculiar spirit of Greek civilization sprang up on the soil of Greece itself, and I do not know that any explanation can be given why it did so. The Greek was not derived from a previous civilization in the sense (or in anything approaching the sense) in which modern civilization is derived from the Greek. A similar contrast may be seen if we compare modern civilization with that which has been another of its main sources: the Jewish. Modern civilization has derived, by an historical tradition and a written record, from the ancient Hebrews, that which the Hebrews themselves derived — whence? Direct from heaven, as they believed, but in any case certainly not by a similar tradition or record from a still earlier past. The fact that modern civilization is in this peculiar sense derived from the past, makes a study of the past indispensable to the understanding of it.

Every civilization consists of two sides, an external and an internal. It consists on the one hand in a certain complex of institutions — political, social, legal, scientific, artistic, religious; and on the other hand in a certain mentality in the men who people it. It is obvious that the former cannot exist without the latter. We have only to imagine the result which would follow from an attempt to impose a system of civilized institutions ready-made upon a society of savages in order to convince ourselves of it. It is not enough for the institutions to be civilized unless the men are so too; that is to say, unless they have acquired a frame of mind and mold of character appropriate to those institutions. Obvious though this truth is, it has often been neglected. Optimistic liberals of the last century, for example, who transplanted the political institutions of parliamentary democracy to diverse lands, did not always realize that the institutions could flourish only in so far as they succeeded in propagating also the appropriate cast of mind and character. And even in those countries in which liberal democracy is native, too little regard has been paid to the fact that the survival of liberal institutions depends on the preservation of the requisite mental and moral character, and its propagation in succeeding generations of citizens.

It is easier to become aware of the distinctive institutions of a civilization than of the distinctive mental character which they presuppose. We know in general what are the institutions characteristic of modern western civilization, but it is harder to realize what is the intellectual and moral constitution of the modern civilized man. The former are before our eyes, but the latter is a part of ourselves. The standards and principles upon which we act and by which we judge are themselves commonly taken for granted and not thought about. For example, the intellectual character which we call common sense is a part of the modern civilized mentality.   Common sense guides the judgments of its possessor.   By applying its standards he will reject *a priori* all superstitious explanations of natural events.   But he will commonly not be aware of the standards which he is applying, or even that he is applying any particular standards at all.   He perceives it to be absurd, for example, that ghosts should exist, or that a crop should be caused to wither by a curse; but he is not consciously aware of the principles which he is applying in making that judgment.   The judgment, nevertheless, springs from a certain definite attitude of mind, characteristic of a definite civilization.   (It is not in every age that those superstitions would have been perceived as absurd.)   Our judgments, actions, and sentiments in every department of life are similarly governed by a constitution of mind, feeling, and moral character, which is what makes us civilized men; or rather (since there is no such thing as civilization in general) civilized modern Europeans or Americans.

I do not, of course, imply that a civilized man has ceased to be a man. He is moved by the passions and instincts which are common to the human race, and shares these with the most primitive of mankind. But his being civilized makes a difference to the way in which he thinks and acts.   Even if it suppresses none of the original store of human motives and adds no fresh one, it operates by disciplining and molding them.   Even if it displaces nothing, it transforms everything; and every account is inadequate which seeks to explain the acts of a civilized man while ignoring his civilization.   There are theories, increasingly numerous in recent times, in which this is denied by implication, or even explicitly.   One class of such theories, often based upon psychology, ignores the cultural differences among men, and claims to find a sufficient explanation of their conduct in the basic minimum of psychical motives which is common to all men.   Another class, while recognizing the importance of varying social environments, yet ignores, or denies, the fundamental distinction between savagery and civilization, and treats civilizations as though they were only different forms of barbarism, explaining, for example, sciences as a modern form of magic, morals as a kind of tabu, religion as a variety of superstition, and so forth.   I shall not undertake the refutation of these theories, but mention them here in order to reject them.

All who are members of modern western civilization share in virtue of that fact certain mental foundations which powerfully affect their thoughts and actions, without their necessarily being conscious of them. These are what constitute modern civilization in its internal aspect, and what was said above of modern civilization in general is true of them: they are in a quite peculiar degree derived from historical sources. The common consciousness of modern civilized men has come to be what it is by assimilating elements from certain past civilizations, principally from the Greek, the Roman, and the Jewish.

To say this is, of course, a commonplace. We are accustomed to being reminded of our "inheritance" from Greece and to hearing talk of the "legacy" of Rome; and this metaphor of inheritance is a very good one, if the word is taken strictly in its legal, not in its biological sense. Some things we derive from our parents as an inseparable consequence of our birth — namely, a certain bodily and mental constitution. The property which we inherit from them is something acquired in addition to this, and transmitted to us by different means. Thus the metaphor brings out the truth that what makes us civilized men is something not innate but acquired, and that it is transmitted not (as, for example, purely racial characteristics are) by birth, but by some other means. But this is still only a metaphor, and I doubt whether all who accord a polite acceptance to such a statement of our relation to these civilizations are aware of all that it means. It means that unless these civilizations had existed and had somehow over the interval of centuries entered into the very structure of our minds, you and I and the next man would not think and act as we do, would not be the creatures that we are, endowed to a greater or less degree (since we are all imperfect specimens) with common sense, a capacity of objective thinking, a certain spirit of tolerance and liberality, a consciousness of individual responsibility — and so on, and so on. It is, of course, a hopeless task to try to enumerate the characters of a civilization in a list of terms.

When the statement is taken seriously, it is likely to arouse objections. "X, who has learned Greek and read Greek authors, may perhaps have absorbed some tinge of Greek ideas; though even he undertook the study too late in life for it to have had more than the most superficial effect in forming him. But what of A and B and C and the millions more, who know nothing about the Greeks? How can they have been influenced by the thoughts of men of whom they have never even heard?" In order to remove this objection, it is necessary to say

a few words on the means which exist for the transmission of the influence of the past.   They could be summed up in a single word:
Education, if that were understood in a broad enough sense, to include
not merely the teaching of school and university, but all the formative
influences which are brought to bear upon a man from his birth until
his death.   Through the earliest instruction in manners and morals
conveyed by his parents, through the literature which he reads, through
the tremendous formative pressure exercised upon him by the public
opinion of the various societies into which he successively enters,
through the necessity imposed upon him of conforming himself to the
institutions among which he grows up — through all these means the
influence of past civilizations operates upon him.   Let us consider a
few examples.   A mother instructs her infant son in manners.   She
teaches him to take off his hat to ladies, and reproves him if he does
not allow precedence to the girls among his companions.   If asked why
she did so, she might reply simply that this was what good manners
demanded; she might give further reasons (and good ones).   But it is,
nevertheless, the truth that the instructions which she gives her son
originate in medieval chivalry.   She may never have heard of the
Middle Ages, but she would never have given that training if she had
not been connected by an unbroken historical tradition with the
medieval civilization.   She herself, by the act of instructing her son,
is continuing the tradition which she has received through a series of
similar acts of instruction of one generation by the preceding.

Or suppose a case not of manners but of morals.   A mother reproves
her child for doing acts of certain kinds, and encourages him to do
certain other acts (and it is superfluous to emphasize the profound
effect which instruction of this kind has in the formation of character).
She may give reasons why these acts are right and those wrong, and
(it must be insisted) they may be good reasons.   But she would certainly not have drawn the line where she does but for the influence of
Christianity.   In this case she is more likely to be aware of the origin of
what she teaches; but whether she is or not, it remains true that Christianity is the source of the moral code characteristic of modern civilization.   Through all the countless channels by which it has exercised its
pervading and penetrating influence, Christianity has been the means
of bringing to bear in the shaping of the minds of modern men not only
the civilization of the Hebrews, but the Greek and Roman elements
which Christianity absorbed.

Or again: one of the earliest things that a child is taught is to speak its native language. The structure and idiom of that language will determine his way of thinking in a manner so profound, yet so subtle, that it is difficult to appreciate it justly. Suppose that the language in question is English. The English language is very largely composed of elements derived from the Latin and the Greek. An English or American child does not have to wait to learn the ancient languages in order to submit his mind to formation by ancient ways of thought. He is forced to do this to some extent in the mere act of acquiring his own language.

I will not multiply examples further, for the reader will readily multiply them for himself. I have mentioned only a few of the countless channels through which past civilizations operate in forming the mentality of modern civilization.

Because this mentality is, in the ways which I have indicated, derived in a peculiar degree from historical sources, an historical study is indispensable to the understanding of it. We cannot comprehend it fully until we have comprehended the elements which have gone to make it up, and have become acquainted with the forces which have stamped its character. The value of the study of the great political philosophies of the European tradition is that it can give this comprehension and acquaintance in one important field of human thought and action. Not, of course, that the works of the theorists have been the sole vehicle by which the influence of the civilizations which they represent has been conveyed. I hope I have said enough to prevent that misconception. The spirit of Greece has exerted its influence not only through the writings of Plato and Aristotle (great though the direct influence of their writings has been), but through the works in every other field in which it found expression: through its poetry, art, and political institutions. But we go to the theories in order to understand the spirit because it is expressed there in intelligible form.

But to understand the "modern mentality" is to understand ourselves. If the study of past political theories contributes to this, it needs no further justification. "Know thyself" was the motto inscribed on the temple at Delphi, by the oracle of which Socrates was dispatched on the quest from which all subsequent European philosophy has sprung.

Perhaps the study may have a further use. It may promote a deeper understanding of all that is involved in being civilized, and remove the temptation to suppose that a civilized man is merely a tame man, differing from the savage only in the way in which the domesticated animal differs from the wild one. If it does so, it will be not irrelevant to the circumstances of the present time, for when we are fighting or working for the preservation of western civilization, it behooves us to understand as well as we can what it is that we are fighting or working for.

CHAPTER TWO

Plato

PLATO was born in Athens, probably in the year 427 B.C., when the civilization of ancient Greece was at its zenith, or perhaps a little past it. The ancient Greek world extended far beyond the boundaries of modern Greece. It covered most of the coastal regions of the Mediterranean and Black seas, from Asia Minor to Marseilles and from Egypt to the mouths of the Danube.

The unit of the political organization of the Greeks was the city, not the nation, as in the modern world. They knew no such thing as a state containing several cities; or rather they knew it as a phenomenon occurring only among "barbarians" — the term by which they designated all people who were not Greeks. Each city was politically independent and self-governing. It was also to a very large extent, though by no means entirely, economically self-sufficient. Different cities varied greatly in the degree in which they were dependent upon imported supplies; but on the whole the degree of self-sufficiency of the ancient Greek city was at least not less than that of the modern European nation. Their consumption of goods was on an incomparably smaller scale than that of the modern world. Their food, dwelling-places, and clothing were extremely simple, and they had very little of the vast mechanical apparatus of modern civilization.

Each city possessed the territory surrounding it, from which it drew its necessary supplies.[1] The land was usually divided into small estates, owned by the citizens. His estate in the country was the citizen's base, but it was not the scene of his principal activities. These were performed in the city, to which he came to perform political, judicial, or military functions, to attend religious celebrations or dramatic

---

[1] These territories varied in size. Attica, the territory of Athens, was 1060 square miles in extent — the size of one of the smaller English counties; and most cities had territories much smaller than this.

performances, to exercise himself in the gymnasia, or simply to converse with his fellow-citizens.   Political constitutions varied greatly from city to city.   In the fifth century before Christ they ranged from extreme oligarchies to extreme democracies.   The degree to which the mass of the citizens participated in the government of their city varied accordingly.   But if a man were to be wholly precluded from participation in the civic activities which I have mentioned; if his whole time were to be engrossed by the getting of a livelihood and the care of his family, he would be deemed by the common judgment of the Greeks to be living a life not befitting a free man at all.

The citizens of a Greek state by no means comprised the whole of its inhabitants.   Not to mention the women, who had no political status, the citizens might well be outnumbered by the resident aliens, serfs, and slaves.   Thus the extremest democracy in the Greek world, in which political power was shared most widely among the citizens, was still by modern standards an oligarchy.   Slavery was an essential feature of Greek civilization, since the labor of the slave gave the citizen the needful leisure for the performance of his (economically unproductive) civic functions.

Although the Greek cities were politically independent of each other, all Greeks shared a strong consciousness of their racial and cultural affinity with one another, and a profound and unquestioning belief in the superiority of Hellenic [1] to other peoples.   They thought of themselves as differing from other peoples in degree rather than in kind of excellence; and hence they implicitly identified the type of Greek manhood with the type of humanity as such.   This sentiment may be compared with that of the white peoples to one another in the modern civilization of the nineteenth century.   In both cases the sentiment of community was compatible with complete political separation, and in neither case did it prevent the outbreak of internecine war between the peoples who recognized themselves to be bearers of a common civilization.

Such a war (the Peloponnesian War) had broken out among the Greek cities about twenty years before Plato's birth.   The protagonists on either side were Athens and Sparta, the two principal states of Greece.   After some truces and many vicissitudes the struggle finally ended, in 404 B.C., with the defeat of Athens.

[1] The ancient Greeks called themselves "Hellenes."

During the course of this war the political life of Greece deteriorated with an astonishing rapidity, and by the time of its conclusion Greek political civilization was manifestly in decay.[1] The disintegrating effect of the war was accentuated by the fact that the antagonists were divided not merely by conflict of interests, but by conflict of "ideologies." Sparta supported the oligarchic, Athens the democratic cause. Each Greek city contained within itself a democratic and an oligarchic party. The side which a city took in the war depended on which party was in the ascendant, and the rival party within it could always rely on support from the other side in its efforts to expel its political opponents from power. Thus the war was not merely a conflict between the Greek states which were ranged on either side; it was a civil conflict also between opposed parties within each state. The unity of each state was disrupted by what the Greeks called "stasis"[2] (faction, or sedition). It is one of the preoccupations of Plato's thought on political matters to find a cure and preventive of "stasis" in states.

Plato was born of an aristocratic Athenian family. Few details are known about his early life, but he doubtless went through the ordinary education of a free-born Athenian boy, which consisted in a twofold course of training in "music" and gymnastic. "Music" included not only the art which we designate by the word, but also the learning by heart and recitation of poetry. The poems of Homer formed the principal basis of this "musical" education, and as these poems are informed by definite moral and religious beliefs, their inculcation served to mold the moral character and sentiments (not merely the esthetic sensibilities) of the pupil (in much the same way as the study of the Bible has influenced more than the literary style of those who have been submitted to its teaching).

We need not ask for what career Plato was destined. His birth settled that. He must have looked forward to a normal participation in the public and political life of Athens.

But during his youth Plato came under the influence of Socrates, one of the most remarkable personalities of whom history bears record. Plato has left a portrait of him in the many dialogues in which he ap-

---

[1] For the history of this war, and its effect upon the political life of Greece, see THUCYDIDES, HISTORY.

[2] For an account of stasis, see THUCYDIDES, Book III, LXXXII–LXXXIV.

pears as the principal character.[1] Socrates was born about the year
469 B.C., he served in the Athenian army in several campaigns in the
Peloponnesian War, he once held political office, but he deliberately
withdrew himself so far as he could from participation in political
affairs, in order to devote himself to the main preoccupation of his life:
philosophical discussion in any company, at any time, and in any place.
In many of his traits, the English character who best stands comparison
with him is Doctor Johnson.   He was grotesquely ugly and entirely
indifferent to his personal appearance; he was endowed with immense
powers of physical endurance and great physical courage; he was both
capable of abstinence and able, without concern, to drink his companions under the table; he was humorous and ironical, passionately fond
of argument, interested in problems of conduct rather than in theory,
possessed of strong moral convictions and entirely careless of the consequences of acting by them, gifted with a power of gaining friendship,
especially of the young, and impervious to the attractions of any save a
city life.   But to describe Socrates thus would be to leave out the most
important thing about him; namely, his consciousness of a divinely
imposed task, which he was continually driven to fulfill.   He was aware
of a mission no less keenly than Bunyan.   It was a mission in the service
of philosophy, not of religion; but he regarded it with a religious seriousness.   The task of his life was to convince men not of sin, but of ignorance.[2]   His method of doing this was the famous "dialectic," by which
he tested the claims of those who thought they knew something, applying a series of questions to elicit a latent contradiction or expose a latent
confusion.   Socrates never claimed to know anything (the "Socratic
irony"), saying that if he were in any way wiser than other men, it was
because he knew his own ignorance, while they did not.   The effect of
his questioning, though intensely irritating to most of his victims, and
shocking to those to whom he seemed to be loosening the roots of the
most sacred and important beliefs, was not skeptical.   It did not lead
to a despair of knowledge, but stimulated thought, and Socrates was
surrounded by a crowd of young followers (often young members of
the Athenian aristocracy) who were fascinated by his method, and
eager to emulate it.   Plato was one of these.

[1] See especially APOLOGY, CRITO, PHAEDO, and SYMPOSIUM.   Xenophon has an
account of him in his MEMORABILIA, and Aristophanes a caricature in his comedy
THE CLOUDS (produced in 423 B.C.)

[2] D. G. RITCHIE, in CHAMBERS' ENCYCLOPAEDIA, s.v. "SOCRATES."

The turning-point in Plato's life came in the year 399, when he was twenty-eight years old. In that year Socrates, then a man of about seventy, was put on his trial before the Athenian courts on charges of disbelieving in the gods of the city, of introducing new deities, and of corrupting the youth. He refused to adopt any of the devices by which he might have secured an acquittal, and delivered an uncompromising defense of his way of life. He was found guilty by a majority of votes and condemned to death. He accepted the sentence with his accustomed serenity, and in the interval which elapsed between his trial and execution refused to countenance the efforts of his friends to contrive his escape.

The real causes of the condemnation of Socrates have never been satisfactorily explained. The polytheistic religion of the Greeks was in general tolerant of heterodoxy. It was regarded as natural that different men should worship different gods; and, if a new deity cropped up, there was usually plenty of room for him in the pagan Pantheon. It has been suggested that political motives underlay the trial. Toward the end of the Peloponnesian War the oligarchic party had seized power in Athens. In 399 the democrats were in control again, and were no doubt disposed to take revenge on their opponents. Socrates himself had abstained from political affairs, but some of the leaders of the oligarchs had been conspicuous members of his company of friends. It may be true that political motives played their part, but the evidence is decisive against the conclusion that the case against Socrates was exclusively, or even primarily, a political one. It is possible that the Athenian people were moved by an instinctive repugnance to a novel principle. They may have recognized obscurely that the way of thinking introduced by Socrates was not one which could take its place in comfortable juxtaposition with the various other religious beliefs of Greece, but that it was destined to undermine the foundations both of the pagan religions and of Greek political life. If the Athenians felt this, their instinct was a true one, as the following pages may help to show.

Plato was profoundly shocked by the death of Socrates. He had no doubt shared the normal Greek attitude of reverence for the laws and constitution of his state, being brought up in the traditional Greek belief that they had been divinely instituted to educate the citizens for the good life, and to secure them the conditions in which it could be led.

But here was a case in which the laws of the state condemned to death
one whom he knew to be "the wisest and justest and best of all the men
whom he had ever known."

Plato was deflected by this experience from pursuing any intention
which he may have held of following a political career in Athens. The
following period of his life is devoted to reflection, literary publication,
and travel. He is said to have visited Africa, Egypt, the Persians, the
Babylonians, and the Hebrews. and Italy and Sicily besides. Some of
the travels ascribed to him are probably fictitious; that to Italy and
Sicily is among those which are certain, and this visit led to friendships
at the court of Dionysius, tyrant of Syracuse, which were later to be
important for him. His literary activity took the form of dialogues, in
which he represented conversations of Socrates with various inter-
locutors. These were probably intended at first as memorials of Socrates; but more and more they became vehicles of Plato's own development of his master's thought, and it is now impossible to distinguish
with certainty between what is Socratic and what Platonic in the
philosophy of the Platonic Socrates.

At a date which cannot be determined precisely, but which must fall
between 388 and 369, Plato took a decisive step: he founded a school of
philosophy, which was called the Academy, after the name of the local-
ity in which it was situated. Plato's school is the parent of all the universities which have been founded since; but in the beginning its organization must have been informal enough. To the eyes of contemporaries it must have closely resembled the band of companions which had
gathered round Socrates and other previous teachers. But in reality
the Academy was founded upon a new idea, which had been ripening
in Plato's mind for perhaps twenty years. He had conceived the possibility of science. Socrates had shown that the knowledge which men
suppose themselves to possess is not really knowledge, but only opinion
or belief. There is no dogma or conviction which cannot be shaken by
well-directed questioning, and the only thing that we can know, in the
strict sense of the word, is that we know nothing. Plato's discovery
was that knowledge in the strict sense of the word can be extended by
the use of a right method beyond the single certainty of our ignorance.
It is possible to attain to positive truths which can be proved, and
thereby made secure against refutation. There can be no doubt that

Plato's inspiration in this matter was derived from mathematics (the geometry later systematized by Euclid was then in an early stage of its development in Greece), and it is by the illustration of mathematics still that we can most easily grasp what he had in mind.   Imagine the case of a man entirely uninstructed in geometry (all readers of this book will have to cast their minds back to their early childhood in order to remember what such a condition is like; but it was the normal condition in which the contemporaries of Plato passed their lives).   Such a man may suppose himself to know many truths, which are in fact capable of geometrical demonstration.   He may be entirely convinced that the two sides of a triangle are together greater than a third, either because he has been told it or because he has had frequent experience of walking from corner to corner of a triangular area.   But however strong his conviction, it is still belief and not knowledge.   But now let the same man be led step by step through the elements of Euclid's geometry, let him be shown the theorem in which the proposition about the sides of the triangle is proved.   He may, if he is still a beginner, read it through once or twice without fully comprehending it; but the moment will come when he "sees" the proof.   From that moment he has knowledge of the proposition, something differing not in degree but in kind from the opinion which he had before.   Once he has an intellectual grasp of the proof, he is able to render an account to any questioner.   The Greek word for "knowledge" is the same as the Greek word for "science"; hence we may say equally well that from this moment he possesses science.

Plato believed that the scientific knowledge attainable in mathematics could be acquired also in other spheres, and he proclaimed it to be the task of the philosopher to acquire it.   In particular he looked forward to the extension of scientific understanding to the sphere of politics and legislation.   In this sphere, he saw, all men were in the same condition in which the man ignorant of geometry is in regard to geometrical truths.   Statesmen and citizens enforce laws, believing (sometimes with an intolerant and bigoted conviction) that they are good; but what they possess in these matters is never more than belief, based on tradition or custom or passion or some other irrational ground. It is little wonder, then, that many laws and constitutions of states are as imperfect as they are found to be.   For their improvement one thing is urgently necessary: that knowledge should take the place of opinion in the determination of what laws are best. Thus the original purpose of the Academy was by no means exclusively "academic." It was to be, among other things, a workshop for the production of that political science which was necessary in order to reform the Greek world.

At about the time of the foundation of the Academy Plato published his greatest work, the dialogue called the *Republic*, in which are set out these ideas about science, and the necessity of its application to politics. (Plato expresses this as the necessity "that philosophers should rule in states."[1]) The *Republic* served thus to give a theoretical justification of the institution which Plato was founding; it was indeed the prospectus of the Academy.[2]

Some years after the foundation of the Academy, Plato received a summons to Syracuse. Dionysius had died and had been succeeded by his young son, Dionysius II, and Plato was invited by his friend, Dion, the son-in-law of the elder Dionysius, to impart philosophical instruction to the young king. He was thus offered an opportunity of putting his ideas into practice, by making a philosopher of one who was already a ruler. Plato went, and failed. Dionysius was unwilling to submit to the arduous discipline which was necessary in order to produce what Plato meant by a philosopher. Plato returned to Athens. He was recalled again to Syracuse some years later, but his mission was again fruitless, and this time perilous to himself. But he escaped and devoted himself to philosophical study and writing, and to the direction of the Academy, until he died in 347 at the age of eighty.

In spite of Plato's failure in Syracuse, the Academy was not entirely barren of direct practical results in the sphere of politics. Cases are recorded in which Greek cities requested, during Plato's lifetime, that a member of the Academy should be sent to them to frame them a constitution. But on the whole Plato's discovery had its greatest effect in other directions than those in which he looked for it. It did not supply statesmen with a handbook of reform; but it was the germ from which that body of knowledge which we call Science eventually grew, and it contained a practical principle also, which was new to the ancient world but became fundamental to the modern; the principle, namely, of the moral responsibility of the individual for his own conduct.[3]

[1] See pp. 84 *et seq.*   [2] WILAMOWITZ-MOELLENDORF, PLATON (1919).
[3] See pp. 109-113, *infra*.

POLITICAL PHILOSOPHY

PLATO'S principal work on political philosophy has a double title: it is called the *Republic, or Concerning Justice*. Whether Plato himself was responsible for the title or not does not matter, for it is an accurate description of the contents of the book. But both the nouns contained in the title require some explanation in order that they may represent the meaning of the Greek.

The word translated "republic" is *politeia*, or "polity." It does not mean "republic" in the narrower modern usage of the term, according to which a republic is a constitution of a particular sort, distinguished from a monarchy. It means constitution in general; republics in the narrow sense, monarchies, and aristocracies are all "polities." Or rather, to speak more accurately, it means political constitution in general, or the constitution of a state. Other forms of society (families, for example, clubs, commercial companies) may have constitutions; indeed, they must have them, since their constitution is what organizes their component members and forms them into the societies. Constitution means nothing more than the way in which individuals are organized in relation to one another to form societies. But not all organizations are political, and not all human societies are states. Plato in the *Republic* is inquiring into the nature of political organization in general, and is asking, "What is it that constitutes a state?" This is clearly the central problem of political philosophy.[1]

Justice

The Greek word translated "justice" is *dikaiosune*. It has a wider application than the English word "justice"; and many passages in Plato's writings will sound strange and will be misleading unless this is remembered. We think of "justice" and "injustice" primarily as qualities displayed in the exercise of a judicial or administrative function. The just judge, for example, is a man who declares the law impartially; an unjust judge is one who inflicts punishment otherwise than in accordance with the deserts of the offender. But the Greeks

[1] This question is discussed further on pp. 43–48, 60–70, *infra*.

extended the term "injustice" to the fault in the offender which made him deserving of punishment. If a judge condemned for theft a man whom he knew to be innocent, we should call the judge "unjust" (and so would Plato); but we should not naturally call the innocent man "just" (as Plato would). If a judge inflicted upon a thief proved guilty the penalty prescribed by law, we should say that he had acted justly; Plato would call the thieving of the accused an act of "injustice." The following example may illustrate the difference of usage. In the conduct of an academic examination, the examiners ought to refrain from favoritism and the candidates from cheating. We should call an examiner "just" who refused to favor, but we should probably use some other term, such as "honest," to describe the candidate who refused to cheat. But the behavior of the latter would be a perfect example of what Plato means by "justice."

Thus justice in Plato means very nearly what we mean by "morality." It is the disposition which makes a man refrain from an act recommended by desire or by his apparent interest, through obedience to a belief that he ought not to perform it.

The foregoing analysis of the meaning of these terms is only preliminary and approximate. Their exact meaning must be gathered from a study of Plato's doctrines. To have comprehended the exact meaning of these, and the other central terms of his philosophy, would be already to have comprehended Plato.

(a) Justice as a Human Virtue

It is Plato's doctrine that justice is a part of human virtue. This doctrine will appear less like a platitude if we perform on the term "virtue" the same operation which was necessary with "justice," and restore to it the meaning which it bore in Greek.

Arete, which is translated "virtue" or, perhaps better, "excellence," is the quality which entitles any thing or person to be called *good*. Things may be good as well as persons. Thus a knife may be a good knife or a bad one, a school may be a good school or a worse one, a horse may be a better horse than another. Whatever it is that makes the knife, school, or horse a *good* knife, school, or horse, that is the virtue, or proper excellence, of the knife, school, or horse.

Men also may be better or worse men, and some may be called good in comparison with others. Virtue will be the quality which the better man possesses in a higher degree than the worse. But when we are speaking of men, a distinction must be made. A man may be good at any of a great variety of things: at carpentry, or boxing, or business, at the arts of medicine or of public speaking. What makes him good at any of these things may certainly be called a kind of virtue, and it is not difficult in each particular case to specify what the virtue in ques tion consists of. What makes a man a good carpenter is his capacity to construct furniture out of wood, what makes him a good doctor is his ability to cure disease; and it is possible in like manner, for every particular thing that a man can be good at, to specify what it is that con stitutes his goodness at it.

Nevertheless, human virtue in the strict sense cannot be identical with any of those kinds of excellence which have hitherto been considered. Human virtue must be what makes a man a good man. These kinds of excellence make their possessor a good doctor, carpenter, boxer, public speaker, as the case may be, but not necessarily a good man. What sort of capacity, then, is it which entitles a man to be called a good man? It is not a superiority in any of those departmental accomplishments which have been mentioned, nor in any of that almost infinite list of departmental accomplishments which it would be possible to mention; for whatever one of these is specified, it will clearly be possible for a person to be as good as you like at this, and at the same time to be a bad man (in the same way in which a good boxer or a good doctor may be at the same time a bad man). Nor does a man become a good man by combining in himself a great number of particular accomplishments, for it is clearly possible to conceive a man who might be a master in a great variety of departments, but who might for all that be a bad man.

One of two things, therefore, is necessary. Either the reality of human virtue must be denied (in this case it would have to be asserted that, though we may still legitimately ascribe to men superiority in departmental excellences, though we may continue to say that X is a good carpenter and Y a better doctor than Z, there is no real sense in which A can be said to be a good *man*, or B a better man than C); or, if human virtue is a real thing, it must be possible to discover in what it consists.

Plato rejects the former alternative and undertakes the task of explaining what human virtue consists in. He divides it into four main constituent elements; namely, into the virtues of Wisdom, Courage, Temperance, and Justice.[1] Whoever has any one of these is to that extent a good man, and whoever has all of them is a wholly good man. Any one of the departmental excellences may be denied of a man without reproach; to say of a man that he is a good doctor but not a good fisherman is a statement of fact, not a criticism. But to deny a man either wisdom, courage, temperance, or justice is necessarily to reproach him, whatever excellences are attributed to him in their stead.

To name, of course, is not to define; and the task still remains of explaining what each of these so-named virtues is. We must confine ourselves here to the last, justice.

The problem, as it presents itself to Plato, is that of distinguishing justice from the departmental goodnesses. It seems at first sight that it should be distinguished from them, as they are distinguished from one another, by having its own particular field of operation. Thus, for example, pugilistic and medical skill both make men "good," each in its own way. If you wish to distinguish these two different goodnesses, you have only to specify what each makes its possessor good *at*. Since we are now told that the goodness called justice is different again from either, it might be thought that it should be distinguished from them in a similar manner; if justice makes a man good, what does it make him good *at*? This question proves incapable of answer, because whatever special field of human activity is selected, it is found to belong to one of the departmental excellences to make a man good at that, and the conclusion seems to follow that justice has no sphere of operation of its own.

This conclusion is drawn in a passage of the *Republic* which exhibits the Socratic dialectic in its most irritating form.

Socrates is discussing with his interlocutor Polemarchus a definition of justice which has been quoted from the poet Simonides, to the effect that the repayment of debts is just. Socrates has exposed some difficulties in the way of taking this as a literal definition and the dialogue proceeds as follows: [2]

---

[1] These have been ever since Plato's time accorded the title of the four cardinal virtues.

[2] REPUBLIC, I, 331–333.

Simonides, then, after the manner of poets, would seem to have spoken darkly of the nature of justice; for he really meant to say that justice is the giving to each man what is proper to him, and this he termed a debt.

That must have been his meaning, he said.

By heaven! I [1] replied: and if we asked him what due or proper thing is given by the art called medicine, and to whom, what answer do you think he would make to us?

He would surely reply that medicine gives drugs and meat and drink to human bodies.

And what due or proper thing is given by the art called cookery, and to what?

Seasoning to food.

And what is that which the art called justice gives, and to whom?

If, Socrates, we are to be guided at all by the analogy of the preceding instances, then justice is the art which gives good to friends and evil to enemies.

That is his meaning, then?

I think so.

And who is best able to do good to his friends and evil to his enemies in time of sickness?

The physician.

Or when they are on a voyage, amid the perils of the sea?

The pilot.

And in what sort of actions or with a view to what result is the just man most able to do harm to his enemy and good to his friend?

In going to war against the one and in making alliances with the other.

But when a man is well, my dear Polemarchus, there is no need of a physician.

No.

And he who is not on a voyage has no need of a pilot?

No.

Then in time of peace justice will be of no use?

I am very far from thinking so.

You think that justice may be of use in peace as well as in war?

Yes.

[1] "I" means Socrates throughout.

Like husbandry for the acquisition of corn?

Yes.

Or like shoemaking for the acquisition of shoes — that is what you mean?

Yes.

And what similar use or power of acquisition has justice in time of peace?

In contracts, Socrates, justice is of use.

And by contracts you mean partnerships?

Exactly.

But is the just man or the skilful player a more useful and better partner at a game of draughts?

The skilful player.

And in the laying of bricks and stones is the just man a more useful or better partner than the builder?

Quite the reverse.

Then in what sort of partnership is the just man a better partner than the harp-player, as in playing the harp the harp-player is certainly a better partner than the just man?

In a money partnership.

Yes, Polemarchus, but surely not in the use of money; for you do not want a just man to be your counsellor in the purchase or sale of a horse; an expert on horses would be better for that, would he not?

Certainly.

And when you want to buy a ship, the shipwright or the pilot would be better?

True.

Then what is that joint use of silver or gold in which the just man is to be preferred?

When you want a deposit to be kept safely.

You mean when money is not wanted for use, but allowed to lie?

Precisely.

That is to say, justice is useful when money is useless?

That is the inference.

And when you want to keep a pruning-hook safe, then justice is useful to the individual and to the state; but when you want to use it, then the art of the vine-dresser?

Clearly.

And when you want to keep a shield or a lyre, and not to use them, you would say that justice is useful; but when you want to use them, then the art of the soldier or the musician?

That must follow.

And so of all other things; — justice is useful when they are useless and useless when they are useful.

That is the inference.

Then justice is not good for much.

The moral of this *reductio ad absurdum* is that justice, if it is to be distinguished from the departmental excellences, must be distinguished from them in a different way from that in which they are distinguished from one another.

Plato's own solution of this problem (which does not appear in that purely destructive piece of argument) is that justice is "architectonic" in relation to the other excellences; i.e., is related to them as the work of the architect, or master-builder, in the construction of a house is related to that of the masons, joiners, wood carvers, sculptors who work under his direction. Each of the subordinate workmen has a particular part of the building under his especial charge, but there is no part of it which is under the especial charge of the master-builder. His charge consists in directing the work of the subordinate workmen. The result of this is that each particular feature of the house is capable of a double excellence (and correspondingly liable to a twofold fault). There is the excellence which it owes to the skill of the particular workman in whose charge it is, and that which is derived from the supervisory skill of the architect. A door, for instance, may be formed with perfect skill. This excellence it owes to the carpenter who made it. But it will need another excellence also. It will need to be proportionate in its dimensions and harmonious in its materials and design with the other features of the building. A door, of however exquisite workmanship, would be bad if it did not satisfy this requirement. This excellence it can derive from the architect's skill alone. Thus, while the architect's skill has no special department, the excellence which is derived from it is present in every department of the building, together with the special excellence peculiar to that part.

Every human action similarly is capable of a twofold excellence, the departmental and the architectonic. For example, of the speech in which Bacon accused Essex,[1] his friend and benefactor, it might be said that it was well done in one sense, i.e., that it was an excellent specimen of forensic art; but that it was ill done in another sense, in view of the ties of obligation by which Bacon was bound to Essex. Bacon's action would then be like the door of exquisite workmanship, which nevertheless ought not to be where it is.   The door exhibits excellence of carpentry, but defect of architecture; and so the speech shows excellence in the departmental art of oratory, but defectiveness in the architectonic art of justice.   It shows its author as a good orator, but not as a good man.

The architectonic nature of justice accounts for that element of restraint which is the first thing apparent in it.   Just as the authority of the architect touches the subordinate craftsmen as a restrictive force, curbing the exuberance of their production, confining their scope, and limiting their freedom in the interest of the design as a whole, so justice operates as a restraint upon a man's particular capacities, withholding him from many things which he has both the desire and the ability to do.

(b) Justice as the Bond of States

It may seem that what has preceded belongs more properly to Plato's moral than to his political philosophy.   But justice is for him not only a part of human virtue.   It is also that quality in men which makes them capable of entering into political relations with one another, and so of forming political societies.   Societies are possible only in so far as each of their individual members exhibits self-restraint toward his fellow members, and refrains from doing or getting all that he has the ability to do or power to get.

This is illustrated by a myth which Plato puts in the mouth of Protagoras, the Sophist.[2]

Once upon a time there were gods only, and no mortal creatures. But when the time came that these also should be created, the gods fashioned them out of earth and fire and various mixtures of both elements in the interior of the earth; and when they were about to bring them into the light of day, they ordered Prometheus and

[1] See Macaulay's essay on Francis Bacon.   [2] PROTAGORAS, 320–322.

Epimetheus to equip them, and to distribute to them severally their proper abilities and powers. Epimetheus said to Prometheus: "Let me distribute, and do you inspect." This was agreed, and Epimetheus made the distribution. There were some to whom he gave strength without swiftness, while he equipped the weaker with swiftness; some he armed, and others he left unarmed; and devised for the latter some other means of preservation, making some large, and having their size as a protection, and others small, whose nature was to fly in the air or burrow in the ground; this was to be their way of escape. Thus did he compensate them with the view of preventing any race from becoming extinct. And when he had provided against their destruction by one another, he contrived also a means of protecting them against the seasons of heaven; clothing them with close hair and thick skins sufficient to defend them against the winter cold and able to resist the summer heat, so that they might have a natural bed of their own when they wanted to rest; also he furnished them with hoofs and hair and hard and callous skins under their feet. Then he gave them varieties of food, — herb of the soil to some, to others fruits of trees, and to others roots, and to some again he gave other animals as food. And some he made to have few young ones, while those who were their prey were very prolific; and in this manner the race was preserved.

Thus did Epimetheus, who, not being very wise, forgot that he had distributed among the brute animals all the qualities which he had to give, — and when he came to man, who was still unprovided, he was terribly perplexed. Now, while he was in this perplexity, Prometheus came to inspect the distribution, and he found that the other animals were suitably furnished, but that man alone was naked and shoeless, and had neither bed nor arms of defence. The appointed hour was approaching when man in his turn was to go forth into the light of day; and Prometheus, not knowing how he could devise his salvation, stole the mechanical arts of Hephaestus and Athene, and fire with them (they could neither have been acquired nor used without fire), and gave them to man. Thus man had the wisdom necessary to the support of life, but political wisdom he had not; for that was in the keeping of Zeus, and the power of Prometheus did not extend to entering into the citadel of heaven, where Zeus dwelt, who moreover had terrible sentinels;

but he did enter by stealth into the common workshop of Athene
and Hephaestus, in which they used to practise their favourite arts,
and carried off Hephaestus' art of working by fire, and also the art
of Athene, and gave them to man.   And in this way man was supplied with the means of life.   But Prometheus is said to have been
afterwards prosecuted for theft, owing to the blunder of Epimetheus.

Now man, having a share of the divine attributes, was at first the
only one of the animals who had any gods, because he alone was of
their kindred; and he would raise altars and images of them.   He
was not long in inventing articulate speech and names; and he also
constructed houses and clothes and shoes and beds, and drew sustenance from the earth.   Thus provided, mankind at first lived
dispersed, and there were no cities.[1]   But the consequence was that
they were destroyed by the wild beasts, for they were utterly weak
in comparison of them, and their art was only sufficient to provide
them with the means of life, and did not enable them to carry on
war against the animals: food they had, but not as yet the art of
government, of which the art of war is a part.   After a while the
desire of self-preservation gathered them into cities; but when they
were gathered together, having no art of government, they evil
intreated one another, and were again in process of dispersion and
destruction.   Zeus feared that the entire race would be extermi-
nated, and so he sent Hermes to them, bearing reverence and justice
to be the ordering principles of cities and the bonds of friendship
and conciliation.   Hermes asked Zeus how he should impart justice
and reverence among men: — Should he distribute them as the
arts are distributed; that is to say, each art to a few men only, one
skilled individual having enough of medicine or of any other art
for many unskilled ones?   "Shall this be the manner in which I am
to distribute justice and reverence among men, or shall I give them
to all?"   "To all," said Zeus; "I should like them all to have a
share; for cities cannot exist, if a few only share in these virtues, as
in the arts.[2]   And further, make a law by my order, that he who
has no part in reverence and justice shall be put to death, for he is
a plague of the state."

[1] That is to say "states," or political societies.   The Greek state was the city, not
the nation.
[2] An important principle is involved in this; cf. pp. 70–72, infra.

Justice is, for Plato, at once a part of human virtue and the bond which joins men together in states. It is an identical quality which makes man good and which makes him social. This identification is the first and fundamental principle of Plato's political philosophy.

It is by no means a platitude, and was denied in many doctrines prevalent in his own day. An opposite doctrine was placed by Plato in the mouths of certain Sophists who appear in some of his dialogues as the opponents of Socrates, and a glance at their doctrines will illustrate Plato's by contrast. They represent the opposition which Plato set himself deliberately to overthrow.

The Sophists admitted that justice, or morality, was essential to the existence of political society; but they denied that it constituted human excellence. They admitted that a man had to limit his individual activities and submit to regulation of his desires if it were to be possible for him to live in society with other men; but they denied that he became a better man by doing so. The following analogy will illustrate their view: Imagine a wild horse, a splendid specimen of its kind, both in physique and spirit. If it is ever to work in a team of other horses, it must be tamed and its spirit curbed. But this domestication does not make it a finer specimen of its type; on the contrary, it makes it a poorer (though a more useful) creature. The curbing of the horse's spirit corresponds to the limitation imposed upon man by the trammels of morality. It is necessary if he is to live as a fellow-citizen with other men; but let us not claim that it heightens his excellence, or (what is the same thing), his proper virtue as a man.

Callicles represents this point of view in the *Gorgias*:[1]

He who would truly live ought to allow his desires to wax to the uttermost, and not to chastise them; but when they have grown to their greatest he should have courage and intelligence to minister to them and to satisfy all his longings. And this I affirm to be natural justice and nobility. To this however the many cannot attain; and they blame the strong man because they are ashamed of their own weakness, which they desire to conceal, and hence they say that intemperance is base. As I have remarked already, they enslave the nobler natures, and being unable to satisfy their pleasures, they praise temperance and justice out of their own cowardice.

[1] GORGIAS, 491–492, 482–484.

❧For if a man had been originally the son of a king, or had a nature capable of acquiring an empire or a tyranny or kingship, what could be more truly base or evil than temperance — to a man like him, I say, who might freely be enjoying every good, and has no one to stand in his way, and yet has admitted custom and reason and the opinion of other men to be lords over him? — must not he be in a miserable plight whom the reputation of justice and temperance hinders from giving more to his friends than to his enemies, even though he be a ruler in his city? Nay, Socrates, for you profess to be a votary of the truth, and the truth is this: — that luxury and intemperance and licence, if they be provided with means, are virtue and happiness — all the rest is a mere bauble, agreements contrary to nature, foolish talk of men, nothing worth. . . .

By the rule of nature, to suffer injustice is the greater disgrace because the greater evil; but conventionally, to do evil is the more disgraceful. For the suffering of injustice is not the part of a man, but of a slave, who indeed had better die than live; since when he is wronged and trampled upon, he is unable to help himself, or any other about whom he cares. The reason, as I conceive, is that the makers of laws are the majority who are weak; and they make laws and distribute praises and censures with a view to themselves and to their own interests; and they terrify the stronger sort of men, and those who are able to get the better of them, in order that they may not get the better of them; and they say, that dishonesty is shameful and unjust; meaning, by the word injustice, the desire of a man to have more than his neighbours; for knowing their own inferiority, I suspect that they are too glad of equality. And therefore the endeavour to have more than the many, is conventionally said to be shameful and unjust, and is called injustice, whereas nature herself intimates that it is just for the better to have more than the worse, the more powerful than the weaker; and in many ways she shows, among men as well as among animals, and indeed among whole cities and races, that justice consists in the superior ruling over and having more than the inferior. For on what principle of justice did Xerxes invade Hellas, or his father the Scythians? (not to speak of numberless other examples). Nay, but these are the men who act according to nature; yes, by Heaven, and according to the law of nature: not, perhaps, according to that artificial law, which we invent and impose upon our fellows, of whom we take the best and strongest from their youth upwards, and tame them like young lions, — charming them with the sound of the voice, and saying to them, that with equality they must be content, and that the equal is the honourable and the just. But if there were a man who had sufficient force, he would shake off and break through, and escape from all this; he would trample under foot all our formulas and spells and charms, and all our laws which are against nature: the slave would rise in rebellion and be lord over us, and the light of natural justice [1] would shine forth.

The Sophist, Thrasymachus, adopts a similar position in the discussion concerning the nature of justice in the *Republic* when he lays down his famous definition "that justice is nothing else than the interest of the stronger." [2]

He expands his definition in a later passage,[3] which makes it clear that his theory is substantially identical with that later revived in the philosophy of Marx. (It is not wholly the same, for Thrasymachus does not assume, as Marx does, that the advantages which a ruling class seeks to secure by legal enactment must be exclusively economic advantages; and there are no doubt other points of difference. But when all allowances have been made, the substantial identity remains.)

ꙮ The different forms of government make laws democratical, aristocratical, tyrannical, with a view to their several interests; and these laws which are made by them for their own interests, are the justice which they deliver to their subjects, and him who transgresses them they punish as a breaker of the law, and unjust. And that is what I mean when I say that in all states there is the same principle of justice, which is the interest of the government; and as the government must be supposed to have power, the only reasonable conclusion is, that everywhere there is one principle of justice, which is the interest of the stronger.

Now I understand you, I said; but whether you are right or not, I will try to discover.

---

[1] What in this passage and in the previous one is called "natural justice" is, of course, simply the negation of justice in the proper sense of the term.

[2] REPUBLIC, I, 338.   [3] *Ibid.*, I, 339.

The implications of the position are later drawn out by Socrates in his interrogation of Thrasymachus as follows: [1]

Well, then, Thrasymachus, I said, suppose you begin at the beginning and answer me. You say that perfect injustice is more gainful than perfect justice?

Yes, that is what I say, and I have given you my reasons.

And what is your view on the following question concerning them? Would you call one of them virtue and the other vice?

Certainly.

I suppose that you would call justice virtue and injustice vice?

What a charming notion! So likely, too, seeing that I affirm injustice to be profitable and justice not.

What else then would you say?

The opposite, he replied.

And would you call justice vice?

No, I would rather say sublime simplicity.

Then would you call injustice malignity?

No, I would rather say prudence.

And do the unjust appear to you to be wise and good?

Yes, he said; at any rate those of them who are able to be perfectly unjust, and who have the power of subduing states and nations; but perhaps you imagine me to be talking of pickpockets. Even this profession if undetected has advantages, though they are not to be compared with those of which I was just now speaking.

I do not think that I misapprehend your meaning, Thrasymachus, I replied; but still I cannot hear without amazement that you class injustice with wisdom and virtue, and justice with the opposite.

Certainly I do so class them.

This, I said, is a more uncompromising position, and it is not easy to know what to say to it; for if the injustice which you were maintaining to be profitable had been admitted by you as by others to be vice and deformity, an answer might have been given to you on received principles; but now I perceive that you will call injustice honourable and strong, and to the unjust you will attribute all the qualities which were attributed by us before to the just, seeing that you do not hesitate to rank injustice with wisdom and virtue.

[1] REPUBLIC, I, 348–349.

You have guessed most infallibly, he said.

Then I certainly ought not to shrink from going through with the argument so long as I have reason to think that you, Thrasymachus, are speaking your real mind; for I do believe that you are now in earnest, and are not amusing yourself at our expense.

The doctrines of Callicles and of Thrasymachus are not identical with one another in all respects, but they agree in the essential point, namely, in asserting that the submission to restraint which membership of political society involves is a diminution and not a heightening of the natural excellence or virtue of man.

This Sophistic doctrine is by no means confined to ancient times. Its affinity with parts of Marxist teaching has already been noticed. It has much in common also with the doctrines of Nietzsche, who expressly claimed spiritual kinship with the Greek Sophists and praised their realism in contrast to the "humbug of the Socratic schools about morality and ideals."

It may be illustrated from Bernard Mandeville's work, *The Fable of the Bees*: "The only useful Passion that man is possessed of toward the Peace and Quiet of a Society is his Fear, and the more you work upon it, the more orderly and governable he'll be." [1] If courage is a virtue and the brave man a better man than the cowardly, then it follows from this doctrine that a man becomes a better citizen by becoming a worse man.

Plato's answer to these opponents depends in part upon the principle that restraint is necessary to perfection. This is true of each of the departmental excellences of which man is capable; no one becomes good at painting or at business or at boxing without submitting to a discipline which imposes a restraint upon the natural impulses. It is true also of the excellence of man in general. He approaches perfection to the degree in which he introduces harmony into his various activities by an architectonic control. But such limitation involves a close restraint of each activity in the interest of the general harmony. A man does not gain a strong personality by "allowing his desires to wax to the uttermost, and not chastising them," any more than he can become a good craftsman by indulging each artistic impulse, as it occurs,

---

[1] The passage occurs in the series of explanatory "Remarks," appended by Mandeville to his poem. See Remark R.

to the limit of its bent.   Though man's submission in society involves restraint, it does not therefore follow that it must impair his individual development; for restraint is essential to his proper individual development.

So far Plato's doctrine is congenial to common sense; the truth which Plato maintains against Callicles is the same as that which inspires the instinctive skepticism of an unsophisticated judgment towards the Nietzschean theories of the Superman.   (Nor, it may be added in parenthesis, is this conformity accidental.   The standards of our common sense have been formed in large measure in the school of Greece, and a grasp of this truth is part of our inheritance from Greece.)

Identification of Moral with Social Restraint

But Plato's doctrine involves more than this.   It implies not only that restraint is necessary for the development of a man's proper excellence, but that this restraint is identical with that imposed upon him by the requirements of political association.   If you would achieve the full virtue of man, that is to say, if you would develop your potentialities as a human being to the perfection for which Nature intended them, then submit them to regulation by law.   By what law?   By the law which binds you together with other members in a political association.

This is the part of Plato which is foreign to modern minds.[1]   Our moral notions are the product of a tradition of over two thousand years [2] which has inculcated the distinction between what is morally right and what is socially expedient.   The state, according to the classical theorists of modern times, exists to enforce the latter, but it is no part of its province to enforce the former.   It exists to make society possible, but not to make men good.

— and Consequently of Ruling with Education

But for Plato the rules which make society possible are identical with

---

[1] Though adherents of the *most* modern tendencies in contemporary politics may find it more congenial.

[2] A tradition of which, in virtue of another side of his doctrine, Plato himself is one of the principal sources.   See pp. 177 *et seq., infra.*

the rules which make men good. Nature has ordained man to be a social animal, and hence has brought it about that the restraints upon the individual's freedom which the requirements of society impose are the very restraints best calculated to develop his individual excellence as a man. Thus the task of the ruler, which is on the one hand to maintain the organization of society, is on the other hand to perfect the nature of the citizens; and the two tasks are not different, but are only two descriptions of the same. To rule is to educate, and education is nothing but the development of the subject into the virtues which his nature has made him capable of. Thus Plato says: "I should wish the citizens to be as readily persuaded to virtue as possible; this will surely be the aim of the legislator in all his laws." Again: "A man should endure all such trials [sc., outlawry and exile] rather than accept such a constitution as will make men worse. . . . Praise laws, therefore, or blame them according as they have this tendency or the reverse." [1] And he puts into the mouth of the dead Dion the following exhortation to the Syracusans, who are about to conclude a civil war by setting up a constitution: "First of all, O Syracusans, accept whatever laws seem to you not calculated to turn your thoughts and passions to the pursuit of profit and wealth. Men possess besides property also bodies and souls. Of these three pay the highest regard to the excellence [i.e., virtue] of the soul, then to the excellence of the body, which is subordinate to that of the soul. Let your regard for property come third and last, for property is subordinate both to the body and the soul." [2]

There is a danger lest, when we read such language, we should mistake it for platitude. We may be tempted to suppose that this is the kind of attitude which everyone would agree in prescribing for the rulers "in an ideal state," but that their aims must be lowered in view of the practical exigencies of the actual world. To suppose this would be to ignore the profound difference which separates Plato from modern philosophy upon this point. For Locke, for example, the virtue of the citizens is not something which even an ideal ruler ought to labor to promote. It is something which lies altogether outside the province of state regulation. The laws of the state, according to Locke, not must, but *ought* to be confined to regulating the property of the sub-

[1] LAWS, VI, 770.
[2] EPISTLES, VIII, 355.

jects; not because their property is more important than their virtue, but because their virtue is regulated by another set of laws.

This identification by Plato of moral with social restraint thus sets him at a wide remove from theories which have prevailed later. This is the pagan Plato. But it is important to guard against misunderstanding of his doctrine. It is misunderstood by most of those critics who accuse him of "idealizing" the state, or of "sacrificing the individual" to it. This accusation would be true only if Plato had taught (as some subsequent philosophers have done) that there was a "good" or an "interest" of the state which might diverge from that of its individual members, and that in cases of divergence the latter should be sacrificed to the former.[1] But Plato's theory is that there is no such divergence. Nature has established such a harmony between the individual and society (she has made him, as Aristotle said later, a "political animal") that his individual good is attained and not sacrificed by submission to the requirements of social life.

Nor must Plato be understood to mean that the laws and regulations imposed by any and every actual state necessarily conduce to the improvement of the individual subjects who are compelled to conform to them. It belongs, indeed, according to him, to the nature of the state to conduce to the individual good. In so far, therefore, as any state realizes its nature as a state, to that degree it must promote the good of its members. But any state may fall short to some degree of realizing its proper nature. There will be perversions and defective specimens among states, just as there are among plants and animals. It is the nature of a state to constitute a certain form of unity among its members. Any organization which can be called a state at all must achieve this unity to a certain degree, but many achieve it only to a very low degree, and it may be that all states fall short of realizing it in the highest degree. So far as any actual state falls short of attaining political unity, to that extent it may be allowed that it will cramp and not develop the virtues of its individual members. Plato's doctrine insists only that it will develop and not cramp them in the precise degree to which it achieves political unity, i.e., realizes its own nature as a state.

[1] There are a few passages in the REPUBLIC in which Plato implies this (Book IV, 419–421; Book V, 462), but they are exceptional.

The Nature of the State

It is important, therefore, for Plato to answer the question: What is the nature of a state? And he proceeds to answer it in the passages which follow. It should be observed that, although he follows a genetic method, and professes to trace the formation of the state from its origin, his purpose is not historical. He does not conceive himself to be describing the actual process by which any particular state was formed. To do this would not fulfill his purpose, because any particular state will fail to conform in some details to the nature of a state. Plato conceives himself to be defining the universal (and, as he would say, eternal) nature which every state possesses in some degree, and in a higher degree the more of a state it is.[1]

Its Origin

A state, I said, arises, as I conceive out of the needs of mankind; no one is self-sufficing, but all of us have many wants. Can any other origin of a state be imagined?

There can be no other.

Then, as we have many wants, and many persons are needed to supply them, one takes a helper for one purpose and another for another; and when these partners and helpers are gathered together in one habitation the body of inhabitants is termed a state.

True, he said.

And they exchange with one another, and one gives and another receives, each under the idea that the exchange will be for his own good.

Very true.

Then, I said, let us begin and create in idea a state. It originates, as it seems, in human necessity.

It must do so, he said.

Now the first and greatest of necessities is food, which is the condition of life and existence.

Certainly.

[1] REPUBLIC, II, 369–372.

🐦 The second is a dwelling, and the third clothing and the like.

True.

And now let us see how our city will be able to supply all these demands: We may suppose that one man is a farmer, another a builder, someone else a weaver — shall we add to them a shoemaker, or perhaps some other purveyor of our bodily wants?

Quite right.

The barest notion of a state might consist of four or five men?

Clearly.

And how will they proceed? Will each bring the result of his labours into a common stock?— the individual farmer, for example, producing for four, and labouring four times as long in the production of food in order to supply others as well as himself; or will he have nothing to do with others and not be at the trouble of producing for them, but provide for himself alone a fourth of the food in a fourth of the time, and in the remaining three fourths of his time be employed in making a house or a coat or a pair of shoes, having no partnership with others, but supplying himself all his own wants?

Adeimantus thought that he should aim at producing food only and not at producing everything.

It is certainly natural I replied that that should be the better way; for while you were speaking I was myself reminded that we are not all born alike; there are diversities of natures among us which are adapted to different occupations.

Very true.

And will you have a work better done when the workman has many occupations or when he has only one?

When he has only one.

Further there can be no doubt that a work is spoilt when not done at the right time?

No doubt.

For business is not disposed to wait until the doer of the business is at leisure; but the doer must order his time to suit his task, not his task to suit his time.

He must.

And if so, we must infer that all things are produced more plentifully and easily and of a better quality when one man does one thing which is natural to him, and does it at the right time, and leaves other things.

Undoubtedly.

Then more than four citizens will be required; for the farmer will not make his own plough or mattock, or other implements of agriculture, if they are to be good for anything. Neither will the builder make his tools — and he too needs many; and in like manner the weaver and shoemaker.

True.

Then carpenters and smiths, and many other artisans will be sharers in our little state, which is already beginning to grow?

True.

Yet even if we add neatherds, shepherds and other herdsmen, in order that our farmers may have oxen to plough with, and builders as well as farmers may have draught cattle, and curriers and weavers fleeces and hides — still our state will not be very large.

That is true, but neither will it be a very small state which contains all these.

Then again there is the situation of the city — to find a place where nothing need be imported is wellnigh impossible.

Impossible.

Then there must be another class of citizens who will bring the required supply from another city?

There must.

But if the trader goes empty-handed, having nothing which they require who would supply his need, he will come back empty-handed.

That is certain.

And therefore what they produce at home must be not only enough for themselves, but such both in quantity and quality as to accommodate those from whom their wants are supplied.

Very true.

Then more farmers and more artisans will be required?

They will.

Not to mention the importers and exporters, who are called merchants?

Yes.

Then we shall want merchants?

We shall.

And if merchandise is to be carried over the sea, skilful sailors will also be needed, and in considerable numbers.

Yes, in considerable numbers.

Then, again, within the city, how will they exchange their productions? For this was our object in forming the community and constituting a state.

Clearly they will buy and sell.

Then they will need a market-place and a money-token for purposes of exchange.

Certainly.

Suppose that a farmer or an artisan brings some production to market, and he comes at a time when there is no one to exchange with him — is he to leave his calling and sit idle in the market-place?

Not at all; he will find people there who, seeing the want, undertake the office of salesman. In well-ordered states they are commonly those who are weakest in bodily strength, and therefore of little use for any other purpose; their duty is to be in the market, and to give money in exchange for goods to those who desire to sell and to take money from those who desire to buy.

This want, then, creates a class of retail-traders in our state...

Yes, he said.

And there is another class of servants, who are not qualified to share in the society by their mental powers, but who have plenty of bodily strength for labour. This accordingly they sell, and are called, if I do not mistake, hired labourers, hire being the name which is given to the price of their labour.

True.

Then hired labourers will help to make up our population?

Yes.

And now, Adeimantus, is our city matured and perfect?

I think so.

Where then is justice, and where is injustice, and with what part of the state did they come in?

I cannot say, Socrates, unless they are to be found in the relations of mutual dependence by which these very persons are bound to one another.

Perhaps you are right in your suggestion, I said; we had better think the matter out and not shrink from the enquiry.

What Plato is investigating in this passage is the nature of political association. This is the central question of political philosophy. What makes a state? A number of individuals? But if I were to select from the telephone directories of the world all subscribers whose surnames begin with the letter L, these individuals would not constitute a state. It is clear that a state is composed of individuals, but of individuals related to one another by a peculiar bond. What is this bond? The bond of local or geographical proximity to one another? That is certainly not a sufficient answer, for if you were to take a pair of compasses and describe a circle at random upon the map of Europe, for example, the circular area marked off would include a collection of individuals related to one another by geographical proximity, but this collection would not form a state. Is the bond that of common race? No; for citizens of different states may be closely akin to one another, and descendants of the most diverse racial stocks may be fellow-members of the same state.

In the passage just quoted Plato has given his preliminary answer to the question: What is the bond uniting individuals in a state? It is the bond of mutual economic dependence which arises from the limited capacity of an individual to supply his own wants, together with the natural diversity in the capacities of individual men, which suits one individual to supply one want and another another.

If we were to take this for Plato's complete answer, we should have to draw two conclusions, the one about the nature of the state, and the other about the virtue of man. About the nature of the state we should have to say that it is, on Plato's view, a purely economic institution, brought into being solely by man's material needs, and constituted exclusively by the system of division of labor which is necessary in order to supply them.

We should have to draw a corresponding conclusion about the nature of human virtue, or at least about that part of human virtue which is denoted by the name of justice. It has already appeared that, upon Plato's view, justice is that quality in the individual which makes possible the association of individuals in states. If states are no more than economic organizations such as that which has been described, then the justice of man will be nothing but the disposition which makes him willing to concentrate his faculties upon the performance of a single specialized economic function. It will differ very little from the

instinct which impels the various classes in a community of ants to devote themselves each to its special task.   Indeed, an ant-heap would
provide a perfect exemplar of justice at work.

This is, of course, not Plato's final answer.   To Adeimantus' suggestion that justice and injustice "are to be found in the relations of
mutual dependence by which these very persons are bound to one
another," Socrates replies, "Perhaps you are right."   These words are
intended, according to Plato's literary usage, to indicate that the
answer is both inadequate and yet true so far as it goes.

It is true so far as it goes, for the system of want and supply, though
it does not exhaust the whole nature of the state, is at least the substructure upon which every state is based.   And an individual's devotion to his vocation, if not the whole of justice, is for Plato at least the
indispensable condition of his being just.

Notice the stress laid by Plato throughout the passage last quoted
upon the words "nature" and "natural."   The Sophists had appealed
to the most persuasive of all arguments in support of their contention
that the rules of morality possess no objective validity; to the argument, namely, that different peoples, brought up in different laws and
customs, recognize different and incompatible obligations.   If canni-
balism and human sacrifice are held in one society to be religious duties,
in another to be abominable impieties, how can the code of either claim
to be valid universally?   The Sophists expressed their conclusion by
saying that all rules of morality are "conventional," not "natural,"
since, if they were natural, they would be necessarily universal.   Plato
is showing that at least some laws (that, for example, of the division
of labor) are natural.   They spring from the very nature of human
society, and must therefore be present in all states.

The Introduction of Luxury and the Origin of War

There follows some further description of the simple life and plain
diet which will characterize such a community; and the description
evokes a protest from Glaucon: [1]

---

[1] REPUBLIC, II, 372–373.

Yes, Socrates, he said, and if you were providing for a city of pigs, [1] how else would you feed the beasts?

But what would you have, Glaucon? I replied.

Why, he said, you should give them the ordinary conveniences of life. People who are to be comfortable are accustomed to lie on sofas, and dine off tables, and they should have sauces and sweets in the modern style.

Yes, I said, now I understand: the question which you would have me consider is, not only how a state but how a luxurious state is created; and possibly there is no harm in this, for in such a state we shall be more likely to see how justice and injustice originate. In my opinion the true and healthy constitution of the state is the one which I have described. But if you wish also to see a state inflamed with fever, I have no objection. It appears, then, that many will not be satisfied with the simpler way of life. They will be for adding sofas, and tables and other furniture; also dainties and perfumes and incense, and courtesans, and cakes, and all these not of one sort only, but in every variety; we must go beyond the necessaries of which I was at first speaking, such as houses and clothes and shoes; the arts of the painter and the embroiderer will have to be set in motion, and gold and ivory and all sorts of materials must be procured.

True, he said.

Then we must enlarge our borders; for the original healthy state is no longer sufficient. Now will the city have to fill and swell with a multitude of callings which are not required by any necessary want; such as the whole tribe of hunters and that of imitators, of whom one large class have to do with forms and colours and another with music — poets and their attendant train of rhapsodists, players, dancers, contractors; also makers of divers kinds of articles, including women's dresses. And we shall want more servants. Will not tutors be also in request, and nurses, wet and dry, tire-women and barbers, as well as confectioners and cooks; and swine-herds, too, who were not needed and therefore had no place in the

[1] The word "pigs" conveys the wrong association to our ears. We regard the pig as a symbol of gluttony, but gluttony is certainly not a fault of the primitive community which Socrates had described. The defect which Glaucon wishes to indicate is that the simplicity of such a life verges on the merely animal; bovine, we should call it, rather than porcine.

former edition of our state, but are needed now?   They must not
be forgotten; and there will be animals of many other kinds, if
people eat them.

Certainly.

And living in this way we shall have much greater need of physicians than before?

Much greater.

And the country which was enough to support the original inhabitants will be too small now, and not enough?

Quite true.

Then a slice of our neighbours' land will be wanted by us for
pasture and tillage, and they will want a slice of ours, if, like ourselves, they exceed the limit of necessity, and give themselves up
to the unlimited accumulation of wealth?

That, Socrates, will be inevitable.

And so we shall go to war, Glaucon, shall we not?

Most certainly, he replied.

Then without determining as yet whether war does good or harm,
thus much we may affirm, that now we have discovered war to be
derived from causes [1] which are also the causes of almost all the
evils in states, private as well as public.

The multiplication of men's wants "beyond the necessary," with the
corresponding increase of the means of supplying them — this is the
process which many writers have seen as the essential process of civilization.[2]   For Plato it represents a disease of human society. He
does not deny the refinement of the tastes which luxury may introduce,
or of the arts which are called into being to satisfy them.   They include music and poetry and painting as well as confectionery and
dressmaking.   Phidias and Sophocles would be among the tribe of new
artists whom the growth of luxury calls into being.   But, Plato says,
this is not part of the state's proper development.   A further development is, indeed, necessary.   The primitive society, which Glaucon
characterized as the city of swine, is not the completed model of a

---

[1] *Sc.*, the feeding of desires beyond the necessary.

[2] *Cf.*, for example, Bertrand Russell: "What is called civilization may be defined
as the pursuit of objects not biologically necessary for survival." PROSPECTS OF
INDUSTRIAL CIVILIZATION (London: 1923), p. 39.

state. But it needs another completion than the mere multiplication and refinement of its wants.

What this completion is to be, will appear in the sequel. It will also appear that the stage of luxury, although in itself a lapse from the true development, is nevertheless necessary in order to evoke the true completion. The proper constitution of the state is called into being by the necessity of curing this "disease."

The latter part of the quotation contains Plato's theory of the origin of war. A state is driven to aggression by its failure to supply its own wants for itself. This failure springs from the breakdown of that system of economic self-sufficiency which constituted the "health" of the original state. Aggression by a state is an effect and a symptom of a disordered, not of a healthy, constitution. It springs from a defect of a state's proper excellence; just as an individual becomes aggressive to other individuals through defect of his proper excellence or virtue.

Plato gives the same name, "justice," to the virtue of a state and to that of an individual. But we must notice (although he does not) that, as he describes them, there is an important difference between them. The just individual abstains from injuring his fellows, but not because his justice renders him self-sufficient and therefore independent of them. On the contrary, his justice is the quality which enables him to take his place as a member within a larger system of mutually dependent units. But Plato never thinks of the state as a unit within a wider system. The justice of the state is the quality which makes it self-sufficient. The just state will indeed avoid injury to other states; but it will do so not by dealing justly with them, but by ceasing to deal with them at all.

Origin of the Class of Guardians

War, in which luxury involves the city, necessitates the introduction of another class:[1]

❧ Our state must once more enlarge; and this time the enlargement will be nothing short of a whole army, which will have to go out and

[1] REPUBLIC, II, 373–374.

fight with the invaders in defence of the wealth and security of the society which has just been described.

Why? he said; are they not capable of defending themselves?

No, I said; not if we were right in the principle which was acknowledged by all of us when we were framing the state; the principle, as you will remember, was that one man cannot practise many arts with success.

Very true, he said.

But is not war an art?

Certainly.

And an art deserving as much care as shoemaking?

By all means.

But the shoemaker was not allowed by us to be a farmer, or a weaver, or a builder — in order that we might have our shoes well made; but to him and to every other worker was assigned one work for which he was by nature fitted, and at that he was to continue working all his life long and at no other; he was not to let opportunities slip, and then he would become a good workman. Now nothing can be more important than that the work of a soldier should be well done. But is war an art so easily acquired that a man may be a soldier who is also a farmer, or shoemaker, or other artisan; although no one in the world would be a good dice or draught player who merely took up the game as a recreation, and had not from his earliest years devoted himself to this and nothing else? The implements of work or sport will not suddenly make a man a skilled workman or athlete, nor be of any use to him who has not learned how to handle them, and has never bestowed any attention upon them. How then will he who takes up a shield or other implement of war become a good fighter all in a day, whether with heavy-armed or any other kind of troops?

Yes, he said, the tools which would teach men their own use would be beyond price.

And the higher the duties of the guardian, I said, the more he will need skill, and art, and application, and leisure from other pursuits?

No doubt, he replied.

Natural Endowments Requisite in a Guardian

Socrates proceeds to argue that this craft of guardianship, like any other special craft, must be pursued by individuals specially qualified for it both by natural endowment and by training.

The natural endowments required are specified in the pages immediately following.[1] They are declared to be the same as those which characterize a good watchdog. The man who is to make a guardian must possess by nature the physical qualities of strength, speed, and sharp-sightedness, and the mental qualities of high spirit, which will make him fierce toward enemies, combined with a gentleness toward those whom it is his business to protect.

Education of Guardians

(a) Music

The training which these guardians will require to fit them for their task is discussed in a long passage immediately following.[2]

Socrates begins by asserting that the education best suited for this purpose is the traditional education of a Greek youth. "What shall their education be? Is it not hard to devise one better than that devised by time itself through a long experience? And that, you know, is gymnastic for the body and music for the soul."

Music, in Greek, is a word of wider significance than in English. It includes poetry, song, and dance. The poems of Homer were the most important single element in the "musical" education of a Greek boy. But, while assenting to the Greek tradition in principle, Plato wishes to reform it in practice. Homer and the other poets upon whom our "musical" training is at present based contain much that is calculated to pervert rather than to educate the young. Hence poetry must be submitted to a censorship designed to expunge everything unsuitable to its educational purpose. There must be expunged all passages which falsify the nature of the gods, by representing them either as

[1] REPUBLIC, II, 374–376.
[2] *Ibid.*, II, 376.

doers of evil or as liable to change; [1] all passages likely to impair the courage of the pupil, by representing death as something fearful; [2] all passages likely to induce intemperance, by painting the delights of indulgence. [3] Dramatic representation is to be sparingly employed, for a guardian is to be trained for the performance of one work, his own, and is not to be habituated to the adoption of a variety of characters. [4] The musical modes and rhythms admitted must be such as to develop in the pupils the characters of sobriety and simplicity. [5]

Plato's theory of "musical" education is summed up as follows: [6]

⁀ But there is no difficulty in seeing that grace or the absence of grace is an effect of good or bad rhythm.

None at all.

And also that good and bad rhythm naturally assimilate to a good and bad style; and that harmony and discord in like manner follow style; for our principle is that rhythm and harmony are regulated by the words, and not the words by them.

Just so, he said, they should follow the words.

And will not the words and the character of the style depend on the temper of the soul?

Yes.

And everything else on the style?

Yes.

Then beauty of style and harmony and grace and good rhythm depend on simplicity — I mean the true simplicity of a rightly and nobly ordered mind and character, not that other simplicity which is only a euphemism for folly?

Very true, he replied.

And if our youth are to do their work in life, must they not make these graces and harmonies their perpetual aim?

They must.

And surely the art of the painter and every other creative and

---

[1] REPUBLIC, II, 377–383.   [2] *Ibid.*, III, 386–388.
[3] *Ibid.*, III, 389–392.   [4] *Ibid.*, III, 392–398.
[5] *Ibid.*, III, 398–400. I need hardly say that the above is not intended as an adequate summary of the discussion, which occupies over twenty pages of Plato's text. I have given the barest minimum which is necessary to the understanding of what follows.
[6] *Ibid.*, III, 401–402.

constructive art are full of them — weaving, embroidery, architecture and every kind of manufacture; also nature, animal and
vegetable — in all of them there is grace or the absence of grace.
And ugliness and discord and inharmonious motion are nearly allied
to ill words and ill nature, as grace and harmony are the twin sisters
of goodness and virtue and bear their likeness.

That is quite true, he said.

But shall our superintendence go no further, and are the poets
alone to be required by us to express the image of the good in their
works, on pain, if they do anything else, of expulsion from our state?
Or is the same control to be extended to other artists, and are they
also to be forbidden to introduce what is evil in character, unre-
strained, mean and deformed into sculptures or buildings or anything else that they make; and is he who cannot conform to this
rule of ours to be prevented from practising his art in our state, lest
the taste of our citizens be corrupted by him?   We would not have
our guardians grow up amid images of deformity, as in some noxious
pasture, and there browse and feed upon many a baneful herb and
flower day by day, little by little, until they silently gather a fester-
ing mass of corruption in their own soul.   Let our artists rather be
those who are gifted to discern the true nature of the beautiful and
graceful; then will our youth dwell in a land of health, amid fair
sights and sounds, and receive good from everything; and beauty,
the effluence of fair works, shall flow into the eye and ear, like a
health-giving breeze from a purer region, and insensibly draw the
soul from earliest years into likeness and sympathy with the beauty
of reason.

There can be no nobler training than that, he said.

And therefore, I said, Glaucon, musical training is a more potent
instrument than any other, because rhythm and harmony find their
way into the inward places of the soul, on which they mightily
fasten, imparting grace, and making the soul of him who is rightly
educated graceful, or of him who is ill-educated ungraceful; and also
because he who has received this true education of the inner being
will most shrewdly perceive omissions or faults in art and nature,
and with a true taste, while he praises and rejoices over and receives
into his soul the good, and becomes noble and good, he will justly
blame and hate the bad, now in the days of his youth, even before

he is able to know the reason why; and when reason comes he will recognize and salute the friend with whom education has made him long familiar.

Yes, he said, I quite agree with you in thinking that our youth should be trained in music and on the grounds which you mention.

(b) Gymnastic

Gymnastic includes the whole education of the body, both in exercise and diet. Its primary object is to produce health in the body, as "musical" education is to produce temperance in the soul. It will do this if it exhibits a simplicity analogous to that demanded in "music."[1] Just as a proper education in music will make judges and law courts superfluous in the state, since the need of them only arises from intemperance in the citizens, so a proper education in gymnastic will put physicians out of employment.[2]

Plato ends by correcting an assumption which he had begun by accepting provisionally; viz., that gymnastic is to be directed exclusively to the training of the body, as music to that of the soul. This is to use gymnastic as athletes use it, whose training is directed solely to bodily strength. In reality the most important effect of gymnastic, as of music, is its effect upon the soul. Gymnastic hardens the character as well as the body, while "music" civilizes; thus both are necessary to develop that double nature, at once fierce and gentle, which a guardian must possess. To do this properly they must be blended in the right proportion; too much gymnastic makes a character too rough, as too much "music" makes it too soft.[3]

And as there are two principles of human nature, one the spirited and the other the philosophical, some God, as I should say, has given mankind two arts answering to them (and only indirectly to the soul and body), in order that these two principles (like the strings of an instrument) may be relaxed or drawn tighter until they are duly harmonized.

That appears to be the intention.

[1] REPUBLIC, III, 403–404.   [2] Ibid., III, 404–410.
[3] Ibid., III, 410–412.

And he who mingles music with gymnastic in the fairest proportions, and best attempers them to the soul, may be rightly called the true musician and harmonist in a far higher sense than the tuner of the strings.

This should suffice to expel a widespread misconception. Modern schemes for "physical culture" or "physical education" are often thought to be eminently Platonic by contrast with the rude sports and violent contests which were held to suffice for the bodily training of schoolboys a hundred years ago. No doubt there is some truth in the claim if we look solely to the attempt to substitute disciplined grace of action for untaught vigor. But in a far more important point the earlier system is more Platonic than the later. A defender of the older system, if he had been called upon to justify the educational value of sports for boys, might say that boys learned by them to take hard knocks without complaint, or to take defeat without sulking and victory without arrogance; or in general that such sports developed manliness of character. This is to adopt the Platonic principle, that the value of bodily exercise lies in its influence on the "soul." But the assumption that bodily fitness or physical grace is an end desirable in itself is not Platonic at all.[1]

Subdivision of the Guardian Class

Education necessarily requires an educator to direct it:[2]

 And such a presiding genius[3] will be always required in our state if the government is to last?
Yes, he will be absolutely necessary.
Such, then, are our principles of nurture and education. Where would be the use of going into further details about the dances of our citizens, or about their hunting and coursing, their gymnastic

[1] Cf. also REPUBLIC, IX, 591; quoted, p. 109, *infra.*
[2] REPUBLIC, III, 412–414.
[3] The reference is to the passage last quoted. Socrates means the man who has the knowledge to "mingle music with gymnastic in the fairest proportions and to attemper them to the soul."

and equestrian contests? For these all follow the general principle, and having found that, we shall have no difficulty in discovering them.

I dare say that there will be no difficulty.

Very good, I said; then what is the next question? Must we not ask who among them are to be rulers and who subjects?

Certainly.

There can be no doubt that the elder must rule the younger.

Clearly.

And that the best of them must rule?

That is also clear.

Now, the best among farmers are those who excel in the qualities of a farmer?

Since, then, these are to be the best among guardians, must they not be those who excel in guarding the state?

Yes.

And to this end they ought to be wise and efficient, and to have a special care of the state?

True.

And a man will be most likely to care about that which he loves?

To be sure.

And he will be most likely to love that which he regards as having the same interests with himself, and that of which the good or evil fortune is supposed by him at any time most to affect his own?

Very true, he replied.

Then there must be a selection. Let us note among the guardians those who in their whole life show the greatest eagerness to do what is for the good of their country, and the greatest repugnance to do what is against her interests.

Those are the right men.

And they will have to be watched at every stage, in order that we may see whether they preserve their resolution, and never, under the influence either of force or enchantment, forget or cast off their sense of duty to the state.

How cast off? he said.

I will explain to you, I replied. A resolution may go out of a man's mind either with his will or against his will; with his will when he gets rid of a falsehood and learns better, against his will whenever he is deprived of a truth.

I understand, he said, the willing loss of a resolution; the meaning of the unwilling I have got to learn.

Why, I said, do you not see that men are unwillingly deprived of good, and willingly of evil? Is not to have lost the truth an evil, and to possess the truth a good? And you would agree that to conceive things as they are is to possess the truth?

Yes, he replied; I agree with you in thinking that men are deprived of truth against their will.

And is not this involuntary deprivation caused either by theft, or force, or enchantment?

Still, he replied, I do not understand you.

I fear that I must have been talking darkly, like the tragedians. I only mean that some men are changed by persuasion and that others forget; argument steals away the hearts of one class, and time of the other; and this I call theft. Now you understand me?

Yes.

Those again who are forced, are those whom the violence of some pain or grief compels to change their opinion.

I understand, he said, and you are quite right.

And you would say with me that the enchanted are those who change their minds either under the softer influence of pleasure, or the sterner influence of fear?

Yes, he said; everything that deceives may be said to enchant.

Therefore, as I was just now saying, we must enquire who are the best guardians of their own conviction that what they think the interest of the state is to be the rule of their lives. We must watch them from their youth upwards, and make them perform actions in which they are most likely to forget or to be deceived, and he who remembers and is not deceived is to be selected, and he who fails in the trial is to be rejected. That will be the way?

Yes.

And there should also be toils and pains and conflicts prescribed for them, in which they will be made to give further proof of the same qualities?

Very right, he replied.

And then, I said, we must try them with enchantments — that is the third sort of test — and see what will be their behaviour: like those who take colts amid noise and tumult to see if they are of a timid nature, so must we take our youth amid terrors of some kind, and again pass them into pleasures, and prove them more thoroughly than gold is proved in the furnace, that we may discover whether they are armed against all enchantments, and of a noble bearing always, good guardians of themselves and of the music which they have learned, and retaining under all circumstances a rhythmical and harmonious nature, such as will be most serviceable to the individual and to the state.   And he who at every age, as boy and youth and in mature life, has come out of the trial victorious and pure, shall be appointed a ruler and guardian of the state; he shall be honoured in life and death, and shall receive sepulture and other memorials of honour, the greatest that we have to give.   But him who fails, we must reject.   I am inclined to think that this is the sort of way in which our rulers and guardians should be chosen and appointed.   I speak generally, and not with any pretension to exactness.

And, speaking generally, I agree with you, he said.

And perhaps the word "guardian" in the fullest sense ought to be applied to this higher class only, who preserve us against foreign enemies and maintain peace among our citizens at home, that the one may not have the will or the others the power, to harm us. The young men whom we before called guardians may be more properly designated auxiliaries and supporters of the principles of the rulers.

I agree with you, he said.

The Possession of Government is the Essential Characteristic of Political Society

It may seem that a disproportionate amount of attention has been devoted to the account of the guardians and their training.   But the space devoted to them is not out of proportion to their importance, for with the introduction of the class of guardians the state has been completed.   They supply an element essential to political society, which was lacking in the primitive city, and which the expansion of the "luxurious city" still failed to supply.

There are two things, in Plato's view, which a political society must possess, and which distinguish it from any other form of society. The first is the presence within the society of a ruling body (or, alternatively, of a ruling individual, for Plato thinks it a matter of secondary importance whether the rulers are one or many), whose special function it shall be to comprehend and to pursue the general interest of the whole. The "first city" constructed by Socrates in the *Republic* [1] (Glaucon's "city of pigs") was not a political society, because it lacked such a class. Each class in that city was devoted to the pursuit of a particular interest (the growing of corn, the construction of houses, the making of shoes, or whatever it might be). The good (indeed, the existence) of the society depended on the maintenance of an organization connecting these various pursuits with one another and preserving harmony and due proportion between them. If this organization was maintained in the "first city," it was maintained by nature and instinct, as a similar organization is maintained in animal and insect societies. Animals have societies, but not states, or political societies. The differentia of political society (which is the society proper to rational creatures) is the substitution for instinct of purposive control. This is achieved by the introduction of a class (the guardian class) whose special function it is to care for the organization of the whole.[2]

The second thing necessary is only the converse of the first. There must be a separate ruling class (or individual); but it must not be devoted to the pursuit of separate class (or individual) interests. If it becomes so, it defeats the end for which it came into being; and a great part of Plato's later regulations in the constitution of his state are designed to remove from the guardians the temptation of private interests which might seduce them from the single-minded pursuit of the public good.[3]

Now that the class of guardians has been introduced, Plato is in a position to sum up his theory of the state in the following passage: [4]

[1] See pp. 43–46, *supra*. [2] Cf. further on this point pp. 70 *et seq.*, *infra*.
[3] See pp. 77, 84, *infra*. [4] REPUBLIC, IV, 427–434 (with omissions).

Completed Constitution of the State

But where, amid all this, is justice? son of Ariston, tell me where. Now that our city has been constituted light a candle and search, and get your brother and Polemarchus and the rest of our friends to help, and let us see where in it we can discover justice and where injustice, and in what they differ from one another, and which of them the man who would be happy should have for his portion, whether seen or unseen by gods and men.

Nonsense, said Glaucon: did you not promise to search yourself, saying that for you not to help justice in her need would be an impiety?

I do not deny that I said so; and as you remind me, I will be as good as my word; but you must join.

We will, he replied.

Well, then, I hope to make the discovery in this way: I mean to begin with the assumption that our state, if rightly ordered, is perfect.

That is most certain.

And being perfect, is therefore wise and brave, temperate and just.[1]

That is likewise clear.

And whichever of these qualities we find in the state, the one which is not found will be the residue?

Very good.

If there were four things, and we were searching for one of them, wherever it might be, the one sought for might be known to us from the first, and there would be no further trouble; or we might know the other three first, and then the fourth would clearly be the one left.

Very true, he said.

And is not a similar method to be pursued about the virtues, which are also four in number?

Clearly.

---

[1] The four cardinal virtues. Plato is working on the assumption that, as a good man will be found to possess these four cardinal constituents of virtue, so a good state will be found to possess them also.

First among the virtues found in the state, wisdom comes into view, and in this I detect a certain peculiarity.

What is that?

The state which we have been describing is said to be wise as being good in counsel?

Very true.

And good counsel is clearly a kind of knowledge, for not by ignorance, but by knowledge, do men counsel well?

Clearly.

And the kinds of knowledge in a state are many and diverse?

Of course.

There is the knowledge of the carpenter; but is that the sort of knowledge which gives a city the title of wise and good in counsel?

Certainly not; that would only give a city the reputation of skill in carpentering.

Then a city is not to be called wise because possessing a knowledge which counsels for the best about wooden implements?

Certainly not.

Nor by reason of a knowledge which advises about brazen pots, he said, nor as possessing any other similar knowledge?

Not by reason of any of them, he said.

Nor yet by reason of a knowledge which cultivates the earth; that would give the city the name of agricultural?

Yes.

Well, I said, and is there any knowledge in our recently-founded state among any of the citizens which advises, not about any particular thing in the state, but about the whole,[1] and considers how a state can best deal with itself and with other states?

There certainly is.

And what is this knowledge, and among whom is it found? I asked.

It is the knowledge of the guardians, he replied, and is found among those whom we were just now describing as perfect guardians.

And what is the name which the city derives from the possession of this sort of knowledge?

The name of good in counsel and truly wise.

[1] For the significance of this phrase, see p. 61, *supra.*

And will there be in our city more of these true guardians or more smiths?

The smiths, he replied, will be far more numerous.

Will not the guardians be the smallest of all the classes who re· ceive a name from the profession of some kind of knowledge?

Much the smallest.

And so by reason of the smallest part or class, and of the knowl· edge which resides in this presiding and ruling part of itself, the whole state, being thus constituted according to nature, will be wise; and this, which has the only knowledge worthy to be called wisdom, has been ordained by nature to be of all classes the least.

Most true.

Thus, then, I said, the nature and place in the state of one of the four virtues has somehow or other been discovered.

And, in my humble opinion, very satisfactorily discovered, he replied.

Again, I said, there is no difficulty in seeing the nature of courage, and in what part that quality resides which gives the name of cou- rageous to the state.

How do you mean?

Why, I said, every one who calls any state courageous or cow- ardly, will be thinking of the part which fights and goes out to war on the state's behalf.

No one, he replied, would ever think of any other.

The rest of the citizens may be courageous or may be cowardly, but their courage or cowardice will not, as I conceive, have the effect of making the city either the one or the other.

Certainly not.

The city will be courageous in virtue of a portion of herself which preserves under all circumstances that opinion about the nature of things to be feared and not to be feared in which our legislator edu- cated them; and this is what you term courage.

I should like to hear what you are saying once more, for I do not think that I perfectly understand you.

I mean that courage is a kind of salvation.

Salvation of what?

Of the opinion respecting things to be feared, what they are and of what nature, which the law implants through education; and I mean by the words "under all circumstances" to intimate that in pleasure or in pain, or under the influence of desire or fear, a man preserves, and does not lose this opinion. Shall I give you an illustration?

If you please.

You know, I said, that dyers, when they want to dye wool for making the true sea-purple, begin by selecting their white colour first; this they prepare and dress with much care and pains, in order that the white ground may take the purple hue in full perfection. The dyeing then proceeds; and whatever is dyed in this manner becomes a fast colour, and no washing either with lyes or without them can take away the bloom. But, when the ground has not been duly prepared, you will have noticed how poor is the look either of purple or of any other colour.

Yes, he said; I know that they have a washed-out and ridiculous appearance.

Then now, I said, you will understand what our object was in selecting our soldiers, and educating them in music and gymnastic; we were contriving influences which would prepare them to take the dye of the laws in perfection, and the colour of their opinion about dangers and of every other opinion was to be indelibly fixed by their nurture and training, not to be washed away by such potent lyes as pleasure — mightier agent far in washing the soul than any soda or lye; or by sorrow, fear, and desire, the mightiest of all other solvents. And this sort of universal saving power of true opinion in conformity with law about real and false dangers I call and maintain to be courage, unless you disagree.

But I agree, he replied; for I suppose that you mean to exclude mere uninstructed courage, such as that of a wild beast or of a slave — this, in your opinion, is not the courage which the law ordains, and ought to have another name.

Most certainly.

Then I may infer courage to be such as you describe?

Why, yes, said I, you may, and if you add the words "of a citizen," you will not be far wrong; — hereafter, if you like, we will carry the examination further, but at present we are seeking not for courage but justice; and for the purpose of our enquiry we have said enough.

You are right, he replied.

Two virtues remain to be discovered in the state — first, temperance, and then justice which is the end of our search.

Very true.

Now, can we find justice without troubling ourselves about temperance?

I do not know how that can be accomplished, he said, nor do I desire that justice should be brought to light and temperance lost sight of; and therefore I wish that you would do me the favour of considering temperance first.

Certainly, I replied, I should not be justified in refusing your request.

Then consider, he said.

Yes, I replied; I will; and as far as I can at present see, the virtue of temperance has more of the nature of harmony and symphony than the preceding.

How so? he asked.

Temperance, I replied, is the ordering or controlling of certain pleasures and desires; this is curiously enough implied in the saying of "a man being his own master"; and other traces of the same notion may be found in language.

No doubt, he said.

There is something ridiculous in the expression "master of himself"; for the master is also the servant and the servant the master; and in all these modes of speaking the same person is denoted.

Certainly.

The meaning is, I believe, that in the human soul there is a better and also a worse principle; and when the better has the worse under control, then a man is said to be master of himself; and this is a term of praise: but when, owing to evil education or association, the better principle, which is also the smaller, is overwhelmed by the greater mass of the worse — in this case he is blamed and is called slave of himself and unprincipled.

Yes, there is reason in that.

And now, I said, look at our newly-created state, and there you will find one of these two conditions realized; for the state, as you will acknowledge, may be justly called master of itself, if the words "temperance" and "self-mastery" truly express the rule of the better part over the worse.

Yes, he said, I see that what you say is true.

Let me further note that the manifold and complex pleasures and desires and pains are generally found in children and women and servants, and in the freemen so called who are of the lowest and more numerous class.

Certainly, he said.

Whereas the simple and moderate desires which follow reason, and are under the guidance of mind and true opinion, are to be found only in a few, and those the best born and best educated.

Very true.

These too, as you may perceive, have a place in our state; and the meaner desires of the many are held down by the virtuous desires and wisdom of the few.

That I perceive, he said.

Then if there be any city which may be described as master of its own pleasures and desires, and master of itself, ours may claim such a designation?

Certainly, he replied.

It may also be called temperate, and for the same reason?

Yes.

And if there be any state in which rulers and subjects will be agreed as to the question who are to rule, that again will be our state?

Undoubtedly.

And the citizens being thus agreed among themselves, in which class will temperance be found — in the rulers or in the subjects?

In both, as I should imagine, he replied.

Do you observe that we were not far wrong in our guess that temperance was a sort of harmony?

Why so?

Why, because temperance is unlike courage and wisdom, each of which resides in a part only, the one making the state wise and the other brave; not so temperance, which extends to the whole, and runs through all the notes of the scale, and produces a harmony of the weaker and the stronger and the middle class, whether you suppose them to be stronger or weaker in wisdom or power or numbers or wealth, or anything else. Most truly then may we deem temperance to be the agreement of the naturally superior and inferior, as to the right to rule of either, both in states and individuals.

I entirely agree with you.

And so, I said, we may consider three out of the four virtues to have been discovered in our state. The last of those qualities which make a state virtuous must be justice, if we only knew what that was.

The inference is obvious.

The time then has arrived, Glaucon, when, like huntsmen, we should surround the cover, and look sharp that justice does not steal away, and pass out of sight and escape us; for beyond a doubt she is somewhere in this country: watch therefore and strive to catch a sight of her, and if you see her first, let me know.

Would that I could! but you should regard me rather as a follower who has just eyes enough to see what you show him — that is about as much as I am good for.

Offer up a prayer with me and follow.

I will, but you must show me the way.

Here is no path, I said, and the wood is dark and perplexing; still we must push on.

Let us push on.

Here I saw something: Hallo! I said, I begin to perceive a track, and I believe that the quarry will not escape.

Good news, he said.

Truly, I said, we are stupid fellows.

Why so?

Why, my good sir, at the beginning of our enquiry, ages ago, there was justice tumbling out at our feet, and we never saw her; nothing could be more ridiculous. Like people who go about looking for what they have in their hands — that was the way with us — we looked not at what we were seeking, but at what was far off in the distance; and therefore, I suppose, we missed her.

What do you mean?

I mean to say that in reality for a long time past we have been talking of justice, and have failed to recognize her.

I grow impatient at the length of your exordium.

Well then, tell me, I said, whether I am right or not: You remember the original principle which we laid down at the foundation of the state, that one man should always practise one thing only, the thing to which his nature was best adapted,[1] — now justice is this principle or a part of it.

Yes, we said that one man should do one thing only.   But we have often said, and often heard others say, that justice is doing one's own business, and not being a busybody.

Yes, we have said so.

Then to do one's own business in a certain way may be assumed to be justice.   Can you tell me whence I derive this inference?

I cannot, but I should like to be told.

Because I think that this is the only virtue which remains in the state when the other virtues of temperance and courage and wisdom are abstracted; and that this is the ultimate cause and condition of the existence of all of them, and while it remains, preserves them also; and we were saying that if the three were discovered by us, justice would be the fourth or remaining one.[2]

That follows of necessity.

.   .   .   .

Think, now, and say whether you agree with me or not.   Suppose a carpenter to be doing the business of a cobbler, or a cobbler of a carpenter; and suppose them to exchange their implements or their duties, or the same person to be doing the work of both, or whatever be the change; do you think that any great harm would result to the state?

Not much.

But when the cobbler or any other man whom nature designed to be a trader, having his heart lifted up by wealth or strength or the number of his followers, or any like advantage, attempts to force his way into the class of warriors, or a warrior into that of legislators and guardians, for which he is unfitted, and either to take the implements or the duties of the other; or when one man is trader, legislator, and

---

[1] See pp. 44–45, *supra.*

[2] The flimsiness of the "argument by residues," which Plato here employs, is apparent.   Plato sometimes supports a conclusion by "logical" arguments of this kind, which in fact do nothing to strengthen it, and can be easily refuted.   But to refute the argument is not to disprove the conclusion, and we may in this case discount the former without prejudice to the latter.

Two further arguments in support of the definition of justice are here omitted.

warrior all in one, then I think you will agree with me in saying that this interchange and this meddling of one with another is the ruin of the state.

Most true.

Seeing then, I said, that there are three distinct classes, any meddling of one with another, or the change of one into another, is the greatest harm to the state, and may be most justly termed evildoing?

Precisely.

And the greatest degree of evil-doing to one's own city would be termed by you injustice?

Certainly.

This then is injustice; and on the other hand when the trader, the auxiliary, and the guardian each do their own business, that is justice, and will make the city just.

I agree with you.

The Class-State

The main thing which differentiates this completed state from the elementary form of society which preceded the outbreak of "luxury" is, as has been seen,[1] the introduction of the two superior classes of the "auxiliaries" and the rulers proper. The completed city is the primitive city with these two classes superimposed upon it; for that economic organization of supply and exchange which formed the constitution of the entire original city must be held to be preserved in the completed city as the constitution of the third class within it.

What is the significance of this change? What new principle has been introduced with the introduction of the two guardian classes? Plato seems at times almost concerned to conceal the fact that any new principle has been introduced at all; he insists so strongly that the specialization of the functions of fighting and ruling in the hands of bodies of men exclusively devoted to these tasks is no more than an ordinary application of the principle of the division of labor, upon which both the primitive city and the luxurious city were founded. But his own doctrine shows this to be false, for he insists no less strongly that the typical

[1] P. 60, *supra.*

characteristic of the completed city is its *threefold* constitution, formed by the three classes of rulers, fighters, and producers, and he has declared with emphasis in the paragraph last quoted [1] that the distinction between the three classes is something different, more essential to the state, and more intimately connected with the true nature of justice, than the previous distinction between the various trades and crafts. An ordinary application of the principle of the division of labor could never have given rise to a threefold constitution of classes at all. Let us suppose for the sake of example that there were twelve or fifteen different trades or professions in the primitive city. The numbers will be greatly increased in the luxurious city, by the subdivision of old trades and the addition of new ones. Let us suppose that they finally reach the number of 117. Now let us suppose two new trades to be added, those of fighting and ruling. If these are special trades *in the same sense in which the others are*, the result of their addition will be simply that the city, which before was organized in 117 divisions, is organized now in 119. The addition of these two professions can give rise to a threefold organization in the city only upon one assumption, namely, that these two professions differ from one another and from all the others in some respect other than that in which the others differ among themselves. Only on such an assumption can Plato be justified in ranking all the other professions together in a single class by contrast with these two.

A closer inspection will show that there is a different principle underlying the specialization of these two classes from that which was applied in specializing the previous trades. The previous specialization depended upon the assumption that men differ in their capacities for various particular accomplishments. This specialization depends upon the assumption that men differ from one another in their capacity for attaining human virtue. The special qualification for membership of the second class is nothing more or less than capacity for the virtue of courage. The special qualification to be a ruler is possession of courage and of the virtue of wisdom in addition.[2]

The result of this is to introduce what did not exist before, not

[1] REPUBLIC, IV, 434; see pp. 69–70, *supra*.

[2] Plato thus refuses to apply to the virtues of wisdom and courage the principle which Protagoras had laid down (p. 34, *supra*) in respect of the virtues of justice and reverence: namely, that they should be shared by all men and not specialized like the arts.

merely a further division of labor, but a distinction of classes.   The word "class" as it is used by some modern political theorists seems full of obscurity.   Even the sense in which we use the word in ordinary language would not be easy to define.   But the sense in which a class distinction may be said to be implied in Plato's political philosophy (though the word is unknown to him) is simple and definite.   It is a distinction of men into ranks in the state according to their superiority or inferiority in respect of human virtue.   The carpenters, doctors, farmers are differentiated from one another by the variety of their several accomplishments, but the members of one profession are not necessarily better than those of the others.   What distinguishes the classes of guardians from all other members of the state is that they are better men.   Their function as members of the superior class is to rule the lower.   That state alone will be what a state should be in which this function is performed by the best men in it.   Thus emerges the distinctive Platonic theory, that the necessary and sufficient qualification for the function of government is superiority of virtue.[1]

In Plato's primitive city men are different, but equal.   In his completed state there is inequality of political status.   It may seem strange that Plato should regard the latter as the superior condition, but inspection may show that he was justified upon his own assumptions. The two higher classes are given means to develop forms of human virtue (political wisdom and civic courage) which were developed not by all, but by none, in the primitive city; and it is better that these should be realized by some than that they should not be realized at all. The members of the subject class themselves have not exchanged a condition of freedom for a condition of servitude; they have exchanged a state of subjection to nature for a state of subjection to wisdom. If we condemn the inequality of Plato's state, it is because we are tacitly comparing it, not with the equality of Plato's primitive state, but with the equality of a state in which all the citizens should realize equally the full human virtue which Plato reserves to a few. To set up such a state as an ideal superior to Plato's presupposes the assumption that all men are naturally equal in respect of their capacity

[1] Not only is a good man qualified by his mere virtue to rule; the exercise of rule will provide him with the proper scope for exercising his virtue.   Contrast the doctrine that "power corrupts those who wield it as much as those who are forced to obey it." BAKUNIN, quoted by I. BERLIN, KARL MARX (London: 1939), p. 205.

for virtue. It was one of Plato's profoundest convictions that this as‚ sum̧ tion is false. Nature, in his view, has made men not only different in respect of their capacities for various accomplishments, she has made them unequal in respect of their capacity for attaining virtue. This being so, it is clearly not only disastrous to the state to place the inferior man in a position for which Nature has not qualified him; it is disastrous also to the welfare of the inferior man, who can enjoy that degree of well-being of which he is capable only by being subjected to guidance by that wisdom in others which Nature has denied to himself.

This is expressed in a later passage of the *Republic*, which contains in a small compass the essence of Plato's doctrine on this point: [1]

The Benefit Which the Individual Subject Derives from the State

❧ And why are mechanical employments and manual arts a reproach? Only because they imply a natural weakness of the higher principle; [2] the individual is unable to rule the creatures within him, [3] but has to serve them, and his great study is how to flatter them.

Such appears to be the reason.

Therefore in order that even these men may be ruled by the same principle which rules in the best men, we say that they ought to be slaves of the best men, in whom the divine element [4] rules; not, as Thrasymachus supposed, to the injury of the slave, but because it is better for anyone to be ruled by knowledge, which is divine. If he has the source of knowledge within himself, that is best of all; but if he has not, it is better that it should rule him from without, in order that all men, being guided by the same principle, may be equals and friends as far as possible.

We shall perhaps estimate more justly the significance of Plato's treatment of the third class if we contrast the status of its members not exclusively with that of the citizens of a modern liberal state, but with

---

[1] REPUBLIC, IX, 590. [2] I.e., the principle of reason in the soul.

[3] I.e., the sensuous passions and appetites. The terms have reference to a simile which has preceded this passage in the REPUBLIC.

[4] *Sc.*, reason.

that of the productive classes in a historical Greek commonwealth. The productive labor in a Greek city was largely performed by sl ves. We shall do more justice to Plato if we think of his third class not as disenfranchised citizens but as emancipated slaves.

It is by no means implied in Plato's theory that the interests of this subject class are to be sacrificed to those of the state. We have quoted a passage [1] in which Plato says of his citizens, "What they think the interest of the state is to be the rule of their lives"; but it is necessary to remember that in this, and in similar passages which might be quoted, Plato is speaking of the ruling class, not of the ruled. The ruled are those whose interests the ruler is to consult (Plato undertook in *Republic*, I, to prove that the aim of the ruler is the good of the governed, as the aim of the doctor is the good of his patients). The good of the subjects and the good of the state are conceived by Plato to be entirely coincident aims. The ruler will necessarily achieve, or fail to achieve, the one in the degree in which he achieves, or fails to achieve, the other. By a bad (i.e., tyrannical) ruler the good of the subjects and the good of the state might be sacrificed together to his own selfish interest; but Plato never conceives that a situation could arise in which the interest of the subjects should conflict with the public interest of the state. He conceives the possibility of such a conflict only in the case of the ruler. In general it will not arise here either; for in general the ruler will realize his proper virtue and attain his proper happiness by performing his duties to the state. But Plato does contemplate the possibility of conflict, and in such cases he requires of the ruler a sacrifice which he never demands of the subject; namely, a sacrifice of his private happiness to the interest of the state. [2]

Class-State, Democracy and Communism

The primitive society of Plato's *Republic* is not a state. It is converted into a state by the development which converts it into the tripartite society which has just been described. The essential thing in this conversion has been the introduction of the function of government.

Plato believes that the exercise of this function must be confined to a special class, because he believes that Nature has confined the capacity of performing it to a few men. There are thus two distinguishable elements in Plato's theory: (1) that the function of government is essential to a state, and (2) that this function must be exercised exclusively by a special class of men within it.

The modern theory of democracy [1] repudiates the latter doctrine, but not the former. It accepts the Platonic doctrine of the state; but, basing itself upon the principle of the equality of men, claims for all citizens an equal right in exercising the function of government.

The Marxian theory repudiates the former part also of Plato's theory; or, to speak more accurately, while admitting that government is essential to a state, it denies that the state is what Plato assumed it to be, namely, the natural and eternal form of human society. It propounds as its ideal a society in which the state shall have "withered away." Before this ideal can be attained, a preliminary stage of the "Dictatorship of the Proletariat," must be gone through. In this stage the state still exists, only control of the function of government has passed from the previous rulers into the hands of the masses. But this stage is only a means to the realization of a form of society from which the state will have disappeared. The Marxian ideal, in other words, is the reversal of the process by which the Platonic state had developed from the primitive society, and the atrophy of the functions which the guardian-class was called into being to perform; whereas the democratic ideal is the wider distribution of these functions. The Marxian demands the expulsion of the guardians; the Democrat, that all citizens should be guardians.

The Ideal State and Real States

Before leaving Plato's account of the completed state, we may raise the question: Does Plato purport in all this to be giving the picture of an ideal or an analysis of the real? Is this intended to be an account of the way in which states ought to be constituted, or an account of what states in the real world actually are?

[1] I wish to emphasize that in what follows I am speaking of the theory of those states in the modern world which are called democracies in contrast with communist or totalitarian countries, and not of democracies in general, not, for example, of the democracies of ancient Greece.

The answer is: It is intended to be both.   It is important for an understanding of Plato to see how this can be so.

(1) It is the picture of an ideal.   In no state that has ever existed has there been a class of men wise enough to comprehend the public inter- est completely or unselfish enough to pursue it unreservedly.

(2) But, unless this ideal were to some degree realized in it, no state could exist at all.   As a matter of historical fact (we may imagine Plato to argue) men are found living in states, not in communities like those of ants or bees in which the organization of the community is out- side the control of any member of it.   In every state there always is a ruler, a government, a ruling class possessed of *some degree* of compre- hension of the organization as a whole, and exercising *some measure* of purposive control of it.   If this were entirely lacking, the society would disintegrate and cease to exist.   It might, no doubt, be replaced by a form of society without government.   But society without government is nowhere in fact actually to be found.   Society without government, Plato might claim, is the mere ideal, the ideal nowhere realized; the constitution of the *republic* is an ideal indeed, but an ideal realized *in some degree* wherever there is a state at all.

Nor, he might continue, is the unselfishness of the ruling class a mere ideal.   No doubt, perfect unselfishness, complete subordination of the particular to the general interest, are nowhere found.   But a ruling class pursuing its particular interests to the complete exclusion of the general interests is not found either in any actual state.   Complete and exclusive selfishness on the part of the rulers necessarily involves the disintegration of political society.   No doubt another form of society might take its place, such a society, for example, as is formed by a slave- holder and his slaves.   But this is not the form of society which is called a state, and societies called states do actually exist.

We said (as Plato himself said when he wrote Book IV of the *Repub- lic*) that the constitution of the state was now complete.   Nevertheless, two important points have been omitted; the one is the most strikingly novel, the other the most profoundly original, of all Plato's political doctrines.[1]

[1] REPUBLIC, III, 416–417, and V, 457–464 (with omissions).

Plato's Novelty. Community of the Guardians in Respect of Families and Property

And not only their education, but their habitations, and all that belongs to them, should be such as will neither impair their virtue as guardians, nor tempt them to prey upon the other citizens. Any man of sense must acknowledge that.

He must.

Then now let us consider what will be their way of life, if they are to realize our idea of them. In the first place, none of them should have any property of his own beyond what is absolutely necessary; neither should they have a private house or store closed against any one who has a mind to enter; their provisions should be only such as are required by trained warriors, who are men of temperance and courage; they should agree to receive from the citizens a fixed rate of pay, enough to meet the expenses of the year and no more; and they will go to mess and live together like soldiers in a camp. Gold and silver we will tell them that they have from God; the diviner metal is within them, and they have therefore no need of the dross which is current among men, and ought not to pollute the divine by any such earthly admixture; for that commoner metal has been the source of many unholy deeds, but their own is undefiled. And they alone of all the citizens may not touch or handle silver or gold, or be under the same roof with them, or wear them, or drink from them. And this will be their salvation, and they will be the saviours of the state. But should they ever acquire homes or lands or moneys of their own, they will become housekeepers and husbandmen instead of guardians, enemies and tyrants instead of allies of the other citizens; hating and being hated, plotting and being plotted against, they will pass their whole life in much greater terror of internal than of external enemies, and the hour of ruin, both to themselves and to the rest of the state, will be at hand. For all which reasons may we not say that thus shall our state be ordered, and that these shall be the regulations appointed by us for our guardians concerning their houses and all other matters?

Yes, said Glaucon.

. . . .

❧ The law, I said, which is the sequel of this and of all that has preceded, is to the following effect, — "that the wives of our guardians are to be common, and their children are to be common, and no parent is to know his own child, nor any child his parent."

Yes, he said, that is a much greater wave [1] than the other; and the possibility as well as the utility of such a law are far more questionable.

I do not think, I said, that there can be any dispute about the very great utility of having wives and children in common; the possibility is quite another matter, and will be very much disputed.

I think that a good many doubts may be raised about both.

You imply that the two questions must be combined, I replied. Now I meant that you should admit the utility; and in this way, as I thought, I should escape from one of them, and then there would remain only the possibility.

But that little attempt is detected, and therefore you will please to give a defence of both.

Well, I said, I submit to my fate. Yet grant me a little favour: let me feast my mind with the dream as day dreamers are in the habit of feasting themselves when they are walking alone; for before they have discovered any means of effecting their wishes — that is a matter which never troubles them and they would rather not tire themselves by thinking about possibilities — they assume that what they desire is already granted to them and proceed with their plan, and delight in detailing what they mean to do when their wish has come true — that is a way which they have of not doing much good to a capacity which was never good for much. Now I myself am beginning to lose heart, and I should like, with your permission, to pass over the question of possibility at present. Assuming therefore the possibility of the proposal, I shall now proceed to enquire how the rulers will carry out these arrangements, and I shall demonstrate that our plan, if executed, will be of the greatest benefit to the state and to the guardians. First of all, then, if you have no objection, I will endeavour with your help to consider the advantages of the measure; and hereafter the question of possibility.

I have no objection; proceed.

---

[1] Socrates has described the difficulties which his argument will have to face, under the image of successive "waves."

First, I think that if our rulers and their auxiliaries are to be worthy of the name which they bear, there must be willingness to obey in the one and the power of command in the other; the guardians must themselves obey the laws, and they must also imitate the spirit of them in any details which are entrusted to their care.

That is right, he said.

You, I said, who are their legislator, having selected the men, will now select the women and give them to them; — they must be as far as possible of like natures with them; and they must live in common houses and meet at common meals. None of them will have anything specially his or her own; they will be together, and will be brought up together, and will associate at gymnastic exercises. And so they will be drawn by a necessity of their natures to have intercourse with each other — necessity is not too strong a word, I think?

Yes, he said; not geometrical, but lovers' necessity, which is far more convincing and constraining to the mass of mankind.

True, I said; and this, Glaucon, like all the rest, must proceed after an orderly fashion; in a city of the blessed, licentiousness is an unholy thing which the rulers will forbid.

Yes, he said, and it ought not to be permitted.

Then clearly the next thing will be to make matrimony sacred in the highest degree, and what is most beneficial will be deemed sacred?

Exactly.

And how can marriages be made most beneficial?

[There follows a discussion of the measures by which the periodic matings of the guardians are to be regulated in order to ensure that the stock shall be maintained at the highest possible degree of purity and perfection.]

Such is the scheme, Glaucon, according to which the guardians of our state are to have their wives and families in common. And now you would have the argument show that this community is consistent with the rest of our polity, and also that nothing can be better — would you not?

Yes, certainly.

Shall we try to find a common basis by asking of ourselves what ought to be the chief aim of the legislator in making laws and in the organization of a state — what is the greatest good, and what is the greatest evil, and then consider whether our previous description has the stamp of the good or of the evil?

By all means.

Can there be any greater evil for a state than discord and distraction and plurality where unity ought to reign? or any greater good than the bond of unity?

There cannot.

And there is unity where there is community of pleasures and pains — where all the citizens are glad or grieved on the same occasions of joy and sorrow?

No doubt.

Yes; and where there is no common but only private feeling a state is disintegrated — when you have one part of the inhabitants triumphing and another plunged in grief at the same events happening to the city or the citizens?

Certainly.

Such differences originate when the terms "mine" and "not mine," "his" and "not his" are not applied identically by the citizens.

Exactly so.

And is not that the best-ordered state in which the greatest number of persons apply the terms "mine" and "not mine" in the same way to the same thing?

Quite true.

Or that again which most nearly approaches to the condition of the individual — as in the body, when but a finger of one of us is hurt, the whole frame, drawn towards the soul as a centre and forming one kingdom under the ruling power therein, feels the hurt and sympathizes all together with the part affected, and we say that the man has a pain in his finger.   And the same is true of any other part of the body, both concerning the pain felt when the part suffers, and the pleasure when it is at ease.

Very true, he replied; and I agree with you that in the best-ordered state there is the nearest approach to this common feeling which you describe.

Then when any one of the citizens experiences any good or evil, the whole state will make his case their own, and will either rejoice or sorrow with him?

Yes, he said, that is what will happen in a well-ordered state.

It will now be time, I said, for us to return to our state and see whether this or some other form is most in accordance with these fundamental principles.

Very good.

Our state like every other has rulers and subjects?

True.

All of whom will call one another citizens?

Of course.

But is there not another name which people give to their rulers in other states?

Generally they call them masters, but in democratic states they simply call them rulers.

And in our state what other name besides that of citizens do the people give the rulers?

They are called saviours and helpers, he replied.

And what do the rulers call the people?

The givers of their wage and maintenance.

And what do they call them in other states?

Slaves.

And what do the rulers call one another in other states?

Fellow-rulers.

And what in ours?

Fellow-guardians.

Did you ever know an example in any other state of a ruler who would speak of one of his colleagues as his friend and of another as not being his friend?

Yes, very often.

And the friend he regards and describes as one belonging to him, and the other as a stranger not belonging to him.

Exactly.

But would any of your guardians think or speak of any other guardian as a stranger?

Certainly he would not; for every one whom they meet will be regarded by them either as a brother or sister, or father or mother, or son or daughter, or as the child or parent of those who are thus connected with him.

Excellent, I said; but let me ask you once more: Shall they be a family in name only; or shall they in all their actions be true to the name? For example, in the use of the word "father," would the care of a father be implied and the filial reverence and duty and obedience to him which the law commands; and is the violator of these duties to be regarded as an impious and unrighteous person who is not likely to receive much good either at the hands of God or of man? Are these to be or not to be the strains which the children will hear repeated in their ears by all the citizens about those who are intimated to them to be their parents and the rest of their kinsfolk?

These, he said, and none other; for what can be more ridiculous than for them to utter the names of family ties with the lips only and not to act in the spirit of them?

Then in our city the language of harmony and concord will be more often heard than in any other. As I was describing before, when any one fares well or ill, the universal word will be "with mine it is well" or "it is ill."

Most true.

And did we not say that community of pleasure and pain was the natural accompaniment of this mode of thinking and speaking?

Yes, and so it is.

Then they will have a common interest in the same thing which they will alike call "my own," and having this common interest they will have a common feeling of pleasure and pain?

Yes, far more so than in other states.

And the reason of this, over and above the general constitution of the state, will be that the guardians will have a community of women and children?

That will be the chief reason.

And this unity of feeling we admitted to be the greatest good, as was implied in our own comparison of a well-ordered state to the relation of the body and the members, when affected by pleasure or pain?

That we acknowledged, and very rightly.

Then the community of wives and children among our auxiliaries is clearly the source of the greatest good to the state?

Certainly.

And this agrees with the other principle which we were affirming

— that the guardians were not to have houses or lands or any other private property; their pay was to be their keep, which they were to receive from the other citizens, and this they were to consume in common; for we intended them to preserve their true character of guardians.

Right, he replied.

Then both our previous regulations concerning their property, and our present regulations concerning their families, as I am saying, tend to make them more truly guardians; they will not tear the city in pieces by differing about "mine" and "not mine"; each man dragging any acquisition which he has made into a separate house of his own, where he has a separate wife and children and private pleasures and pains; but all will be affected as far as may be by the same pleasures and pains because they are all of one opinion about what is near and dear to them, and therefore they all tend towards a common end.

Since this theory is often referred to as "Plato's theory of communism," it is well to consider briefly to what extent it properly deserves that name. For this purpose it will be necessary to distinguish Plato's treatment of the family from his treatment of property.

(a) Family

In respect of wives and children Plato's is definitely a system of "communism," in the sense of common ownership. No guardian will be able to say of any wife or child, "She, or he, is mine"; but all guardians will be able to say of all wives and children, "They are ours."

Plato states that the object of this system is to promote the unity of the city by extending to its members that community of interest and sentiment which unites the members of a single family. Its direct result could be only to promote such unity among members of the governing class with one another, since there is no indication that the system of common families is to be extended to other classes in the state. But Plato believes that the only source from which disunity in the state can spring is disunity within the governing class. "If they are free from dissension, there is no fear of the rest of the city quarrelling either with them or with one another." [1] "Is it not a universal fact, that a change in any constitution originates in those who hold office when dissension arises actually within the governing power; while, so long as they are of one mind, however few they may be, the city cannot be changed?" [2] So far is Plato from holding the doctrine of the "Class war." [3]

(b) Property

But it is only to a very small extent that Plato recommends common ownership of property. Such small amount of property as consists of articles required for daily use is indeed to be retained by the guardians, and is to be owned by them in common. But all other property, all money and all land, that is to say, all capital, is not to be owned in common by the guardians, for it is not to be owned by them at all. It will be owned by members of the third class,[4] and will be owned by them individually, not in common. The common ownership of the means of production, which is the principle of modern communism, thus does not occur in Plato's thought at all.

Plato's guardians are not to own property in common, but to renounce it in common. This renunciation likewise supplies a bond of unity to the state, but a bond this time to unite the governing with the subject class. If the governors had property, they would have private economic interests of their own which might compete with those of their subjects. Remove these interests, and they can have no motive to use their power for any end except their subjects' welfare.

Plato's Originality: Philosophers to Rule

We have now to consider the most profoundly original doctrine of Plato's entire political theory, the doctrine that states should be gov-

[1] REPUBLIC, V, 465.   [2] Ibid., VIII, 545.

[3] I mean by this the doctrine which finds the original cause of revolutions and changes of constitution in the antagonism between classes. Whatever may be the truth in later periods of history, it seems that Plato's is the more accurate analysis of the historical causes of revolutions in the city-states of ancient Greece.

[4] This fact may remind us to avoid the natural, but disastrous, inclination to think of Plato's third class as a "proletariat." The third class includes capital as well as labor.

erned by philosophers.   We will first quote the passages in which Plato himself expounds the doctrine,[1] and others in which he elucidates his conception of a philosopher; and shall endeavor later to explain the significance of the doctrine.[2]

❧ Let me next endeavour to show what is that fault in states which is the cause of their present maladministration, and what is the least change which will enable a state to pass into the truer form; and let the change, if possible, be of one thing only, or, if not, of two; at any rate, let the changes be as few and slight as possible.

Certainly, he replied.

I think, I said, that there might be a reform of the state if only one change were made, which is not a slight or easy though still a possible one.

What is it? he said.

Now then, I said, I go to meet that which I liken to the greatest of the waves;[3] yet shall the word be spoken, even though the wave break and drown me in laughter and dishonour; and do you mark my words.

Proceed.

I said: Until philosophers[4] are kings, or the kings and princes of the world have the spirit and power of philosophy, and political greatness and wisdom meet in one, and those numerous natures who pursue either to the exclusion of the other are forcibly restrained from doing so, cities will never have rest from their evils, — no, nor the human race, as I believe, — and then only will this our state have a possibility of life and behold the light of day.   Such was the thought, my dear Glaucon, which I would fain have uttered if it had not seemed too extravagant; for to be convinced that in no other state can there be happiness private or public is indeed a hard thing.

There follows a description of the true philosopher, who is distin-

---

[1] REPUBLIC, V, 473, and VI, 497–501.
[2] See p. 99, *infra*.   [3] See p. 78, *supra*, note.
[4] The literal meaning of the word "philosopher" is "lover of wisdom, or knowledge."   Exactly what Plato understands by the term will not become clear until later.   But the reader should free his mind from preconceptions derived from its specialized modern usage.   Cf. p. 99, *infra*.

guished from those who falsely lay claim to the title. The general experience that philosophers are either noxious or useless is accounted for by the fact that no state, as states are now constituted, provides a soil in which the philosophic nature can flourish. The result is that some whom Nature intended for philosophers are corrupted, and that the few who resist corruption can do so only by isolating themselves from the influences of their society, and so rendering themselves useless to it.

True Nature of a Philosopher

The causes why philosophy is in such an evil name have now been sufficiently explained: the injustice of the charges against her has been shown — is there anything more which you wish to say?

Nothing more on that subject, he replied; but I should like to know which of the governments now existing is in your opinion the one adapted to her.

Not any of them, I said; and that is precisely the accusation which I bring against them — not one of them is worthy of the philosophic nature, and hence that nature is warped and estranged; — as the exotic seed which is sown in a foreign land becomes denaturalized, and is wont to be overpowered and to lose itself in the new soil, even so this growth of philosophy, instead of persisting, degenerates and receives another character. But if philosophy ever finds in the state that perfection which she herself is, then will be seen that she is in truth divine, and that all other things, whether natures of men or institutions, are but human; — and now I know that you are going to ask what that state is:

No, he said; there you are wrong, for I was going to ask another question — whether it is the state of which we are the founders and inventors,[1] or some other?

Yes, I replied, ours in most respects; but you may remember my saying before, that some living authority would always be required in the state having the same idea of the constitution which guided you when as legislator you were laying down the laws.

That was said, he replied.

[1] I.e., the state which has been constructed in the earlier portion of the REPUBLIC.

⁊❧ Yes, but not in a satisfactory manner; [1] you frightened us by inter-
posing objections, which certainly showed that the discussion would
be long and difficult; and what still remains is the reverse of easy.

What is there remaining?

The question how the study of philosophy may be so ordered as
not to be the ruin of the state. All great attempts are attended with
risk; "hard is the good," as men say.

Still, he said, let the point be cleared up, and the enquiry will then
be complete.

I shall not be hindered, I said, by any want of will, but, if at all,
by a want of power: my zeal you may see for yourselves; and please
to remark in what I am about to say how boldly and unhesitatingly
I declare that states should pursue philosophy, not as they do now,
but in a different spirit.

In what manner?

At present, I said, the students of philosophy are quite young;
beginning when they are hardly past childhood they embark on the
most difficult part of philosophy (I mean dialectic) in the time which
intervenes before they set up in business and housekeeping; thereafter even those of them who are reputed to have most of the philosophic spirit take themselves off. In after life when invited by some
one else, they may, perhaps, go and hear a lecture, and about this
they make much ado, for philosophy is not considered by them to
be their proper business: at last, when they grow old, in most cases
they are extinguished more truly than Heracleitus' sun, inasmuch
as they never light up again. [2]

But what ought to be their course?

Just the opposite. In childhood and youth their study, and what
philosophy they learn, should be suited to their tender years: during
this period while they are growing up towards manhood, the chief
and special care should be given to their bodies that they may have
them to use in the service of philosophy; as life advances and the

---

[1] Plato is referring back to the passage (REPUBLIC, III, 412; quoted on pp. 57 *et
seq.*, *supra*) in which he declared that it would be necessary to select from among
the guardians a smaller sub-class who should be the rulers in the strictest sense.
What was there omitted and is here supplied is the explanation that the essential
qualification of this select class is their possession of that power of scientific insight
which makes a man a philosopher.

[2] Heracleitus said that the sun was extinguished every evening and relighted every
morning. [Tr.]

intellect begins to mature, let them increase the gymnastics of the
soul; but when the strength of our citizens fails and is past civil and
military duties, then let them range at will and engage in no other
serious labour, as we intend them to live happily here, and to crown
this life with a similar happiness in another.

How truly in earnest you are, Socrates! he said; I am sure of that;
and yet most of your hearers, if I am not mistaken, are likely to be
still more earnest in their opposition to you, and will never be convinced; Thrasymachus least of all.

Do not make a quarrel, I said, between Thrasymachus and me,
who have recently become friends, although, indeed, we were never
enemies; for I shall go on striving to the utmost until I either con-
vert him and other men, or do something which may profit them
against the day when they live again, and hold the like discourse in
another state of existence.

You are speaking of a time which is not very near.

The interval, I replied, is as nothing in comparison with eternity.
Nevertheless, I do not wonder that the many refuse to believe; for
they have never seen that of which we are now speaking realized;
they have seen only a conventional imitation of philosophy, consisting of words artificially brought together, not like these of ours having a natural unity. But a human being who in word and work is
perfectly moulded, as far as he can be, into the proportion and likeness of virtue — such a man ruling in a city which bears the same
image, they have never yet seen, neither one nor many of them —
do you think that they ever did?

No, indeed.

No, my friend, and they have seldom, if ever, heard free and noble
sentiments; such as men utter when they are earnestly and by every
means in their power seeking after truth for the sake of knowledge,
while they look coldly on the subtleties of controversy, of which the
end is opinion and strife, whether they meet with them in the courts
of law or in society.

They are strangers, he said, to the words of which you
speak.

And this was what we foresaw, and this was the reason why truth
forced us to admit, not without fear and hesitation, that neither cities nor states nor individuals will ever attain perfection until the

small class of philosophers whom we termed useless but not corrupt are providentially compelled, whether they will or not, to take care of the state, and until a like necessity be laid on the state to obey them; or until kings, or if not kings, the sons of kings or princes, are divinely inspired with a true love of true philosophy. That either or both of these alternatives are impossible, I see no reason to affirm: if they were so, we might indeed be justly ridiculed as dreamers and visionaries. Am I not right?

Quite right.

If then, in the countless ages of the past, or at the present hour in some foreign clime which is far away and beyond our ken, the perfected philosopher is or has been or hereafter shall be compelled by a superior power to have the charge of the state, we are ready to assert to the death, that this our constitution has been, and is — yea, and will be whenever the Muse of Philosophy is queen. There is no impossibility in all this; that there is a difficulty, we acknowledge ourselves.

My opinion agrees with yours, he said.

But do you mean to say that this is not the opinion of the multitude?

I should imagine not, he replied.

O my friend, I said, do not attack the multitude: they will change their minds, if, not in an aggressive spirit, but gently and with the view of soothing them and removing their dislike of over-education, you show them your philosophers as they really are and describe as you were just now doing their character and profession, and then mankind will see that he of whom you are speaking is not such as they supposed — if they view him in this light, they will surely change their notion of him, and answer in another strain. Who can be at enmity with one who loves them, who that is himself gentle and free from envy will be jealous of one in whom there is no jealousy? Nay, let me answer for you, that in a few this harsh temper may be found but not in the majority of mankind.

I quite agree with you, he said.

And do you not also think, as I do, that the harsh feeling which the many entertain towards philosophy originates in the pretenders, who rush in uninvited, and are always abusing them, and finding fault with them, who make persons instead of things the theme of their conversation? and nothing can be more unbecoming in philosophers than this.

It is most unbecoming.

For he, Adeimantus, whose mind is fixed upon true being, has surely no time to look down upon the affairs of earth, or to be filled with malice and envy, contending against men; his eye is ever directed towards things fixed and immutable, which he sees neither injuring nor injured by one another, but all in order moving according to reason; these he imitates, and to these he will, as far as he can, conform himself. Can a man help imitating that with which he holds reverential converse?

Impossible.

And the philosopher, holding converse with the divine order, becomes orderly and divine, as far as the nature of man allows; but like everyone else, he will suffer from detraction.

Of course.

And if a necessity be laid upon him of fashioning, not only himself, but human nature generally, whether in states or individuals, into that which he beholds elsewhere, will he, think you, be an unskilful artificer of justice, temperance, and every civil virtue?

Anything but unskilful.

And if the world perceives that what we are saying about him is the truth, will they be angry with philosophy? Will they disbelieve us, when we tell them that no state can be happy which is not designed by artists who imitate the heavenly pattern?

They will not be angry if they understand, he said. But how will they draw out the plan of which you are speaking?

They will begin by taking the state and the manners of men, from which, as from a tablet, they will rub out the picture, and leave a clean surface. This is no easy task. But whether easy or not, herein will lie the difference between them and every other legislator, — they will have nothing to do either with individual or state, and will inscribe no laws, until they have either found, or themselves made, a clean surface.

They will be very right, he said.

Having effected this, they will proceed to trace an outline of the constitution?

No doubt.

And when they are filling in the work, as I conceive, they will often turn their eyes upwards and downwards: I mean that they will first look at absolute justice and beauty and temperance, and again at the human copy; and will mingle and temper the various elements of character into the image of true manhood, taking as their guide what Homer called "divine" and "godlike" in the characters of men.

Very true, he said.

And one feature they will erase, and another they will put in, until they have made the ways of men, as far as possible, agreeable to the ways of God?

Indeed, he said, in no way could they make a fairer picture.

And now, I said, we are beginning to persuade those whom you described as rushing at us with might and main, that the painter of constitutions is such an one as we were praising; at whom they were so very indignant because to his hands we committed the state; and are they growing a little calmer at what they have just heard?

Much calmer, if there is any sense in them.

Why, where can they still find any ground for objections? Will they doubt that the philosopher is a lover of truth and being?

They would not be so unreasonable.

Or that his nature, being such as we have delineated, is akin to the highest good?

Neither can they doubt this.

But again, will they tell us that such a nature, placed under favorable circumstances, will not be perfectly good and wise if any ever was? Or will they prefer those whom we have rejected?

Surely not.

Then will they still be angry at our saying, that, until philosophers bear rule, states and individuals will have no rest from evil, nor will this our imaginary state ever be realized?

I think that they will be less angry.

The following passage illustrates by an analogy the process of enlightenment or conversion by which, according to Plato's conception, a man becomes a philosopher: [1]

[1] REPUBLIC, VII, 514-521.

The Making of a Philosopher: Analogy of the Cave

❧ And now, I said, let me show in a figure how far our nature is enlightened or unenlightened; — Behold! human beings living in an underground cave, which has a mouth open towards the light and reaching all along the cave; here they have been from their child-hood, and have their legs and necks chained so that they cannot move, and can only see before them, being prevented by the chains from turning round their heads.   Above and behind them a fire is blazing at a distance, and between the fire and the prisoners there is a raised way; and you will see, if you look, a low wall built along the way, like the screen which marionette players have in front of them, over which they show the puppets.

I see.

And do you see, I said, men passing along the wall carrying all sorts of vessels, and statues and figures of animals made of wood and stone and various materials, which appear over the wall?   Some of them are talking, others silent.

You have shown me a strange image, and they are strange prisoners.

They are like ourselves, I replied.   In the first place, they see only their own shadows, or the shadows of one another, which the fire throws on the opposite wall of the cave?

True, he said; how could they see anything but the shadows if they were never allowed to move their heads?

And of the objects which are being carried in like manner they would only see the shadows?

Yes, he said.

And if they were able to converse with one another, would they not suppose that what they saw were the real objects them-selves?

Inevitably.

And suppose further that the prison had an echo which came from the other side, would they not be sure to fancy when one of the passers-by spoke that the voice which they heard came from the passing shadow?

No question, he replied.

To them, I said, the truth would be literally nothing but the shadows of the artificial objects.

That is certain.

And now look again, and see what will naturally follow if the prisoners are released and disabused of their error. At first, when any of them is liberated and compelled suddenly to stand up and turn his neck round and walk and look towards the light, he will suffer sharp pains; the glare will distress him, and he will be unable to see the realities of which in his former state he had seen the shadows; and then conceive some one saying to him, that what he saw before was an illusion, but that now, when he is approaching nearer to being and his eye is turned towards more real existence, he has a truer vision, — what will be his reply? And you may further imagine that his instructor is pointing to the objects as they pass and requiring him to name them, — will he not be perplexed? Will he not fancy that the shadows which he formerly saw are truer than the objects which are now shown to him?

Far truer.

And if he is compelled to look straight at the light, will he not have a pain in his eyes which will make him turn away to take refuge in the objects of vision which he can see, and which he will conceive to be in reality clearer than the things which are now being shown to him?

True, he said.

And suppose, once more, that he is reluctantly dragged up a steep and rugged ascent, and held fast until he is forced into the presence of the sun himself, is he not likely to be pained and irritated? When he approaches the light his eyes will be dazzled, and he will not be able to see anything at all of what are now called realities.

Not all in a moment, he said.

He will require to grow accustomed to the sight of the upper world. And first he will see the shadows best, next the reflections of men and other objects in the water, and then the objects themselves; then he will gaze upon the light of the moon and the stars and the spangled heaven; and he will see the sky and the stars by night better than the sun or the light of the sun by day?

Certainly.

Last of all he will be able to see the sun, and not mere reflections

✍of it in the water, but he will see it in its own proper place, and not in another; and he will contemplate it as it is.

Certainly.

He will then proceed to argue that it is the sun that gives the season and the years, and governs all that is in the visible world, and is in a certain way the cause of all the things which he and his fellows have been accustomed to behold?

Clearly, he said, he would first see the sun and then reason about it.

And when he remembered his old habitation, and the wisdom of the cave and his fellow-prisoners, do you not suppose that he would felicitate himself on the change, and pity them?

Certainly, he would.

And if they were in the habit of conferring honours among themselves on those who were quickest to observe the passing shadows and to remark which of them went before, and which followed after, and which were together; and who were therefore best able to draw conclusions as to the future, do you think that he would care for such honours and glories, or envy the possessors of them? Would he not say with Homer,

"Better to be the poor servant of a poor master," and to endure anything, rather than think as they do and live after their manner?

Yes, he said, I think that he would rather suffer anything than entertain these false notions and live in this miserable manner.

Imagine once more, I said, such an one coming suddenly out of the sun to be replaced in his old situation; would he not be certain to have his eyes full of darkness?

To be sure, he said.

And if there were a contest, and he had to compete in measuring the shadows with the prisoners who had never moved out of the cave, while his sight was still weak, and before his eyes had become steady (and the time which would be needed to acquire this new habit of sight might be very considerable), would he not be ridiculous? Men would say of him that he had gone up only to return with his eyesight ruined; and that it was better not even to think of ascending; and if any one tried to loose another and lead him up to the light, let them only catch the offender, and they would put him to death.

No question, he said.

This entire allegory, I said, you may now append, dear Glaucon, to the previous argument; the prison-house is the visible world, the light of the fire is the sun, and you will not misapprehend me if you interpret the journey upwards to be the ascent of the soul into the intellectual world according to my poor belief, which, at your desire, I have expressed — whether rightly or wrongly God knows. But, whether true or false, my opinion is that in the world of knowledge the idea of good appears last of all, and is seen only with an effort; and, when seen, is also inferred to be the universal author of all things beautiful and right, parent of light and of the lord of light [1] in this visible world, and the immediate source of reason and truth in the intellectual; and that this is the power upon which he who would act rationally either in public or private life must have his eye fixed.

I agree, he said, as far as I am able to understand you.

Moreover, I said, you must not wonder that those who attain to this beatific vision are unwilling to descend to human affairs; for their souls are ever hastening into the upper world where they desire to dwell; which desire of theirs is very natural, if our allegory may be trusted.

Yes, very natural.

And is there anything surprising in one who passes from divine contemplations to human ills, making ridiculous blunders; if, while his eyes are blinking and before he has become accustomed to the surrounding darkness, he is compelled to fight in courts of law, or in other places, about the images or the shadows of images of justice, and is endeavouring to meet the conceptions of those who have never yet seen absolute justice?

Anything but surprising, he replied.

Any one who has common sense will remember that the bewilderments of the eyes are of two kinds, and arise from two causes, either from coming out of the light or from going into the light, which is true of the mind's eye, quite as much as of the bodily eye; and he who remembers this when he sees any one whose vision is perplexed and weak, will not be too ready to laugh; he will first ask whether that soul of man has come out of the brighter life, and is unable to

[1] I.e., the sun.

to see because unaccustomed to the dark, or having turned from dark‹› ness to the day is dazzled by excess of light.   And he will count the one happy in his condition and state of being, and he will pity the other; or, if he have a mind to laugh at the soul which comes from below into the light, there will be more reason in this than in the laugh which greets him who returns from above out of the light into the cave.

That, he said, is a very just distinction.

But then, if I am right, certain professors of education must be wrong when they say that they can put a knowledge into the soul which was not there before, like sight into blind eyes.

They undoubtedly say this, he replied.

Whereas our argument shows that the power and capacity of learning exists in the soul already; and that just as the eye was unable to turn from darkness to light without the whole body, so too the instrument of knowledge can only by the movement of the whole soul be turned from the world of becoming into that of being,[1] and learn by degrees to endure the sight of being, and of the brightest and best of being, or in other words, of the good.

Very true.

And must there not be some art which will effect conversion in the easiest and quickest manner; not implanting the faculty of sight, for that exists already, but has been turned in the wrong direction, and is looking away from the truth?

Yes, he said, such an art may be presumed.

And whereas the other so-called virtues of the soul seem to be akin to the bodily excellencies, for they are not originally innate but are implanted later by habit and exercise, the virtue of wisdom belongs to a divine organ, which never loses its power, but becomes either useful and profitable or useless and hurtful according to the direction towards which it is turned, and by this conversion is rendered useful and profitable; or, on the other hand, hurtful and useless.   Did you never observe the narrow intelligence flashing from the keen eye of a clever rogue — how eager he is, how clearly his paltry soul sees the way to his end; he is the reverse of blind,

[1] The "world of becoming" is the mutable world of sensible things, the "world of being" the immutable world of intelligible "ideas," which it is the task of philosophy to discern.

but his keen eye-sight is forced into the service of evil, and he is mischievous in proportion to his cleverness?

Very true, he said.

But what if there had been a chiselling of such natures in the days of their youth; and they had been severed from those sensual pleasures, such as eating and drinking, which belong to the world of becoming, and which like leaden weights drag them down and turn the vision of their souls upon the things that are below — if, I say, they had been released from these impediments and turned in the opposite direction, the very same faculty in them would have seen the truth as keenly as they see what their eyes are turned to now.

Very likely.

Yes, I said; and there is another thing which is likely, or rather a necessary inference from what has preceded, that neither the uneducated and uninformed of the truth, nor yet those who never make an end of their education, will be able ministers of state; not the former, because they have no single aim in their life which shall be the rule of all their actions, private as well as public; nor the latter, because they will not act at all except upon compulsion, fancying that they are already dwelling apart in the islands of the blest.

Very true, he replied.

Then, I said, the business of us who are the founders of the state will be to compel the best minds to attain that knowledge which we have already shown to be the greatest of all — they must continue to ascend until they arrive at the good; but when they have ascended and seen enough we must not allow them to do as they do now.

What do you mean?

I mean that they remain in the upper world: but this must not be allowed; they must be made to descend again among the prisoners in the cave, and partake of their labours and honours, whether they are worth having or not.

But is not this unjust? he said; ought we to give them a worse life, when they might have a better?

You have again forgotten, my friend, I said, what is the purpose of law. It does not aim at making any one class in the state happy above the rest, but contrives the happiness of the state as a whole, holding the citizens together by persuasion and necessity, making them benefactors of the state, and therefore benefactors of one another. It is the law which produces such men in the state, not in order to set them free to follow their own inclinations, but to use them as its instruments in binding the state together.

True, he said, I had forgotten.

Observe, Glaucon, that there will be no injustice in compelling the philosophers who grow up in our state to have a care for the others and to guard them; we shall explain to them that in other states, men of their sort are not obliged to share in the toils of politics: and this is reasonable, for they grow up at their own sweet will, and the government would rather not have them. Being self-taught, they cannot be expected to show any gratitude for a culture which they have never received. But we have brought you into the world to be rulers of the hive, kings of yourselves and of the other citizens, and have educated you far better and more perfectly than they have been educated, and you are better able to share in the double duty. Wherefore each of you, when his turn comes, must go down to the general underground abode, and get the habit of seeing in the dark. When you have acquired the habit, you will see ten thousand times better than the inhabitants of the cave, and you will know what the several images are, and what they represent, because you have seen the beautiful and just and good in their truth. And thus our state, which is also yours, will be a reality, and not a dream only, and will be administered in a spirit unlike that of other states, in which men fight with one another about shadows only and are distracted in the struggle for power, which in their eyes is a great good. Whereas the truth is that the state in which the rulers are most reluctant to govern is always the best and most quietly governed, and the state in which they are most eager, the worst.

Quite true, he replied.

And will our pupils, when they hear this, refuse to take their turn at the toils of state, when they are allowed to spend the greater part of their time with one another in the heavenly light?

Impossible, he answered; for they are just men, and the commands which we impose upon them are just; there can be no doubt that every one of them will take office as a stern necessity, and not after the fashion of our present rulers of state.

Yes, my friend, I said; and there lies the point. You must contrive for your future rulers another and a better life than that of a ruler, and then you may have a well-ordered state; for only in the state which offers this, will they rule who are truly rich, not in silver and gold, but in virtue and wisdom, which are the true blessings of life. Whereas if they go to the administration of public affairs, poor and hungering after their own private advantage, thinking that hence they are to snatch the chief good, order there can never be; for they will be fighting about office, and the civil and domestic broils which thus arise will be the ruin of the rulers themselves and of the whole state.

Most true, he replied.

And the only life which looks down upon the life of political ambition is that of true philosophy. Do you know of any other?

Indeed, I do not, he said.

And those who govern ought not to be lovers of the task? For, if they are, there will be rival lovers, and they will fight.

No question.

Who then are those whom we shall compel to be guardians? Surely they will be the men who are wisest about affairs of state, and by whom the state is best administered, and who at the same time have other honours and another and a better life than that of politics?

To understand this doctrine of Plato's that the philosopher should rule, we must realize what Plato meant by a philosopher. He meant nothing so specialized as we mean by the term. When we speak of a philosopher, we generally have in mind the contrast between philosophy and science. But Plato does not mean to use the word in this narrow and exclusive sense. He means by "philosopher" a man possessed of the power of scientific thought, and it must be remembered that the very notion of *science* was new in the world when Plato wrote, and that Plato's work itself is the principal source from which both our notion of science and our science have been derived.

What is science? According to Plato, science is simply genuine knowledge, and I have genuine knowledge always and only when I can give a *proof* or produce a reason. If I cannot, I may still have the strongest possible belief, and what I believe may be in fact correct, but I do not know it, I have no science, and am no philosopher. Sup-

posing I have never studied geometry, I may still be perfectly certain
of many geometrical truths.   I may believe that any two sides of a
triangle are together greater than a third with a conviction so entire
that it has never occurred to me to doubt it.   I may act implicitly
upon this conviction when I have to choose the shortest route between
one corner and another of a triangular area.   But I do not *know* it
until I have comprehended the geometrical theorem in which it is
demonstrated.   When I do this, I have not merely a higher degree of
certainty; I have a different kind of certainty.   Those who have never
had a mathematical education go to their graves without knowing it in
this sense.   The proportion of such people has become smaller through
Plato's influence, for it is mainly through Plato that mathematics became, and has remained, an essential part of education.   But in
Plato's time mathematics itself was only in process of being born,
knowledge of it was confined to a few philosophers, and most people
in this as in all other matters were limited to the condition of belief.

It was the task of philosophy, according to Plato, not only in mathematics, but in every sphere, to substitute knowledge for belief.   Plato
is himself the first philosopher to give proofs, reasons, demonstrations,
arguments for his conclusions.   They are sometimes wire-drawn and
fallacious, but we shall pardon him the more readily for that when we
compare them with the systems of his predecessors.   They delivered
their systems in the form of dogma or of myth.   They may have been
works of great genius; they may have been true.   But they were believed, not known; asserted, not proved; systems of dogma, not of
science.

The laws and customs which regulate men's conduct in society are
dogmas for most of those who live under them.   They yield them an
unreasoning assent, and it may be an implicit obedience.   Here, as
elsewhere, it is the task of philosophy to substitute knowledge for belief, to discover the reasons for these rules and to approve or judge
them in the light of reason.   Nothing can illustrate the position more
clearly than a slight adaptation of a metaphor which Plato himself
employs in the passage from his dialogue, *The Statesman*, which I shall
quote immediately.[1]

Suppose a doctor, not an empiric who has learned by trial and error
that certain kinds of treatment have had beneficial results in certain

[1] P. 105, *infra*.

kinds of cases, but a scientific physician who understands the reasons which make some treatments beneficial and others the reverse; suppose that such a doctor is necessitated to go away on a long journey, leaving his patients behind him without an expert attendant to whom they can turn in his absence. He will provide for them in his absence by leaving them a code of rules for their observance in all the varying contingencies which he can foresee. The patients will believe in these rules and will apply them, and will no doubt generally benefit by doing so; that is to say, they will be better off with these rules to guide them than they would be without any guidance at all. But if the question is asked, whether they are better off under these rules than they would be under the personal charge of the physician himself, if he returned, there can be only one answer. In the first place, the rules are necessarily fallible by reason of their generality. No rule which can be expressed in the formula: "In such and such circumstances always take such and such measures" is ever right in one hundred per cent of cases. In ninety-nine per cent of cases it may be beneficial; but in the hundredth case, which no general rule can cover, it will be harmful. Whereas a science which is alive in the intelligence of a person does not suffer from this inflexibility of the general rule, it can be applied to the treatment of each individual case upon its merits. There is also a second, and still more important, advantage to be derived from the personal presence of the physician. The rules will require to be preserved against the dangers of oblivion and of insensible corruption in the course of time. If no physician is present, the task of preservation must be in the hands of men who do not understand the reasons of the rules which they are to preserve. But such men will necessarily be unable to distinguish what is essential in the rules from what is merely accidental, or the spirit from the letter. It is inevitable that after a sufficient lapse of time such guardians, however faithful, will be found tenaciously clinging to unimportant details of the formulae, while unconsciously distorting them in other respects from their original purpose. However well-devised the rules may have been at their original institution, no safeguard can preserve them in their integrity over a long period of time unless their preservation is committed to the charge of a man who understands the grounds for them.

Now, to apply the analogy: the citizens of an ordinary state are in a position like that of the patients of the absentee physician; the laws which they obey are like the rules which he left behind on his departure. No doubt they may be beneficial on the whole, and infinitely better than no laws. But to ask whether it would not be better that philosophers should be kings, is to ask whether it would not be better that there should be present in the state a man, or body of men, who understand the reasons which make them beneficial. The answer must be "yes" to such a question, on both of the two grounds mentioned in the analogy. Only a man possessed of such understanding can apply the true spirit of the law to the individual cases which the letter of it does not provide for; and only he can be trusted to preserve its essence unchanged through change of time and circumstance.

Notice the statement, toward the end of the passage quoted, that the philosophers in their period of withdrawal from the task of governing enjoy "a better life than that of the statesman." Life in the state is not, then, after all, the best and highest life for man. On the significance of this admission, which runs counter to much that Plato says elsewhere, some further comments are made below.[1]

The Philosopher is Above the Law

STRANGER.[2] Do you think that the multitude in a state can attain political science?

YOUNGER SOCRATES. Impossible.

STRANGER. But, perhaps, in a city of a thousand men, there would be a hundred, or say fifty, who could?

YOUNGER SOCRATES. In that case political science would certainly be the easiest of all sciences; there could not be found in a city of that number as many really first-rate draught-players, if judged by the standard of the rest of Hellas, and there would certainly not be as many kings. For kings we may truly call those who possess royal science, whether they rule or not, as was shown in the previous argument.

STRANGER. Thank you for reminding me; and the consequence

---

[1] Page 225.

[2] The following passage is taken from THE STATESMAN (Jowett's translations of Plato, third edition, 1892, pp. 292–297), a dialogue written later than the REPUBLIC. The persons in the dialogue are Socrates the Younger, and a stranger, who may be taken to represent the views of Plato himself.

is that any true form of government can only be supposed to be the government of one, two, or, at any rate, of a few.

YOUNGER SOCRATES. Certainly.

STRANGER. And these, whether they rule with the will, or against the will, of their subjects, with written laws or without written laws, and whether they are poor or rich, and whatever be the nature of their rule, must be supposed, according to our present view, to rule on some scientific principle; just as the physician, whether he cures us against our will or with our will, and whatever be his mode of treatment, — incision, burning, or the infliction of some other pain, — whether he practises out of a book or not out of a book, and whether he be rich or poor, whether he purges or reduces in some other way, or even fattens his patients, is a physician all the same, so long as he exercises authority over them according to rules of art, if he only does them good and heals and saves them. And this we lay down to be the only proper test of the art of medicine, or of any other art of command.

YOUNGER SOCRATES. Quite true.

STRANGER. Then that can be the only true form of government in which the governors are really found to possess science, and are not mere pretenders, whether they rule according to law or without law, over willing or unwilling subjects, and are rich or poor themselves — none of these things can with any propriety be included in the notion of the ruler.

YOUNGER SOCRATES. True.

STRANGER. And whether with a view to the public good they purge the State by killing some, or exiling some; whether they reduce the size of the body corporate by sending out from the hive swarms of citizens, or, by introducing persons from without, increase it; while they act according to the rules of wisdom and justice, and use their power with a view to the general security and improvement, the city over which they rule, and which has these characteristics, may be described as the only true State. All other governments are not genuine or real, but only imitations of this, and some of them are better and some of them are worse; the better are said to be well governed, but they are mere imitations like the others.

YOUNGER SOCRATES. I agree, Stranger, in the greater part of what you say; but as to their ruling without laws — the expression has a harsh sound.

STRANGER. You have been too quick for me, Socrates; I was just going to ask you whether you objected to any of my statements. And now I see that we shall have to consider this notion of there being good government without laws.

YOUNGER SOCRATES. Certainly.

STRANGER. There can be no doubt that legislation is in a manner the business of a king, and yet the best thing of all is not that the law should rule, but that a man should rule supposing him to have the wisdom of a king. Do you see why this is?

YOUNGER SOCRATES. Why?

STRANGER. Because the law does not perfectly comprehend what is noblest and most just for all and therefore cannot enforce what is best. The differences of men and actions, and the endless irregular movements of human things, do not admit of any universal and simple rule. And no art whatsoever can lay down a rule which will last for all time.

YOUNGER SOCRATES. Of course not.

STRANGER. But the law is always striving to make one; — like an obstinate and ignorant tyrant, who will not allow anything to be done contrary to his appointment, or any question to be asked — not even in sudden changes of circumstances, when something happens to be better than what he commanded for some one.

YOUNGER SOCRATES. Certainly; the law treats us all precisely in the manner which you describe.

STRANGER. A perfectly simple principle can never be applied to a state of things which is the reverse of simple.

YOUNGER SOCRATES. True.

STRANGER. Then if the law is not the perfection of right, why are we compelled to make laws at all? The reason of this has next to be investigated.

YOUNGER SOCRATES. Certainly.

STRANGER. Let me ask, whether you have not meetings for gymnastic contests in your city, such as there are in other cities, at which men compete in running, wrestling, and the like?

YOUNGER SOCRATES. Yes; they are very common among us.

STRANGER. And what are the rules which are enforced on their

20 pupils by professional trainers or by others having similar authority? Can you remember?

YOUNGER SOCRATES. To what do you refer?

STRANGER. The training-masters do not issue minute rules for individuals, or give every individual what is exactly suited to his constitution; they think that they ought to go more roughly to work, and to prescribe generally the regimen which will benefit the majority.

YOUNGER SOCRATES. Very true.

STRANGER. And therefore they assign equal amounts of exercise to them all; they send them forth together, and let them rest together from their running, wrestling, or whatever the form of bodily exercise may be.

YOUNGER SOCRATES. True.

STRANGER. And now observe that the legislator who has to preside over the herd, and to enforce justice in their dealings with one another, will not be able, in enacting for the general good, to provide exactly what is suitable for each particular case.

YOUNGER SOCRATES. He cannot be expected to do so.

STRANGER. He will lay down laws in a general form for the majority, roughly meeting the cases of individuals; and some of them he will deliver in writing, and others will be unwritten; and these last will be traditional customs of the country.

YOUNGER SOCRATES. He will be right.

STRANGER. Yes, quite right; for how can he sit at every man's side all through his life, prescribing for him the exact particulars of his duty? Who, Socrates, would be equal to such a task? No one who really had the royal science, if he had been able to do this, would have imposed upon himself the restriction of a written law.

YOUNGER SOCRATES. So I should infer from what has now been said.

STRANGER. Or rather, my good friend, from what is going to be said.

YOUNGER SOCRATES. And what is that?

STRANGER. Let us put to ourselves the case of a physician, or trainer, who is about to go into a far country, and is expecting to be a long time away from his patients — thinking that his instructions *will not be remembered unless they are written down, he will leave notes of them for the use of his pupils or patients.

YOUNGER SOCRATES. True.

STRANGER. But what would you say, if he came back sooner than he had intended, and, owing to an unexpected change of the winds or other celestial influences, something else happened to be better for them, — would he not venture to suggest this new remedy, al‧ though not contemplated in his former prescription? Would he persist in observing the original law, neither himself giving any new commandments, nor the patient daring to do otherwise than was prescribed, under the idea that this course only was healthy and medicinal, all others noxious and heterodox? Viewed in the light of science and true art, would not all such enactments be utterly ridiculous?

YOUNGER SOCRATES. Utterly.

STRANGER. And if he who gave laws, written or unwritten, determining what was good or bad, honourable or dishonourable, just or unjust, to the tribes of men who flock together in their several cities, and are governed in accordance with them; if, I say, the wise legislator were suddenly to come again, or another like to him, is he to be prohibited from changing them? — would not this prohibition be in reality quite as ridiculous as the other?

YOUNGER SOCRATES. Certainly.

STRANGER. Do you know a plausible saying of the common people which is in point?

YOUNGER SOCRATES. I do not recall what you mean at the moment.

STRANGER. They say that if any one knows how the ancient laws may be improved, he must first persuade his own State of the improvement, and then he may legislate, but not otherwise.

YOUNGER SOCRATES. And are they not right?

STRANGER. I dare say. But supposing that he fails to persuade, and uses violence to enforce the better, is this a kind of violence properly deserving the name? Or rather, before you answer, let me ask the same question in reference to our previous instances.

YOUNGER SOCRATES. What do you mean?

STRANGER. Suppose that a skilful physician has a patient, of whatever sex or age, whom he compels against his will to do some

⮞thing for his good which is contrary to the written rules; is this properly to be called a use of violence? Would you ever dream of calling it a violation of the art, or a breach of the laws of health? Nothing could be more unjust than for the patient to whom such violence is applied, to charge the physician who practises the violence with wanting skill or aggravating his disease.

YOUNGER SOCRATES. Most true.

STRANGER. In the political art error is not called disease, but evil, or vice, or injustice.

YOUNGER SOCRATES. Quite true.

STRANGER. And when the citizen, contrary to law and custom, is compelled to do what is juster and better and nobler than he did before, the last and most absurd thing which he could say about such violence is that he has incurred disgrace or evil or injustice at the hands of those who compelled him.

YOUNGER SOCRATES. Very true.

STRANGER. And shall we say that the violence, if exercised by a rich man, is just, and if by a poor man, unjust? May not any man, rich or poor, with or without laws, with the will of the citizens or against the will of the citizens, do what is for their interest? Is not this the true principle of government, according to which the wise and good man will order the affairs of his subjects? As the pilot, by watching continually over the interests of the ship and of the crew, — not by laying down rules, but by making his art a law, — preserves the lives of his fellow-sailors, even so, and in the self-same way, may there not be a true form of polity created by those who are able to govern in a similar spirit, and who show a strength of art which is superior to the law? Nor can wise rulers ever err while they observing the one great rule of distributing justice to the citizens with intelligence and skill, are able to preserve them, and, as far as may be, to make them better from being worse.

YOUNGER SOCRATES. No one can deny what has been now said.

STRANGER. Neither, if you consider, can any one deny the other statement.

YOUNGER SOCRATES. What was it?

STRANGER. We said that no great number of persons, whoever they may be, can attain political knowledge, or order a State wisely, but that the true government is to be found in a small body, or in an individual.

The wealth of doctrine packed into this passage makes adequate comment impossible here.   One conclusion which emerges from it is that no law can have any authority which it does not derive from reason.   In this respect laws are like the general rules and prescriptions which the absentee doctor leaves behind him.   These rules possess authority for the patients because they are supposed to be justified by reasons which the doctor can see, although the patient himself cannot.   But suppose that at any time it should appear in respect of any such rule that this supposition is false, and that the reasons supposed do not sufficiently justify it.   It will lose immediately all claim to the submission of the subject.   For him to continue to obey it in the absence of such reasons, would be the sign only of an irrational and slavish superstition.   It would be similarly superstitious to respect the authority of a law on any ground for which no reason can be given. Only a philosopher, of course, is capable of discerning the reasons of laws, and only he therefore has the right of judging whether any law is rationally justified or not.   But he has the right of calling any law to the bar of reason, and of refusing his allegiance to it if it cannot prove its claim.

Plato was not a revolutionary, but this is the germ of a doctrine which has inspired revolutions since Plato's time.   It is easy to discern its identity, for example, with the doctrine of the sovereignty of reason, which was propounded by the philosophers of the French "Enlightenment," and which led them to refuse assent to any law resting upon mere authority, whether of church or king or historical tradition.   To point out an identity is not of course to deny a difference, but it would be too great a task to try to trace the differences between the two doctrines, derived from the two thousand years which intervened between them.

Nevertheless, one important difference may be mentioned, which may perhaps account for the revolutionary effect of the doctrine in its modern form.   Plato believed that the capacity to achieve scientific insight into the principles according to which men ought to be governed was confined by nature to very few;[1] the modern rationalist philosophers believed that it was shared equally by all.

[1] See p. 102, *supra*.

The Philosopher in a Corrupt State has Access to a Rule of Conduct Independent of the Law of His State

The Philosopher, we have been told, has the insight needed in order to mould states as they ought to be. We are now told that, even though he be denied the opportunity of reforming his state, the same insight will at least serve to provide him with a standard for the ordering of his own conduct.[1]

꙳ From what point of view, then, and on what ground can we say that a man is profited by injustice or intemperance or other baseness, which will make him a worse man, even though he acquire money or power by his wickedness?

From no point of view at all.

What shall he profit, if his injustice be undetected and unpunished? He who is undetected only gets worse, whereas he who is detected and punished has the brutal part of his nature silenced and humanized; the gentler element in him is liberated, and his whole soul is perfected and ennobled by the acquirement of justice and temperance and wisdom, more than the body ever is by receiving gifts of beauty, strength, and health, in proportion as the soul is more honourable than the body.

Certainly, he said.

To this nobler purpose the man of understanding will devote the energies of his life. And in the first place, he will honour studies which impress these qualities on his soul, and will disregard others?

Clearly, he said.

In the next place, he will regulate his bodily habit and training, and so far will he be from yielding to brutal and irrational pleasures, that he will regard even health as quite a secondary matter; his first object will be not that he may be fair or strong or well, unless he is likely thereby to gain temperance, but he will always desire so to attemper the body as to preserve the harmony of the soul?

Certainly he will, if he has true music in him.

And in the acquisition of wealth there is a principle of order and harmony which he will also observe; he will not allow himself to be

[1] REPUBLIC, IX, 591–592.

dazzled by the foolish applause of the world, and heap up riches to his own infinite harm?

Certainly not, he said.

He will look at the city which is within him,[1] and take heed that no disorder occur in it, such as might arise within from superfluity or want; and upon this principle he will regulate his property and gain or spend according to his means.

Very true.

And for the same reason, he will gladly accept and enjoy such honours as he deems likely to make him a better man, but those, whether public or private, which are likely to disorder his life, he will avoid.

Then, if that is his motive, he will not take part in public affairs.

By the dog of Egypt, he will! in the city which is his own he certainly will, though in the land of his birth perhaps not, unless by some divine chance.

I understand; you mean that he will be a ruler in the City of which we are the founders,[2] and which exists in idea only; for I do not believe that there is such an one anywhere on earth?

In heaven, I replied, there is laid up a pattern of it, methinks, which he who desires may behold, and beholding, may give a right constitution to his own soul. But whether such a one exists, or ever will exist in fact, is no matter; for he will live after the manner of that city and of no other.

I think so, he said.

There is a danger lest the importance of the latter part of this passage may be ignored, because it sounds so like a platitude. But it sounds platitudinous only because it is familiar. To comprehend it truly, we must see it with Plato's eyes, as something new, important, and revolutionary.

Consider the position from which Plato starts. Men live in states, and each state has its own "Nomos." This Greek word is translated "Law," but it means both law and custom without distinction. The Nomos of his state provides for each man a standard of what he ought to do, which is independent of what he wants to do. Without such a

---

[1] I.e., the constitution of his soul.
[2] I.e., the ideal city, sketched in the REPUBLIC.

standard, there could be no distinction between what a man wants and what he ought to do. There would be no motive for any action except that he wanted at the time to do it, and, although there might be conflict of desire with desire, there could be no such thing as moral conflict, which is the opposition between what is wanted and what ought to be done. The Nomos of the city prescribes to men a standard of conduct which involves a restraint of their appetites and impulses, by calling upon them to do what they do not want to do. It becomes an effective motive in determining their actions by the instruments of punishment and reward, honor and disgrace; but, above all, by education. The process of education consists in imbuing the young citizen with the spirit of the Nomos, so that he imposes its standard upon his own actions, and no longer requires to be restrained by force or urged on by reward.[1] Hence arise moral distinctions. An act is good or bad as it conforms or not to the Nomos, and a man acquires virtue in proportion as his soul is informed by its spirit.

It would be a mistake to criticize this as a humdrum notion of morality, as though it made virtue consist in the passive acceptance of a set of rules. The Nomos may well set a standard only to be approached by arduous effort and only to be attained by an heroic virtue. Leonidas and the other heroes of Greek history were not doing more than fulfilling the Nomos of their states.

But the Nomos of his state is the only standard of right conduct which a man possesses, and this standard itself will be a better or a worse one according as the state is healthy or corrupt. Thus a man may lack virtue from either of two causes. He may fail to live up to the Nomos of his state, and for this he will be culpable. Or he may be born into an inferior state, of which the Nomos itself is defective or corrupt. He will then be fated to fall short of virtue, and his case will admit neither of blame nor of remedy. Thus the possibility of a man's attaining virtue depends on the fulfillment of conditions which are not in his power, and no man born in a bad state can be held responsible for not being good.

The Greek world, on the whole, acquiesced in this conclusion. They believed that the constitutions of states were given them by superhuman beings, or by lawgivers divinely inspired, and hence that a good Nomos was, in the literal sense, a gift of the gods, and not in

[1] He is, in one of the senses which that phrase can bear, a law to himself.

human power to secure; and they accepted the consequence that a man's chance of acquiring virtue was dependent on the luck of his birth.[1] Plato's originality appears at the point at which he reacts against this view. The power of reason, he declares ("the Philosopher" is the figure in which he embodies this conception), enables a man to control his destiny and puts into his own power the conditions necessary for the attainment of virtue.

It can do this in either of two ways: (1) The philosopher can attain to knowledge which will enable him to plan good constitutions upon rational principles. Thus mankind need no longer wait upon the caprice of divine benefaction in order to ensure to themselves conditions in which the attainment of virtue will be possible. It is only necessary that philosophers should be placed in the positions of power, and a good city can be constructed according to reason.[2]

But the difficulty presents itself: What likelihood is there that this union of knowledge with power will ever be achieved? The science of the philosopher which qualifies him to use power is of no use at all in helping him to attain it. It has appeared that the formation of constitutions can be transferred from chance to reason, granted the prior condition that philosophers become kings; but the fulfillment of this prior condition depends itself upon chance. Hence Plato is driven to surrender the contention that his ideal state is capable of realization — "unless by chance or by some divine inspiration."

(2) But in a sense Plato may be said to snatch his greatest victory out of the ruins of this defeat. In the passage last quoted [3] he has admitted that the philosopher's ability to construct a state in reality will in all human probability remain ineffective; *but*, he continues, the idea of the state, although unrealized, will serve him as a standard by which to guide his private conduct, however bad may be the state in which he is actually born. "Whether such an one exists, or ever will exist in fact, is no matter; for he will live after the manner of that city and of no other." If this is true, then the philosopher, at least, is no longer dependent for his standard upon the Nomos of the state in

---

[1] Cf. the story related of Themistocles. A man from Seriphos (an insignificant island in the Aegean) declared that he deserved no praise for the great things which he had done, since he would never have achieved that greatness if he had been born in Seriphos. Themistocles replied: "I would not have achieved it if I had been born in Seriphos; but you would not have achieved it if you had been born in Athens."

[2] See pp. 84 *et seq.*, *supra*.   [3] Pp. 109 *et seq.*, *supra*.

which he is born. He need not wait for the foundalion of good states in order to secure to himself the conditions of a good life. He has a standard of which no historical accident can deprive him; and in consequence a responsibility from which no historical accident can absolve him.

It is probable that in the subsequent history of western civilization the latter doctrine has been even of more importance than the former. Until very recent times the classical theory and the normal practice of the western world have been based on the assumption that all men have that freedom and that responsibility which Plato discovered in the person of the Philosopher.

For Further Reading

Translations

There is a translation of the complete works, with the exception of the *Letters*, by Benjamin Jowett (third edition; Oxford: Clarendon Press, 1925, 5 vols.). This is the translation used in the present book and is probably the best for an English reader. A. D. Lindsay's translation of the *Republic* (New York: E. P. Dutton and Company, 1908; now also published in Everyman's Library) is more accurate, but less fluent.

Works of Plato which are of most importance for his political theory are the following dialogues: *Crito, Republic, Statesman* (from 291 to the end), and *Laws* (but this last work is too long to be recommended). See also Letters 7 and 8 (translated by L. A. Post in *Thirteen Epistles of Plato* [Oxford: Oxford University Press, 1925]). R. W. Livingston's *Plato: Portrait of Socrates* (Oxford: Clarendon Press, 1938) contains Jowett's translations of the following dialogues: *Apology, Crito*, and *Phaedo*, with introduction and notes for the English reader.

Commentaries and General Works

Barker, Ernest, greek political theory; plato and his predecessors. New York: The Macmillan Company, 1919.
Crossman, R. H. S., plato today. New York: Oxford University Press, 1939.
   A first-rate popular work, which occasionally distorts Plato by interpreting him in the light of contemporary political controversies.

GROTE, GEORGE, PLATO AND THE OTHER COMPANIONS OF SOCRATES. London: Murray, 1867. 4 vols. Especially vol. III, chaps. 33 and 34.

> *Rather old, but a work of considerable force. It contains a vigorous criticism of Plato's doctrines from the point of view of a nineteenth-century individualist and utilitarian.*

JOSEPH, HORACE W. B., ESSAYS IN ANCIENT AND MODERN PHILOSOPHY, chaps. I–V. New York: Oxford University Press, 1935.

> *Acute and ingenious studies in the* REPUBLIC: *sometimes too ingenious, and more difficult than Plato, but very valuable to a reader who is willing to chew his* REPUBLIC.

NETTLESHIP, R. L., LECTURES ON THE REPUBLIC OF PLATO (LORD CHARNWOOD, editor). New York: The Macmillan Company, 1936.

NETTLESHIP, R. L., THEORY OF EDUCATION IN PLATO'S REPUBLIC. With an introduction by SPENCER LEESON. New York: Oxford University Press, 1935.

PATER, WALTER, PLATO AND PLATONISM.

> *Several editions.*

TAYLOR, ALFRED E., PLATO: THE MAN AND HIS WORK. New York: Dial Press, 1927.

Social and Political Background

See note at end of next chapter.

CHAPTER THREE

Aristotle

LIFE OF ARISTOTLE

ARISTOTLE was born at Stagira, a Greek colony on the Macedonian coast, in the year 384 B.C., and lived there until his eighteenth year. In 367 he migrated to Athens in order to study philosophy under Plato. Plato was at that time absent on his second visit to Syracuse,[1] but on his return Aristotle became his pupil, and remained a member of the Academy for nearly twenty years.

In 347 Plato died, leaving the direction of the Academy in the hands of his nephew, Speusippus. Aristotle then departed from Athens, and took up his abode with Hermeias, the despot of the town of Atarneus in Asia Minor, who had been his pupil formerly in Athens. Three years later, Hermeias was treacherously killed. Aristotle fled to Mitylene, in the island of Lesbos, taking with him Pythias, the sister or niece of Hermeias, whom he married.

Two years later, in 342 B.C., Aristotle was invited by Philip, king of Macedonia, to undertake the education of his son Alexander, later called "the Great," who was then thirteen years old. When Alexander set out on his expedition to Asia in 334, Aristotle departed from Macedonia and returned to Athens. He opened a school of philosophy called, from the name of a temple in its vicinity, "the Lyceum." He had been head of this for twelve years when, in 322, the anti-Macedonian party came into power in Athens, and, among other measures, prepared to bring an accusation of impiety against him. He fled from Athens, and died in the same year at Chalcis in Euboea.

The greatness of Aristotle is exhibited not in his life, but in his writings. He was a master in almost every department of knowledge, except mathematics. His works cover the spheres of theology, metaphysics, ethics, economics, politics, aesthetics, and physics; they com-

---

[1] See p. 24, *supra.*

prise studies of every department of the natural world. He founded the science of logic, and thus fixed the meaning of the terms which we still employ for the conduct of almost any piece of abstract thinking.[1] There is probably no parallel in the history of mankind either to the vastness of his intellectual achievement or to the extent of its subsequent influence.

In his early period at the Academy Aristotle wrote dialogues on the Platonic model, of which only fragments have been preserved. But the main body of his work is composed in the form of treatises, put together without pretensions to literary style or literary arrangement, and intended primarily to serve as a basis of instruction, a kind of lecture notes, in the activity of teaching in which he was engaged without interruption throughout his life.

I have prefixed a brief account of Aristotle's life, but his biography throws, on the whole, singularly little light upon the understanding of his thought. This is not to say that his thought underwent no development; but its development seems to have been unaffected either by vicissitudes of his personal experience or by historical events in the contemporary world. Aristotle was a pure theorist, as Plato never was. This statement does not mean that his thought was detached from historical influences. He might have thought himself that it was so, but to the backward gaze of the historian he appears as the most Greek of all Greek thinkers, and the essential spirit of Greece finds its completest philosophical expression in his works. But the spirit which he expresses (at least in his political works) is that of the classical age of Greece, which was past before he was born. He is unaffected by the movements of his own time, and detached from contemporary happenings. His lifetime coincided with the period in which the Greek cities lost their independence. The author of this change was Philip, king of Macedon, who succeeded to the throne in 360, and after twenty-two years of aggression, encroachment and intrigue, overcame the last resistance of the Greeks at the battle of Chaeronea in 338. Philip then prepared to execute his great design of leading the united forces of Greece against the Persian Empire, which extended from India to the Mediterranean coasts of Asia Minor. He was as-

[1] Essence, substance, accident, subject and predicate, category, genus and general, species and special, universal and particular, are all technical terms of the Aristotelian logic. Most of them have found their way into English through Latin translations of the Greek words.

sassinated in 336, but his design was executed by his son Alexander the Great, who had conquered half the known world when he died in 323 at the age of 32.   His successors divided his empire, and his death marks the beginning of what is called the "Hellenistic Age," in which the unit of political organization was no longer the city-state, but the empire.   In spite of his close connection with the kings of Macedon, Aristotle shows no awareness of the importance of the revolution which they brought about.   He writes the political philosophy of the city-state as though it were eternal, instead of being a phenomenon peculiar to an age which had already passed away.

There is, nevertheless, one fact in Aristotle's life which is of great importance for the understanding of his philosophy; namely, the fact that for nearly twenty years of his life, from the age of seventeen to that of thirty-six, he was a member of Plato's Academy.   The influence of this long and intimate relationship upon the formation of Aristotle's thought can hardly be overestimated.   He is permeated by Platonism to a degree in which perhaps no great philosopher besides him has been permeated by the thought of another.   This does not mean, of course, that Aristotle agreed with every doctrine of Plato.   On the contrary, his disagreements with Plato are both violent and notorious, and they have sometimes misled subsequent generations [1] (as they probably misled Aristotle himself) into overlooking their far more fundamental agreement.

POLITICAL PHILOSOPHY

In political philosophy two striking points of difference are that Aristotle criticizes Plato's most novel doctrine [2] and rejects his most original one.[3]   His criticism of Plato's argument for "communism" in respect of families and property is contained in his *Politics*, Book II, chapters 1–5; this difference is of smaller importance than the other, and may almost be called a difference on a point of detail.   It is more

---

[1] Cf. the often-repeated saying that men are born either Aristotelians or Platonists — as though these two philosophies represented opposite poles of thought.   Similarly, the adherents of Roman Catholic and of Protestant Christianity have regarded one another as opposite extremes, but become conscious of their affinities with each other when both are faced with systems of belief which are not Christian at all.

[2] See pp. 77 *et seq., supra.*   [3] See pp. 84 *et seq., supra.*

important that Aristotle rejects the principle of Plato's claim that philosophers should be kings. He does not reject his discovery of the nature of scientific knowledge, nor his belief that the pursuit of such knowledge is the proper task of the philosopher; but he introduces a distinction, which had been unknown to Plato, between the theoretical and the practical exercise of reason. Scientific knowledge is possible only of what is necessary and universal. Necessity and universality are found in the realm of nature, which is, therefore, the proper object of theoretical knowledge; but they are not found in the realm of human affairs, which is the field of practical activity. Hence the scientific knowledge which is the peculiar possession of the philosopher gives him an ever profounder comprehension of the principles of the natural universe, but no especial understanding of the principles which should govern men's conduct. Thus, it does not specially qualify its owner to be a ruler.

To know in any individual situation what is the right thing to be done, and hence to be able to direct and rule the conduct of others for the best: this is a matter not of science, but of *judgment*.[1] It is not to be acquired by study, but rather by moral discipline, practice, and experience. It is a faculty like that by which a man of educated taste can judge individual works of art. If he is a good judge, he is likely to be right; but his judgment is not a matter of science, it cannot be demonstrated by necessary reasoning. Nor could he have acquired this faculty of judgment by a theoretical study of artistic principles, but only by a long acquaintance with actual works of art. The prime qualification for a statesman, therefore, is not philosophy, but practical wisdom.

Aristotle's own treatise on *Politics* is a work of just such practical reason. It is a handbook for the statesman, containing the wisdom distilled, as it were, from the collective political experience of the Greek states. Hegel says of Plato's *Republic* that it does no more than represent the theory implicit in the practical morality and political life of Greece. This saying is by no means wholly true of Plato, for it ignores the new element which Plato introduced; namely, the Platonic doctrine of the sovereignty of reason. But it is very nearly true

---

[1] Strictly speaking it should be said "this is a matter not of science in Plato's sense of the word," for Aristotle does not deny the term "practical science" to such exercise of judgment.

if applied to the *Politics* of Aristotle. This book is, if a single book can be, the classical representation of Greek political thought. There is a passage, even in Aristotle, in which a new and revolutionary doctrine intrudes itself, but it is not actually in the *Politics*.[1]

The Nature of the State [2]

Every state is a community of some kind, and every community is established with a view to some good; for mankind always act in order to obtain that which they think good. But, if all communities aim at some good, the state or political community, which is the highest of all, and which embraces all the rest, aims at good in a greater degree than any other, and at the highest good.

Some people think that the qualifications of a statesman, king, householder, and master are the same, and that they differ, not in kind, but only in the number of their subjects. For example, the ruler over a few is called a master; over more, the manager of a household; over a still larger number, a statesman or king, as if there were no difference between a great household and a small state. The distinction which is made between the king and the statesman is as follows: When the government is personal, the ruler is a king; when, according to the rules of the political science, the citizens rule and are ruled in turn, then he is called a statesman.

But all this is a mistake; for governments differ in kind, as will be evident to any one who considers the matter according to the method which has hitherto guided us. As in other departments of science, so in politics, the compound should always be resolved into the simple elements or least parts of the whole. We must therefore look at the elements of which the state is composed, in order that we may see in what the different kinds of rule differ from one another, and whether any scientific result can be attained about each one of them.

He who thus considers things in their first growth and origin, whether a state or anything else, will obtain the clearest view of them. In the first place there must be a union of those who cannot exist without each other; namely, of male and female, that the race

[1] See p. 173, *infra*.   [2] POLITICS, Book I, chaps. 1-2.

may continue (and this is a union which is formed, not of deliberate purpose, but because, in common with other animals and with plants, mankind have a natural desire to leave behind them an image of themselves), and of natural ruler and subject, that both may be preserved. For that which can foresee by the exercise of mind is by nature intended to be lord and master, and that which can with its body give effect to such foresight is a subject, and by nature a slave; hence master and slave have the same interest. Now, nature has distinguished between the female and the slave. For she is not niggardly, like the smith who fashions the Delphian knife for many uses; she makes each thing for a single use, and every instrument is best made when intended for one and not for many uses. But among barbarians [1] no distinction is made between women and slaves, because there is no natural ruler among them: they are a community of slaves, male and female. Wherefore the poets say, —

"It is meet that Hellenes should rule over barbarians";

as if they thought that the barbarian and the slave were by nature one.

Out of these two relationships between man and woman, master and slave, the first thing to arise is the family, and Hesiod is right when he says, —

"First house and wife and an ox for the plough,"

for the ox is the poor man's slave. The family is the association established by nature for the supply of men's everyday wants, and the members of it are called by Charondas "companions of the cupboard," and by Epimenides the Cretan, "companions of the manger." But when several families are united, and the association aims at something more than the supply of daily needs, the first society to be formed is the village. And the most natural form of the village appears to be that of a colony from the family, composed of the children and grandchildren, who are said to be "suckled with the same milk." And this is the reason why Hellenic states were originally governed by kings; because the Hellenes were under royal rule before they came together, as the barbarians still are. Every family is ruled by the eldest, and therefore in the colonies of the family the

[1] The Greeks described all non-Greek peoples by this term.

kingly form of government prevailed because they were of the same blood. As Homer says:

"Each one gives law to his children and to his wives."

For they lived dispersedly, as was the manner in ancient times. Wherefore men say that the Gods have a king, because they themselves either are or were in ancient times under the rule of a king. For they imagine, not only the forms of the Gods, but their ways of life to be like their own.

When several villages are united in a single complete community, large enough to be nearly or quite self-sufficing, the state comes into existence, originating in the bare needs of life, and continuing in existence for the sake of a good life. And therefore, if the earlier forms of society are natural, so is the state, for it is the end of them, and the nature of a thing is its end. For what each thing is when fully developed, we call its nature, whether we are speaking of a man, a horse, or a family. Besides, the final cause and end of a thing is the best, and to be self-sufficing is the end and the best.

Hence it is evident that the state is a creation of nature, and that man is by nature a political animal. And he who by nature and not by mere accident is without a state, is either a bad man or above humanity; he is like the

"Tribeless, lawless, hearthless one,"

whom Homer denounces — the natural outcast is forthwith a lover of war; he may be compared to an isolated piece at draughts.

Now, that man is more of a political animal than bees or any other gregarious animals is evident. Nature, as we often say, makes nothing in vain, and man is the only animal whom she has endowed with the gift of speech. And whereas mere voice is but an indication of pleasure or pain, and is therefore found in other animals (for their nature attains to the perception of pleasure and pain and the intimation of them to one another, and no further), the power of speech is intended to set forth the expedient and inexpedient, and therefore likewise the just and the unjust. And it is a characteristic of man that he alone has any sense of good and evil, of just and unjust, and the like, and the association of living beings who have this sense makes a family and a state.

Further, the state is by nature clearly prior to the family and to the individual, since the whole is of necessity prior to the part; for example, if the whole body be destroyed, there will be no foot or hand, except in an equivocal sense, as we might speak of a stone hand; for when destroyed the hand will be no better than that. But things are defined by their working and power; and we ought not to say that they are the same when they no longer have their proper quality, but only that they have the same name. The proof that the state is a creation of nature and prior to the individual is that the individual, when isolated, is not self-sufficing; and therefore he is like a part in relation to the whole. But he who is unable to live in society, or who has no need because he is sufficient for himself, must be either a beast or a god: he is no part of a state. A social instinct is implanted in all men by nature, and yet he who first founded the state was the greatest of benefactors. For man, when perfected, is the best of animals, but, when separated from law and justice, he is the worst of all; since armed injustice is the more dangerous, and he is equipped at birth with arms, meant to be used by intelligence and virtue, which he may use for the worst ends. Wherefore, if he have not virtue, he is the most unholy and the most savage of animals, and the most full of lust and gluttony. But justice is the bond of men in states, for the administration of justice, which is the determination of what is just, is the principle of order in political society.

"Hence it is evident that the state is a creation of nature, and that man is by nature a political animal." Aristotle's starting-point is the same as Plato's; he begins by attempting to refute the Sophistic doctrine [1] that the institutions of political society are the product of "convention," not of "nature." This meant that submission to the laws of the state was something cramping to the individual's natural development. He might submit to the curb through fear of punishment or hope of reward, or, more commonly, through an unreflective acquiescence in the traditions in which he had grown up. But, once he reflected, it must become clear to him that there was no *reason* why he should submit. The only reason which could govern the acts of a rational being is the reason that such and such an act is for his own good. If it appears that submission to laws is directly inimical to his

[1] Cf. pp. 35 *et seq., supra.*

own good, such a reflection dissolves at once the power of the traditional beliefs that he ought to do such and such actions and refrain from such and such others. Such traditions have power only so long as they are unquestioned. He will have no motive any longer for doing what the law prescribes and for refraining from what it forbids, unless he is subject to some force superior to his own which is able to deter him by the threat of penalties or induce him by the promise of rewards Thus the effect of the Sophistic doctrine was to strip the law of the state of all moral authority. It may still be prudent to obey it, if there exists a power which makes obedience worth while; but obedience in itself is an evil, and no clear-headed man would choose it except under promise of compensation, either in the form of a reward or of avoidance of a greater evil.

In opposition to a doctrine such as that just outlined, Aristotle, like Plato, seeks to re-establish the moral authority of political laws. He wishes to show that the belief in which the orthodox good citizen lives, that he ought to obey the laws even in cases where he has no reward to hope for and no punishment to fear — that this belief is not dispelled but confirmed by rational reflection. Rational reflection could confirm it only by showing that such obedience is for the agent's own good; for Aristotle fully believes that there can be for a rational creature no moral obligation except that of promoting his own good. Hence he has to show that, in spite of appearances to the contrary, the submission to law which membership in a state involves is in itself a good and not an evil; not a loss which may be counterbalanced by a greater gain, but in itself a gain. These consequences are contained in the Aristotelian principle that the state is natural.

The main argument of this passage, which is somewhat elliptically expressed, is as follows: No one would maintain of the *family* that it is anything but natural. It would not occur to the most ingenious Sophist to suggest that that was an institution deliberately invented and imposed upon men from without; it is so clearly the natural expression of his native instincts. *Therefore* it does not thwart human growth but fosters it: it is like a nest, not like a cage. But the state is the logical development of the family, since the state alone achieves completely what the family aims at and achieves partly — namely, "self-sufficiency," or ability to stand on its own feet. That the individual is not self-sufficient is the very reason which makes the family necessary to him.   But the family in turn, though it achieves a degree of self-sufficiency which the individual cannot, is still dependent upon support from without.   The same natural necessity which makes individuals combine in a family makes families combine to form a village and villages in their turn to form a state.   The state has, therefore, the same title to be called "natural" that the family has; it is the fulfillment of the natural process, not a departure from it.   It also, therefore, must be regarded as a means of fostering, not of thwarting, the development of man as an individual.

One important step Aristotle does not argue, but takes for granted. It might be admitted that the state is necessary in order to supply man's animal needs; but, nevertheless, that the restrictions imposed by it are trammels upon the free development of his higher nature. It might be held that man is *condemned* to live as a member of a state, not indeed by any human artifice or design, but by the fate which has condemned him to inhabit an animal body.   This is a view which became general later; it is a view which is found in one remarkable passage in Aristotle himself; [1] but it is not the view of Aristotle's *Politics*. According to the view of this book the state is natural not only in the sense that it supplies man's animal requirements, but also in the further sense that it supplies the nurture and the environment for the development of his higher nature.   "Higher nature" is a vague phrase, but its meaning is not vague for Aristotle.   Man's higher nature, that which distinguishes him from all other animals, is his possession of the faculty of reason, and it is only the state which can give scope for the exercise of this.   The lower forms of society, the village, for example, prove inadequate *not only* because they do not adequately supply the needs of man's animal nature, but also because they do not supply the needs of his rational nature.   These latter can be supplied only in a political, as distinct, for example, from a merely economic society; and man's rational nature finds its proper development only in a political, as distinct from an economic, activity.

Thus, although the state is natural to man in precisely the same sense in which the beehive is natural to the bee, the state differs from the beehive because man's nature differs from the bee's in being rational.   The hive is governed by laws, as the state is; but the bees do not live a political life, because they do not understand the laws which

govern them.   It is an essential part of the political life of men that
they should reason with one another about the laws by which they are
governed; and its essential condition that the ruler should justify his
orders rationally, not impose them by an arbitrary fiat, and that the
subject should be persuaded, not terrified, into acceptance.

   The word "political" has become so narrow in its significance to us
that it may sound absurd that Aristotle should conceive it as the end
and *raison d'être* of the state to make a "political life" possible for its
members.   The phrase "public life" represents his meaning better.
Public life included for him not only the activity of politics in the narrower sense, but the performance of all the functions of government,
legislature, administration, and judicial decision.   It included also
participation in the enjoyment of art and the practice of religion, which
in the Greek world were public functions, not private experiences.
Public life in this sense is what the state exists to make possible; and
when it is understood in its full extension, it appears less odd that
Aristotle should have identified this life with the "good life" for man.

The Function of a State[1]

   A state exists for the sake of a good life, and not for the sake of
life only: if life only were the object, slaves and brute animals might
form a state, but they cannot, for they have no share in happiness
or in a life of free choice.   Nor does a state exist for the sake of alliance and security from injustice, nor yet for the sake of exchange
and mutual intercourse; for then the Tyrrhenians and the Cartha-
ginians, and all who have commercial treaties with one another,
would be the citizens of one state.   True, they have agreements
about imports, and engagements that they will do no wrong to one
another, and written articles of alliance.   But there are no magistracies common to the contracting parties who will enforce their
engagements; different states have each their own magistracies.
Nor does one state take care that the citizens of the other are such
as they ought to be, nor see that those who come under the terms of
the treaty do no wrong or wickedness at all, but only that they do
no injustice to one another.   Whereas those who care for good government take into consideration virtue and vice in states.   Whence

[1] POLITICS, Book III, chap. 9.

it may be further inferred that virtue must be the care of a state which is truly so called, and not merely enjoys the name: for without this end the community becomes a mere alliance which differs only in place from alliances of which the members live apart; and law is only a convention, "a surety to one another of justice," as the sophist Lycophron says, and has no real power to make the citizens good and just.

This is obvious; for suppose distinct places, such as Corinth and Megara, to be brought together so that their walls touched, still they would not be one city, not even if the citizens had the right to inter-marry, which is one of the rights peculiarly characteristic of states. Again, if men dwelt at a distance from one another, but not so far off as to have no intercourse, and there were laws among them that they should not wrong each other in their exchanges, neither would this be a state. Let us suppose that one man is a carpenter, another a husbandman, another a shoemaker, and so on, and that their number is ten thousand: nevertheless, if they have nothing in common but exchange, alliance, and the like, that would not constitute a state. Why is this? Surely not because they are at a distance from one another: for even supposing that such a community were to meet in one place, but that each man had a house of his own, which was in a manner his state, and that they made alliance with one another, but only against evil-doers; still an accurate thinker would not deem this to be a state, if their intercourse with one another was of the same character after as before their union. It is clear then that a state is not a mere society, having a common place, established for the prevention of mutual crime and for the sake of exchange. These are conditions without which a state cannot exist; but all of them together do not constitute a state, which is a community of families and aggregations of families in well-being, for the sake of a perfect and self-sufficing life. Such a community can only be established among those who live in the same place and intermarry. Hence arise in cities family connexions, brotherhoods, common sacrifices, amusements which draw men together. But these are created by friendship, for the will to live together is friendship. The end of the state is the good life, and these are the means towards it. And the state is the union of families and villages in a perfect and self-sufficing life, by which we mean a happy and honourable life.

Our conclusion, then, is that political society exists for the sake of noble actions, and not of mere companionship. Hence they who contribute most to such a society have a greater share in it than those who have the same or a greater freedom or nobility of birth but are inferior to them in political virtue; or than those who exceed them in wealth but are surpassed by them in virtue.

This passage brings out clearly the fundamental difference by which Aristotle's (and Plato's) theory of the state's function is separated from, say, Locke's. Locke's theory is important because it is an expression of the principles by which the policies of liberalism in England and of republicanism in America have been inspired. According to Locke, the function of the state (or of what he calls "Civil Society") is limited to the preservation of the rights of its members against infringement by others. Each individual has a right to security of his person and his property and to liberty of action in so far as he does not use this liberty to infringe the rights of others. The task of the state is to repress by the use of force any violation of these rights, to deter any man from injuring another in respect of his person, property, or freedom, or to punish where it is not successful in deterring. It is this and nothing more; a state exceeds its legitimate function if it endeavors to go beyond these limits.

This limitation of the state's functions is precisely what Aristotle is attacking here. The theory which he rejects is identical in many respects with Locke's. That the government shall *not* "see that those who come under the terms of the treaty do no wrong or wickedness at all," but only "that they shall do no wickedness to one another" — this is the very limitation which Locke places on its power. "A mere society, having a common place, established for the prevention of mutual crime and for the sake of exchange," a community in which "each man had a house of his own which was in a manner his city," [1] and of which the members have "made alliance with one another, but only against those who commit injury" — these phrases are tolerably exact descriptions of civil society as Locke thought it ought to be.

Such a society, Aristotle says, must indeed form the groundwork of every state: "These are conditions without which a state cannot exist"; but a society which was no more than this would not deserve the name of a state at all. Why not? Because it would be restricted from

[1] Cf. "An Englishman's house is his castle."

performing that service to its citizens which it is the chief end of a state to perform — the service of making them good men, or (the same thing) of educating them to virtue. The bad actions of a man which do not infringe the rights of his neighbor are just as vicious as those which do. A state is doing only half its duty which sets itself to curb the latter but ignores the former. Above all, a state should be concerned with the characters of its citizens, not merely with their overt actions. To deter a criminal from committing a crime by fear of a penalty is to leave the criminal as bad a man as he was before. A state which does not care how good or bad its citizens are so long as they do not commit criminal actions is not performing the proper function of a state. "Those who care for good government take into consideration virtue and vice in states. Whence it may be further inferred that virtue must be the care of a state which is truly so called, and not merely enjoys the name."

"Education" is the name which Aristotle (and Plato) give to the process of making men good, or of training them to virtue. It has a wider significance than our word, in proportion as his notion of virtue was a wider one than ours; and we may sum up in a sentence the vital difference between Aristotle and Locke by saying that, whereas for Locke education was not a function of the state, for Aristotle it was its principal function. The object of its institutions should be to train men to goodness, not only to intellectual, but to moral and physical excellence, and not only during childhood, but during the whole course of their lives. The state should be the school of the citizen.

It is worth while inquiring what provision Locke thought should be made for the education of the citizens of a civil society, especially for their training in moral virtue. He can hardly have thought that men are born good, or that they grow into goodness naturally and without discipline. But, if the state is not to undertake their training, what agency is to be responsible for it? A Roman Catholic theorist would have no difficulty in answering this question. He would restrict the state's action in much the same way in which Locke had done, and would consign the training of men to virtue to the care of another agency — the church. But this could not be the answer of Locke, the Protestant. He does not make education a public care at all, whether of the state or of the church. He leaves it to the free discretion of each individual citizen to bring up his own children as he will.

Locke, I believe, never faces the question of what is to happen if the individual citizens are unable or unwilling to provide an educational discipline such as will make their children good men. In his time the individual family was in a great number of cases a genuinely educational institution, exercising a disciplinary and formative influence upon its members, imbuing them with the religion of Protestant Christianity and moulding them according to the principles of Christian morality. He assumed that what was true in his time would be true of all times; that what was true of the Christian family was true of the family as such; that any man, if he were left free to bring up his children as he would, would bring them up in some manner similar to this. Thus he could divest the state of the function of educating, because he assumed that the private individual both would and could undertake it. So long as the assumption is justified, he has an answer to Aristotle's criticism: the state can afford to be indifferent to the virtue of its citizens, because that is cared for elsewhere. But, if it is not, it would be harder to justify the indifference of the state.

The falsification of Locke's assumption gives rise to a difficulty not only in political theory, but also in the political practice of those liberal states which are founded on Lockian principles. They have been driven already since Locke's day to undertake the intellectual education of their children, through the inability of the individual parent to provide it. If the inability of the private home to provide training of character drives the state to undertake this part of education also, it will have lost its liberal character and become a different form of polity.

Nature and Justification of Slavery[1]

❧ Seeing then that the state is made up of households, before speaking of the state we must speak of the management of the household. The parts of household management correspond to the persons who compose the household, and a complete household consists of slaves and freemen. Now we should begin by examining everything in its fewest possible elements; and the first and fewest possible parts of a family are master and slave, husband and wife, father and children. We have therefore to consider what each of

[1] POLITICS, Book I, chaps. 3–5 and 13.

these three relations is and ought to be: — I mean the relation of
master and servant, the marriage relation (the conjunction of man
and wife has no name of its own), and thirdly, the procreative relation (this also has no proper name). And there is another element
of a household, the so-called art of getting wealth, which, according
to some, is identical with household management, according to
others, a principal part of it; the nature of this art will also have to
be considered by us.

Let us first speak of master and slave, looking to the needs of
practical life and also seeking to attain some better theory of their
relation than exists at present. For some[1] are of opinion that the
rule of a master is a science, and that the management of a household, and the mastership of slaves, and the political and royal rule,
as I was saying at the outset,[2] are all the same. Others affirm that
the rule of a master over slaves is contrary to nature, and that the
distinction between slave and free-man exists by law only, and not
by nature; and being an interference with nature is therefore unjust.

Property is a part of the household, and the art of acquiring
property is a part of the art of managing the household; for no man
can live well, or indeed live at all, unless he be provided with necessaries. And as in the arts which have a definite sphere the workers
must have their own proper instruments for the accomplishment of
their work, so it is in the management of a household. Now, instruments are of various sorts; some are living, others lifeless; in the
rudder, the pilot of a ship has a lifeless, in the look-out man, a living
instrument; for in the arts the servant is a kind of instrument.
Thus, too, a possession is an instrument for maintaining life. And
so, in the arrangement of the family, a slave is a living possession,
and property a number of such instruments; and the servant is himself an instrument which takes precedence of all other instruments.
For if every instrument could accomplish its own work, obeying
or anticipating the will of others, like the statues of Daedalus, or the
tripods of Hephaestus, which, says the poet,

"of their own accord entered the assembly of the Gods;"

if, in like manner, the shuttle would weave and the plectrum touch
the lyre without a hand to guide them, chief workmen would not

[1] Plato in THE STATESMAN, 258E–259D. [Tr.]   [2] P. 119, *supra.*

want servants, nor masters slaves. Here, however, another distinction must be drawn: the instruments commonly so called are instruments of production, whilst a possession is an instrument of action. The shuttle, for example, is not only of use; but something else is made by it, whereas of a garment or of a bed there is only the use. Further, as production and action are different in kind, and both require instruments, the instruments which they employ must likewise differ in kind. But life is action and not production, and therefore the slave is the minister of action. Again, a possession is spoken of as a part is spoken of; for the part is not only a part of something else, but wholly belongs to it; and this is also true of a possession. The master is only the master of the slave; he does not belong to him, whereas the slave is not only the slave of his master, but wholly belongs to him. Hence we see what is the nature and office of a slave; he who is by nature not his own but another's man, is by nature a slave; and he may be said to be another's man who, being a human being, is also a possession. And a possession may be defined as an instrument of action, separable from the possessor.

But is there any one thus intended by nature to be a slave, and for whom such a condition is expedient and right, or rather is not all slavery a violation of nature?

There is no difficulty in answering this question, on grounds both of reason and of fact. For that some should rule and others be ruled is a thing not only necessary, but expedient; from the hour of their birth, some are marked out for subjection, others for rule.

And there are many kinds both of rulers and subjects (and that rule is the better which is exercised over better subjects — for example, to rule over men is better than to rule over wild beasts; for the work is better which is executed by better workmen, and where one man rules and another is ruled, they may be said to have a work); for in all things which form a composite whole and which are made up of parts, whether continuous or discrete, a distinction between the ruling and the subject element comes to light. Such a duality exists in living creatures, but not in them only; it originates in the constitution of the universe; even in things which have no life there is a ruling principle, as in a musical mode. But we are wandering from the subject. We will therefore restrict ourselves to the living creature, which, in the first place, consists of soul and body; and of these two, the one is by nature the ruler, and the other the subject. But then we must look for the intentions of nature in things which retain their nature, and not in things which are corrupted. And therefore we must study the man who is in the most perfect state both of body and soul, for in him we shall see the true relation of the two; although in bad or corrupted natures the body will often appear to rule over the soul, because they are in an evil and unnatural condition. At all events we may firstly observe in living creatures both a despotical and a constitutional rule; for the soul rules the body with a despotical rule, whereas the intellect rules the appetites with a constitutional and royal rule. And it is clear that the rule of the soul over the body, and of the mind and the rational element over the passionate, is natural and expedient; whereas the equality of the two or the rule of the inferior is always hurtful. The same holds good of animals in relation to men; for tame animals have a better nature than wild, and all tame animals are better off when they are ruled by man; for then they are preserved. Again, the male is by nature superior, and the female inferior; and the one rules, and the other is ruled; this principle, of necessity, extends to all mankind. Where then there is such a difference as that between soul and body, or between men and animals (as in the case of those whose business is to use their body, and who can do nothing better), the lower sort are by nature slaves, and it is better for them as for all inferiors that they should be under the rule of a master. For he who can be, and therefore is, another's, and he who participates in rational principle enough to apprehend, but not to have, such a principle, is a slave by nature. Whereas the lower animals cannot even apprehend a principle; they obey their instincts. And indeed the use made of slaves and of tame animals is not very different; for both with their bodies minister to the needs of life. Nature would like to distinguish between the bodies of freemen and slaves, making the one strong for servile labour, the other upright, and although useless for such services, useful for political life in the arts both of war and peace. But the opposite often happens — that some have the souls and others have the bodies of freemen. And doubtless if men differed from one another in the mere forms of their bodies as much as the statues of the Gods do from men, all would acknowledge that the inferior class should be slaves of the superior. And if this is true of the body, how much more just that a similar distinction should exist in the soul. But the beauty of the body is seen, whereas the beauty of the soul is not seen. It is clear, then, that some men are by nature free, and others slaves, and that for these latter slavery is both expedient and right.

. . . .

Thus it is clear that household management attends more to men than to the acquisition of inanimate things, and to human excellence more than to the excellence of property which we call wealth, and to the virtue of freemen more than to the virtue of slaves. A question may indeed be raised, whether there is any excellence at all in a slave beyond and higher than merely instrumental and ministerial qualities — whether he can have the virtues of temperance, courage, justice, and the like; or whether slaves possess only bodily and ministerial qualities. And, whichever way we answer the question, a difficulty arises; for, if they have virtue, in what will they differ from freemen? On the other hand, since they are men and share in rational principle, it seems absurd to say that they have no virtue. . . . The virtue of the slave is relative to a master. Now, we determined that a slave is useful for the wants of life, and therefore he will obviously require only so much virtue as will prevent him from failing in his duty through cowardice or lack of self-control. Some one will ask whether, if what we are saying is true, virtue will not be required also in the artisans, for they often fail in their work through the lack of self-control. But is there not a great difference in the two cases? For the slave shares in his master's life; the artisan is less closely connected with him, and only attains excellence in proportion as he becomes a slave. The meaner sort of mechanic has a special and separate slavery; and whereas the slave exists by nature, not so the shoemaker or other artisan. It is manifest, then, that the master ought to be the source of such excellence in the slave, and not a mere possessor of the art of mastership which trains the slave in his duties. Wherefore they are mistaken who forbid us to converse with slaves and say that we should employ command only, for slaves stand even more in need of admonition than children.

Aristotle's justification of slavery is the same in principle as Plato's justification of the permanent subjection of the producing class.[1]   A man needs slaves in order to develop the moral and intellectual excellences of which he is capable.   The development of these demands leisure,[2] and is incompatible with the performance of necessary and menial labors.   A man can no more live the good life without slaves than he can produce music without an instrument.   Thus slavery is justified from the point of view of the master by the exercise of virtue which it makes possible for him.

But it is justified also from the point of view of the slave.   If the slave had by nature an equal capacity with his master for the virtues which can be exercised in leisure, then indeed it would be unjust that his development should be stunted in order that another's should be perfected; and the enslavement of men possessing such capacities is accordingly condemned by Aristotle as unnatural.   But there are men lacking such capacities, men who in any case could not perform more than menial and mechanical functions.   Such men are better as slaves, for, in being subject to direction by a master of moral and intellectual excellence, they benefit from those excellences at second hand.   A slave by nature, for example, will never have the true virtue of temperance, i.e., the capacity of governing his appetites by his reason; but he can acquire a kind of derivative temperance by submitting his conduct in a childlike trust to the control of a temperate master.   The choice for him is not between the inferior and the perfect form of human virtue; it is between the inferior form and none.   Nothing in this passage is more striking than the contrast which Aristotle draws between the situation of the slave and that of the mechanical laborer who is not a slave. The comparison is to the disadvantage of the latter.   "The slave shares in his master's life; the artisan is less closely connected with him, *and only attains excellence* [or virtue] *in proportion as he becomes a slave.*"

This is an austere theory.   The master is justified in using the services of slaves for one end only: not in order to increase his wealth or comfort or power as such, but solely in order to enable him to attain to the exercise of human virtue.   If he fails to do this, the slave loses the one advantage which slavery contains for him, namely guidance of his life by one of superior virtue to himself, and the relation ceases to be one of mutual benefit.

[1] See p. 73, *supra.*   [2] See pp. 168 *et seq., infra.*

The theory rests obviously upon two great assumptions: namely, that men are divided by nature in respect of their capacities for virtue, and that it is possible to determine to which class any given individual belongs. Aristotle recognizes some of the difficulties of the latter task; he never questions the truth of the former assumption.

Notice, by the way, that this is a theory of household, not of industrial, slavery. What is the essential difference between the two things? It is given in the distinction which Aristotle draws [1] between action and production. There are instruments of action, as there are instruments of production. (A sword is an example of the former, a chisel of the latter; for one makes something with a chisel, but does something with a sword.) Now, a slave is a living instrument, but, Aristotle adds, an instrument of action, not of production. It is true that the line between the two kinds of slavery cannot be drawn absolutely, since there must be production in a household, at least in a household of the sort which Aristotle has in mind. Clothes will have to be woven, furniture made, food produced, and slaves will have these tasks assigned to them. But in a household production is subordinate to use, and is limited to the supply of what the household needs for the maintenance of its life. Industrial production has no such limit. It is not a means to an end, but is itself an end; or rather, its end is wealth-getting, which imposes no limit. Thus the factory slave is essentially an instrument of production, but the household slave only *per accidens*, in so far as production is necessary to the maintenance of the household's life, which consists in "action, and not production." [2]

Theory of Property and Wealth [3]

Let us now inquire into property generally, and into the art of getting wealth, in accordance with our usual method, for a slave has been shown to be a part of property. The first question is whether the art of getting wealth is the same with the art of managing a household or a part of it, or instrumental to it; and if the last, whether in the way that the art of making shuttles is instrumental to the art of weaving, or in the way that the casting of bronze is instrumental to the art of the statuary, for they are not instrumental in

[1] P. 131, *supra*.   [2] P. 131, *supra*.
[2] POLITICS, Book I, chaps. 8–9 (with omissions).

ᴣᴥthe same way, but the one provides tools and the other material; and by material I mean the substratum out of which any work is made; thus wool is the material of the weaver, bronze of the statuary. Now it is easy to see that the art of household management is not identical with the art of getting wealth, for the one uses the material which the other provides. For the art which uses household stores can be no other than the art of household management. There is, however, a doubt whether the art of getting wealth is a part of household management or a distinct art. If the getter of wealth has to consider whence wealth and property can be procured, but there are many sorts of property and riches, then are husbandry, and the care and provision of food in general, parts of the wealth-getting art or distinct arts?

.　　.　　.　　.　　.　　.　　.　　.　　.　　.　　.　　.　　.

Of the art of acquisition there is one kind which by nature is a part of the management of a household, in so far as the art of household management must either find ready to hand, or itself provide, such things necessary to life, and useful for the community of the family or state, as can be stored. They are the elements of true riches; for the amount of property which is needed for a good life is not unlimited, although Solon in one of his poems says that —

"No bound to riches has been fixed for man."

But there is a boundary fixed, just as there is in the other arts; for the instruments of any art are never unlimited, either in number or size, and riches may be defined as a number of instruments to be used in a household or in a state. And so we see that there is a natural art of acquisition which is practised by managers of households and by statesmen, and what is the reason of this.

There is another variety of the art of acquisition which is commonly and rightly called an art of wealth-getting, and has in fact suggested the notion that riches and property have no limit. Being nearly connected with the preceding, it is often identified with it. But though they are not very different, neither are they the same. The kind already described is given by nature, the other is gained by experience and art.

Let us begin our discussion of the question with the following considerations:

Of everything which we possess there are two uses: both belong to the thing as such, but not in the same manner, for one is the proper, and the other the improper or secondary use of it. For example, a shoe is used for wear, and is used for exchange; both are uses of the shoe. He who gives a shoe in exchange for money or food to him who wants one, does indeed use the shoe as a shoe, but this is not its proper or primary purpose, for a shoe is not made to be an object of barter. The same may be said of all possessions, for the art of exchange extends to all of them, and it arises at first from what is natural, from the circumstance that some have too little, others too much.

Hence we may infer that retail trade is not a natural part of the art of getting wealth; had it been so, men would have ceased to exchange when they had enough. In the first community, indeed, which is the family, this art is obviously of no use, but it begins to be useful when the society increases. For the members of the family originally had all things in common; later, when the family divided into parts, the parts shared in many things, and different parts in different things, which they had to give in exchange for what they wanted, a kind of barter which is still practised among barbarous nations who exchange with one another the necessaries of life and nothing more; giving and receiving wine, for example, in exchange for corn, and the like. This sort of barter is not part of the wealth-getting art and is not contrary to nature, but is needed for the satisfaction of men's natural wants. The other or more complex form of exchange grew, as might have been inferred, out of the simpler. When the inhabitants of one country became more dependent on those of another, and they imported what they needed, and exported what they had too much of, money necessarily came into use. For the various necessaries of life are not easily carried about, and hence men agreed to employ in their dealings with each other something which was intrinsically useful and easily applicable to the purposes of life, for example, iron, silver, and the like. Of this the value was at first measured simply by size and weight, but in process of time they put a stamp upon it, to save the trouble of weighing and to mark the value.

When the use of coin had once been discovered, out of the barter of necessary articles arose the other art of wealth-getting, namely, retail trade; which was at first probably a simple matter, but became more complicated as soon as men learned by experience whence and by what exchanges the greatest profit might be made. Originating in the use of coin, the art of getting wealth is generally thought to be chiefly concerned with it, and to be the art which produces riches and wealth; having to consider how they may be accumulated. Indeed, riches is assumed by many to be only a quantity of coin, because the arts of getting wealth and retail trade are concerned with coin. Others maintain that coined money is a mere sham, a thing not natural, but conventional only, because, if the users substitute another commodity for it, it is worthless, and because it is not useful as a means to any of the necessities of life, and indeed, he who is rich in coin may often be in want of necessary food. But how can that be wealth of which a man may have a great abundance and yet perish with hunger, like Midas in the fable, whose insatiable prayer turned everything that was set before him into gold?

Hence men seek after a better notion of riches and of the art of getting wealth than the mere acquisition of coin, and they are right. For natural riches and the natural art of wealth-getting are a different thing; in their true form they are part of the management of a household; whereas retail trade is the art of producing wealth, not in every way, but by exchange. And it is thought to be concerned with coin; for coin is the unit of exchange and the measure or limit of it. And there is no bound to the riches which spring from this art of wealth-getting. As in the art of medicine there is no limit to the pursuit of health, and as in the other arts there is no limit to the pursuit of their several ends, for they aim at accomplishing their ends to the uttermost (but of the means there is a limit, for the end is always the limit), so, too, in this art of wealth-getting there is no limit of the end, which is riches of the spurious kind, and the acquisition of wealth.

But the art of wealth-getting which consists in household management, on the other hand, has a limit; the unlimited acquisition of wealth is not its business. And, therefore, in one point of view, all riches must have a limit; nevertheless, as a matter of fact, we find the opposite to be the case; for all getters of wealth increase their hoard of coin without limit. The source of the confusion is the near connexion between the two kinds of wealth-getting; in either, the instrument is the same, although the use is different, and so they pass into one another; for each is a use of the same property, but with a difference: accumulation is the end in the one case, but there is a further end in the other. Hence some persons are led to believe that getting wealth is the object of household management, and the whole idea of their lives is that they ought either to increase their money without limit, or at any rate not to lose it. The origin of this disposition in men is that they are intent upon living only, and not upon living well; and, as their desires are unlimited, they also desire that the means of gratifying them should be without limit. Those who do aim at a good life seek the means of obtaining bodily pleasures; and, since the enjoyment of these appears to depend on property, they are absorbed in getting wealth: and so there arises the second species of wealth-getting. For, as their enjoyment is in excess, they seek an art which produces the excess of enjoyment; and, if they are not able to supply their pleasures by the art of getting wealth, they try other arts, using in turn every faculty in a manner contrary to nature. The quality of courage, for example, is not intended to make wealth, but to inspire confidence; neither is this the aim of the general's or of the physician's art; but the one aims at victory and the other at health. Nevertheless, some men turn every quality or art into a means of getting wealth; this they conceive to be the end, and to the promotion of the end they think all things must contribute.

Thus, then, we have considered the art of wealth-getting, which is unnecessary, and why men want it; and also the necessary art of wealth-getting, which we have seen to be different from the other, and to be a natural part of the art of managing a household, concerned with the provision of food, not, however, like the former kind, unlimited, but having a limit.

Aristotle's doctrine of property is contained in his definition of wealth as "a store of *instruments* to be used in a household or in a state." The essential thing about an instrument is that its dimensions are limited by the function for which it is intended. A hammer must be heavy in order to serve its purpose; but the object of the hammer-maker will not therefore be to make it as heavy as possible. The same function of the hammer which demands weight also sets a limit to the weight required; and the good hammer-maker will observe this limit.

If wealth is an instrument, then the art of acquiring wealth will be subject to the same limitations as the art of making hammers, and to acquire too much wealth will be as gross an error as to make a hammer too heavy.

The end to which wealth is an instrument is the "good life," whether within the household or in the state. The use of the instrument for the achievement of that end belongs to the arts of household-management and statesmanship respectively, as the proper use of the hammer belongs to the art of carpentry. The art of acquiring wealth is in its proper (or, as Aristotle says, its "natural") condition only when it is subject to these latter arts, and aims at producing not the *greatest* amount of wealth, but the *right* amount.

But the art of acquisition may free itself from subjection to the end to which it should be subservient; it then becomes the "unnatural" form of acquisition. This pursues wealth as an end in itself; and since there is nothing now to determine when the right amount has been attained (or nothing except the man's desires, which are insatiable), the pursuit is limitless.

This notion that there is a limit to the amount of wealth which it is right for a man to possess, and that the proper limit is fixed by the function to which it is instrumental, was inherited from Aristotle by the Middle Ages. It gave way to the Lockian doctrine, according to which the sole condition of the rightful ownership of wealth was that it should have been justly earned; granted that condition to have been fulfilled, there was no limit to the extent to which wealth might be rightfully increased.[1]

---

[1] I should perhaps add that there is in these chapters of Aristotle another and less valuable doctrine mixed up with that which I have quoted. Aristotle draws a second distinction between natural and unnatural acquisition, not this time with reference to the end which the wealth acquired is to serve, but with reference to the source from which it is derived. According to this distinction, the art of getting wealth from land, whether from crops or from animals, is natural; the art of getting it by exchange of commodities for profit, and above all by usury, is unnatural. This is more of a prejudice than a theory. It was inherited with the theory by the Middle Ages.

CITIZENSHIP[1]

Definition of a Citizen

He who would inquire into the essence and attributes of various kinds of government must first of all determine "What is a state?" At present this is a disputed question. Some say that the state has done a certain act; others no, not the state, but the oligarchy or the tyrant. And the legislator or statesman is concerned entirely with the state; a constitution or government being an arrangement of the inhabitants of a state. But a state is composite, like any other whole made up of many parts; — these are the citizens, who compose it. It is evident, therefore, that we must begin by asking, Who is the citizen, and what is the meaning of the term? For here again there may be a difference of opinion. He who is a citizen in a democracy will often not be a citizen in an oligarchy. Leaving out of consideration those who have been made citizens, or who have obtained the name of citizen in any other accidental manner, we may say, first, that a citizen is not a citizen because he lives in a certain place, for resident aliens and slaves share in the place; nor is he a citizen who has no legal right except that of suing and being sued; for this right may be enjoyed under the provisions of a treaty. Nay, resident aliens in many places do not possess even such rights completely, for they are obliged to have a patron, so that they do but imperfectly participate in citizenship, and we call them citizens only in a qualified sense, as we might apply the term to children who are too young to be on the register, or to old men who have been relieved from state duties. Of these we do not say quite simply that they are citizens, but add in the one case that they are not of age, and in the other, that they are past the age, or something of that sort; the precise expression is immaterial, for our meaning is clear. Similar difficulties to those which I have mentioned may be raised and answered about deprived citizens and about exiles. But the citizen whom we are seeking to define is a citizen in the strictest sense, against whom no such exception can be taken, and his special char-

---

[1] POLITICS, Book III, chap. I (with omissions), 4, 5; Book VII, chaps. 9 and 14.

acteristic is that he shares in the administration of justice, and in offices.

.   .   .   .

He who has the power to take part in the deliberative or judicial administration of any state is said by us to be a citizen of that state; and, speaking generally, a state is a body of citizens sufficing for the purposes of life.

.   .   .   .

There is a point nearly allied to the preceding: Whether the virtue of a good man and a good citizen is the same or not.   But, before entering on this discussion, we must certainly first obtain some general notion of the virtue of the citizen.   Like the sailor, the citizen is a member of a community.   Now, sailors have different functions, for one of them is a rower, another a pilot, and a third a look-out man, a fourth is described by some similar term; and while the precise definition of each individual's virtue applies exclusively to him, there is, at the same time, a common definition applicable to them all.   For they have all of them a common object, which is safety in navigation.   Similarly, one citizen differs from another, but the salvation of the community is the common business of them all.   This community is the constitution; the virtue of the citizen must therefore be relative to the constitution of which he is a member.   If, then, there are many forms of government, it is evident that there is not one single virtue of the good citizen which is perfect virtue. But we say that the good man is he who has one single virtue which is perfect virtue.   Hence it is evident that the good citizen need not of necessity possess the virtue which makes a good man.

The same question may also be approached by another road, from a consideration of the best constitution.   If the state cannot be entirely composed of good men, and yet each citizen is expected to do his own business well, and must therefore have virtue, still, inasmuch as all the citizens cannot be alike, the virtue of the citizen and of the good man cannot coincide.   All must have the virtue of the good citizen — thus, and thus only, can the state be perfect; but they will not have the virtue of a good man, unless we assume that in the good state all the citizens must be good.

Again, the state, as composed of unlikes, may be compared to the living being: as the first elements into which a living being is resolved are soul and body, as soul is made up of rational principle and appetite, the family of husband and wife, property of master and slave, so of all these, as well as other dissimilar elements, the state is composed; and, therefore, the virtue of all the citizens cannot possibly be the same, any more than the excellence of the leader of a chorus is the same as that of the performer who stands by his side. I have said enough to show why the two kinds of virtue cannot be absolutely and always the same.

But will there then be no case in which the virtue of the good citizen and the virtue of the good man coincide? To this we answer that the good *ruler* is a good and wise man, and that he who would be a statesman must be a wise man. And some persons say that even the education of the ruler should be of a special kind; for are not the children of kings instructed in riding and military exercises? As Euripides says:

"No subtle arts for me, but what the state requires."

As though there were a special education needed by a ruler. If then the virtue of a good ruler is the same as that of a good man, and we assume further that the subject is a citizen as well as the ruler, the virtue of the good citizen and the virtue of the good man cannot be absolutely the same, although in some cases they may; for the virtue of a ruler differs from that of a citizen. It was the sense of this difference which made Jason say that "he felt hungry when he was not a tyrant," meaning that he could not endure to live in a private station. But, on the other hand, it may be argued that men are praised for knowing both how to rule and how to obey, and he is said to be a citizen of approved virtue who is able to do both. Now if we suppose the virtue of a good man to be that which rules, and the virtue of the citizen to include ruling and obeying, it cannot be said that they are equally worthy of praise. Since, then, it is sometimes thought that the ruler and the ruled must learn different things and not the same, but that the citizen must know and share in them both, the inference is obvious. There is, indeed, the rule of a master, which is concerned with menial offices, — the master need not know how to perform these, but may employ others in the execution of them: the other would be degrading; and by the other I mean the power actually to do menial duties, which vary much in character and are executed by various classes of slaves, such, for example, as handicraftsmen, who, as their name signifies, live by the labour of their hands: — under these the mechanic is included. Hence in ancient times, and among some nations, the working classes had no share in the government — a privilege which they only acquired under the extreme democracy. Certainly the good man and the statesman and the good citizen ought not to learn the crafts of inferiors except for their own occasional use; if they habitually practise them, there will cease to be a distinction between master and slave.

This is not the rule of which we are speaking; but there is a rule of another kind, which is exercised over freemen and equals by birth — a constitutional rule, which the ruler must learn by obeying, as he would learn the duties of a general of cavalry by being under the orders of a general of cavalry, or the duties of a general of infantry by being under the orders of a general of infantry, and by having had the command of a regiment and of a company. It has been well said that "he who has never learned to obey cannot be a good commander." The two are not the same, but the good citizen ought to be capable of both; he should know how to govern like a freeman, and how to obey like a freeman — these are the virtues of a citizen. And, although the temperance and justice of a ruler are distinct from those of a subject, the virtue of a good man will include both; for the virtue of the good man who is free and also a subject, e.g. his justice, will not be one, but will comprise distinct kinds, the one qualifying him to rule, the other to obey, and differing as the temperance and courage of men and women differ. For a man would be thought a coward if he had no more courage than a courageous woman, and a woman would be thought loquacious if she imposed no more restraint on her conversation than the good man; and indeed their part in the management of the household is different, for the duty of the one is to acquire, and of the other to preserve. Practical wisdom only is characteristic of the ruler; it would seem that all other virtues must equally belong to ruler and subject. The virtue of the subject is certainly not wisdom, but only true opinion; he may be compared to the maker of the flute, while his master is like the flute-player or user of the flute.

From these considerations may be gathered the answer to the

question, whether the virtue of the good man is the same as that of the good citizen, or different, and how far the same, and how far different.

. . . .

There still remains one more question about the citizen: Is he only a true citizen who has a share of office, or is the mechanic to be included? If they who hold no office are to be deemed citizens, not every citizen can have this virtue of ruling and obeying; for this man is a citizen. And if none of the lower class are citizens, in which part of the state are they to be placed? For they are not resident aliens, and they are not foreigners. May we not reply, that as far as this objection goes there is no more absurdity in excluding them than in excluding slaves and freedmen from any of the above-mentioned classes? It must be admitted that we cannot consider all those to be citizens who are necessary to the existence of the state; for example, children are not citizens equally with grown-up men, who are citizens absolutely, but children, not being grown up, are only citizens on a certain assumption. Nay, in ancient times, and among some nations, the artisan class *were* slaves or foreigners, and therefore the majority of them are so now. The best form of state will not admit them to citizenship; but if they are admitted, then our definition of the virtue of a citizen will not apply to every citizen, nor to every free man as such, but only to those who are freed from necessary services. The necessary people are either slaves who minister to the wants of individuals, or mechanics and labourers who are the servants of the community. These reflections carried a little further will explain their position; and indeed what has been said already is of itself, when understood, explanation enough.

Since there are many forms of government there must be many varieties of citizens, and especially of citizens who are subjects; so that under some governments the mechanic and the labourer will be citizens, but not in others, as, for example, in aristocracy or the so-called government of the best (if there be such a one), in which honours are given according to virtue and merit; for no man can practise virtue who is living the life of a mechanic or labourer. In oligarchies the qualification for office is high, and therefore no labourer can ever be a citizen; but a mechanic may, for an actual majority of them are rich. At Thebes there was a law that no man could hold office

who had not retired from business for ten years. But in many
states the law goes to the length of admitting aliens; for in some
democracies a man is a citizen though his mother only be a citizen;
and a similar principle is applied to illegitimate children; the law is
relaxed when there is a dearth of population. But when the number
of citizens increases, first the chi.dren of a male or a female slave
are excluded; then those whose mothers only are citizens; and at
last the right of citizenship is confined to those whose fathers an.l
mothers are both citizens.

Hence, as is evident, there are different kinds of citizens; and
he is a citizen in the highest sense who shares in the honours of the
state. Compare Homer's words, "like some dishonoured stranger"
he who is excluded from the honours of the state is no better than
an alien. But when this exclusion is concealed, then the object
is that the privileged class may deceive their fellow inhabitants.

As to the question whether the virtue of the good man is the
same as that of the good citizen, the considerations already adduced
proved that in some states the good man and the good citizen are
the same, and in others different. When they are the same, it is
not every citizen who is a good man, but only the statesman and
those who have or may have, alone or in conjunction with others,
the conduct of public affairs.[1]

.   .   .   .

Having determined these points, we have in the next place to
consider whether all ought to share in every sort of occupation.
Shall every man be at once husbandman, artisan, councillor, judge,
or shall we suppose the several occupations just mentioned assigned
to different persons? or, thirdly, shall some employments be assigned to individuals and others common to all? The same arrangement, however, does not occur in every constitution; as we were
saying, all may be shared by all, or not all by all, but only some by
some; and hence arise the differences of constitutions, for in democracies all share in all, in oligarchies the opposite practice prevails.
Now, since we are here speaking of the best form of government,

[1] The reason for this is given on p. 144, *supra*, where it is said that of all the members of a state, the ruler alone has to exercise practical wisdom. Practical wisdom is
part of the virtue of a man, and no man can be called wholly good who does not profess
it. Yet a member who is not a ruler can dispense with it; i.e., he can be a perfectly
good citizen without being a perfectly good man.

☛i.e., that under which the state will be most happy (and happiness, as has been already said, cannot exist without virtue), it clearly follows that in the state which is best governed and possesses men who are just absolutely, and not merely relatively to the principle of the constitution, the citizens must not lead the life of mechanics or tradesmen, for such a life is ignoble and inimical to virtue. Neither must they be husbandmen, since leisure is necessary both for the development of virtue and the performance of political duties.

. . . .

Since every political society is composed of rulers and subjects, let us consider whether the relations of one to the other should interchange or be permanent. For the education of the citizens will necessarily vary with the answer given to this question. Now, if some men excelled others in the same degree in which gods and heroes are supposed to excel mankind in general (having in the first place a great advantage even in their bodies, and secondly in their minds), so that the superiority of the governors was undisputed and patent to their subjects, it would clearly be better that once for all the one class should rule and the others serve. But since this is unattainable, and kings have no marked superiority over their subjects, such as Scylax affirms to be found among the Indians, it is obviously necessary on many grounds that all the citizens alike should take their turn of governing and being governed. Equality consists in the same treatment of similar persons, and no government can stand which is not founded upon justice. For if the government be unjust every one in the country unites with the governed in the desire to have a revolution, and it is an impossibility that the members of the government can be so numerous as to be stronger than all their enemies put together. Yet that governors should excel their subjects is undeniable. How all this is to be effected, and in what way they will respectively share in the government, the legislator has to consider. The subject has been already mentioned. Nature herself has provided the distinction when she made a difference between old and young within the same species, of whom she fitted the one to govern and the other to be governed. No one takes offence at being governed when he is young, nor does he think himself better than his governors, especially if he will enjoy the same privilege when he reaches the required age.

We conclude that from one point of view governors and governed are identical, and from another different. And therefore their education must be the same and also different. For he who would learn to command well must, as men say, first of all learn to obey. As I observed in the first part of this treatise, there is one rule which is for the sake of the rulers and another rule which is for the sake of the ruled; the former is a despotic, the latter a free government. Some commands differ not in the thing commanded, but in the intention with which they are imposed. Wherefore, many apparently menial offices are an honour to the free youth by whom they are performed; for actions do not differ as honourable or dishonourable in themselves so much as in the end and intention of them. But since we say that the virtue of the citizen and ruler is the same as that of the good man, and that the same person must first be a subject and then a ruler, the legislator has to see that they become good men, and by what means this may be accomplished, and what is the end of the perfect life.

Aristotle is entirely at one with Plato in the belief that the one thing necessary to qualify a man to be a ruler is superiority in virtue. The converse of this is that it is only in ruling that the whole of human virtue is called into play. "Practical wisdom" is a human virtue which can be exercised fully only in the activity of ruling. Aristotle differs from Plato in that he denies that the capacity of practical wisdom is the exclusive possession of a certain few individuals. At any given time, some of the citizens must be ruling and the others subject, but theirs is not a permanent subjection. Their subjection is the apprenticeship which qualifies them in their turn to rule. If a man were excluded from all prospect of succeeding to the ruling position, he would not, according to Aristotle's definition, be a citizen at all. "It is obviously necessary that all the citizens alike should take their turn of governing and being governed. Equality consists in the same treatment of similar persons, and no government can stand which is not founded upon justice."

But it would be grossly erroneous on the strength of these words to imagine Aristotle an apostle of equalitarian democracy. Justice demands equal treatment, certainly; but only of those who are equal in virtue. The equality which Aristotle demands is confined to the members of the citizen body. But far the larger number of the residents within a state would be excluded from this body: not only the slaves, the resident aliens, and the women, but also the mechanics and tradesmen, "for such a life is ignoble, and inimical to virtue," and even the husbandmen, "since leisure is necessary both for the development of virtue and the performance of political duties."

In order to see Aristotle in his proper relation to Plato, it is necessary to realize that Aristotle's citizen body corresponds solely to Plato's two classes of guardians. Aristotle is objecting to the erection of a distinction within the guardian class. The whole of those who form the "third class" of Plato's state would be excluded by Aristotle altogether from the citizen body. In regard to these, it is Plato, and not Aristotle, whose thought is the more progressive. The condition of the "third class" in Plato's state is far enough from according with any notions of the equality of man, but it is significant of Plato that he strives to make them, the manufacturers and farmers, the producers of wealth, an organic part of the state to which they belong. Aristotle is content to leave them as instruments, not members, of the state: "Mechanics, or any other class which is not a producer of virtue, have no share in the state."[1]

It is odd that it seems never to have occurred to Aristotle that the same argument which he brings against the proposal to exclude some citizens from rule might have been turned with equal force against the proposal to exclude some men from citizenship. "If some men excelled others in the same degree in which gods and heroes are supposed to excel mankind in general (having in the first place a great advantage even in their bodies, and secondly in their minds), so that the superiority of the governors was undisputed and patent to their subjects, it would clearly be better that once for all the one class should rule and the others serve. But since this is unattainable, and kings have no marked superiority over their subjects, ... it is obviously necessary on many grounds that all the citizens alike should take their turn of governing and being governed." Is there, then, this "patent and undisputed superiority," this gulf as obvious as that between gods and men, clearly dividing a class of men who are fitted by nature to

[1] POLITICS, Book VII, chap. 9; not included in the part selected for quotation.

be citizens from a vastly larger class of men who are not? Apparently Aristotle was convinced that there was.

(It is necessary to enter a warning similar to that which was necessary with Plato.[1] The "mechanics" whom Aristotle would exclude from citizenship are not to be thought of as a "proletariat." The term includes the industrialist as well as the laborer, and there is no reason why the unenfranchised "mechanic" should not be wealthier than the citizen — as, indeed, he often was in Greek states. "The actual majority of them are rich"[2]).

Types of Constitutions [3]

~ Having determined these questions, we have next to consider whether there is only one form of government or many, and if many, what they are, and how many, and what are the differences between them.

A constitution is the arrangement of magistracies in a state, especially of the highest of all. The government is everywhere sovereign[4] in the state, and the constitution is in fact the government. For example, in democracies the people are supreme, but in oligarchies, the few; and, therefore, we say that these two forms of government also are different: and so in other cases.

First, let us consider what is the purpose of a state, and how many forms of government there are by which human society is regulated. We have already said, in the first part of this treatise, when discussing household management and the rule of a master, that man is by nature a political animal. And therefore, men, even when they do not require one another's help, desire to live together; not but that they are also brought together by their common interests in proportion as they severally attain to any measure of well-being. This is certainly the chief end, both of individuals and of states. And also for the sake of mere life (in which there is possibly some noble element so long as the evils of existence do not greatly overbalance the good) mankind meet together and maintain

---

[1] See p. 84 *n.* 4, *supra.* [2] Aristotle, quoted p. 145, *supra.*

[3] POLITICS, Book III, chaps. 6–7.

[4] "Supreme" would be a less misleading translation. See pp. 160 *et seq., infra.* The Greek word is the same as that which is translated "supreme" in the following sentence. and elsewhere.

the political community. And we all see that men cling to life even at the cost of enduring great misfortune, seeming to find in life a natural sweetness and happiness.

There is no difficulty in distinguishing the various kinds of authority; they have been often defined already in discussions outside the school. The rule of a master, although the slave by nature and the master by nature have in reality the same interests, is nevertheless exercised primarily with a view to the interest of the master, but accidentally considers the slave, since, if the slave perish, the rule of the master perishes with him. On the other hand, the government of a wife and children and of a household, which we have called household management, is exercised in the first instance for the good of the governed or for the common good of both parties, but essentially for the good of the governed, as we see to be the case in medicine, gymnastic, and the arts in general, which are only accidentally concerned with the good of the artists themselves. For there is no reason why the trainer may not sometimes practise gymnastics, and the helmsman is always one of the crew. The trainer or the helmsman considers the good of those committed to his care. But, when he is one of the persons taken care of, he accidentally participates in the advantage, for the helmsman is also a sailor, and the trainer becomes one of those in training. And so in politics: when the state is framed upon the principle of equality and likeness, the citizens think that they ought to hold office by turns. Formerly, as is natural, every one would take his turn of service; and then again, somebody else would look after his interest, just as he, while in office, had looked after theirs. But nowadays, for the sake of the advantage which is to be gained from the public revenues and from office, men want to be always in office. One might imagine that the rulers, being sickly, were only kept in health while they continued in office; in that case we may be sure that they would be hunting after places. The conclusion is evident: that governments which have a regard to the common interest are constituted in accordance with strict principles of justice, and are therefore true forms; but those which regard only the interest of the rulers are all defective and perverted forms, for they are despotic, whereas a state is a community of freemen.

Having determined these points, we have next to consider how many forms of government there are, and what they are; and in the first place what are the true forms, for, when they are determined, the perversions of them will at once be apparent. The words constitution and government have the same meaning, and the government, which is the supreme authority in states, must be in the hands of one, or of a few, or of the many. The true forms of government, therefore, are those in which the one, or the few, or the many, govern with a view to the common interest; but governments which rule with a view to the private interest, whether of the one, or of the few, or of the many, are perversions. For the members of a state, if they are truly citizens, ought to participate in its advantages. Of forms of government in which one rules, we call that which regards the common interests, kingship or royalty; that in which more than one, but not many, rule, aristocracy; and it is so called, either because the rulers are the best men, or because they have at heart the best interests of the state and of the citizens. But when the citizens at large administer the state for the common interest, the government is called by the generic name, — a constitution. And there is a reason for this use of language. One man or a few may excel in virtue; but as the number increases it becomes more difficult for them to attain perfection in every kind of virtue, though they may in military virtue, for this is found in the masses. Hence in a constitutional government the fighting-men have the supreme power, and those who possess arms are the citizens.

Of the above-mentioned forms, the perversions are as follows: — of royalty, tyranny; of aristocracy, oligarchy; of constitutional government, democracy. For tyranny is a kind of monarchy which has in view the interest of the monarch only; oligarchy has in view the interest of the wealthy; democracy, of the needy: none of them the common good of all.

Aristotle does not adhere consistently to this use of the term "democracy." In other parts of his work he uses it in a general, not, as here, in a bad sense. In its wider sense it means simply "government by the many"; not necessarily "government by the many in a sectional interest."

A Defense of Popular Supremacy[1]

❧ The principle that the multitude ought to be supreme rather than the few best is one that is maintained, and, though not free from difficulty, yet seems to contain an element of truth. For the many, of whom each individual is but an ordinary person, when they meet together may very likely be better than the few good, if regarded not individually but collectively, just as a feast to which many contribute is better than a dinner provided out of a single purse. For each individual among the many has a share of virtue and prudence, and when they meet together, they become in a manner one man, who has many feet, and hands, and senses; that is a figure of their mind and disposition. Hence the many are better judges than a single man of music and poetry; for some understand one part, and some another, and among them they understand the whole. There is a similar combination of qualities in good men, who differ from any individual of the many, as the beautiful are said to differ from those who are not beautiful, and works of art from realities, because in them the scattered elements are combined, although, if taken separately, the eye of one person or some other feature in another person would be fairer than in the picture.

Whether this principle can apply to every democracy, and to all bodies of men, is not clear. Or rather, by heaven, in some cases it is impossible of application; for the argument would equally hold about brutes; and wherein, it will be asked, do some men differ from brutes? But there may be bodies of men about whom our statement is nevertheless true. And if so, the difficulty which has been already raised, and also another which is akin to it — viz. what power should be assigned to the mass of freemen and citizens, who are not rich and have no personal merit — are both solved. There is still a danger in allowing them to share the great offices of state, for their folly will lead them into error, and their dishonesty into crime. But there is a danger also in not letting them share, for a state in which many poor men are excluded from office will necessarily be full of enemies. The only way of escape is to assign to them some deliberative and judicial functions. For this reason

[1] POLITICS, Book III, chap. II.

Solon and certain other legislators give them the power of electing
to offices, and of calling the magistrates to account, but they do not
allow them to hold office singly. When they meet together, their
perceptions are quite good enough, and combined with the better
class they are useful to the state (just as impure food when mixed
with what is pure sometimes makes the entire mass more wholesome than a small quantity of the pure would be), but each individual, left to himself, forms an imperfect judgement.

On the other hand, the popular form of government involves
certain difficulties. In the first place, it might be objected that he
who can judge of the healing of a sick man would be one who could
himself heal his disease, and make him whole — that is, in other
words, the physician; and so in all professions and arts. As, then,
the physician ought to be called to account by physicians, so ought
men in general to be called to account by their peers. But physicians are of three kinds: — there is the ordinary practitioner, and
there is the physician of the higher class, and thirdly the intelligent
man who has studied the art: in all arts there is such a class; and
we attribute the power of judging to them quite as much as to
professors of the art. Secondly, does not the same principle apply
to elections? For a right election can only be made by those who
have knowledge; those who know geometry, for example, will choose
a geometrician rightly, and those who know how to steer, a pilot;
and, even if there be some occupations and arts in which private
persons share in the ability to choose, they certainly cannot choose
better than those who know. So that, according to this argument,
neither the election of magistrates, nor the calling of them to account,
should be entrusted to the many. Yet possibly these objections
are to a great extent met by our old answer, that if the people are
not utterly degraded, although individually they may be worse
judges than those who have special knowledge, as a body they are
as good or better. Moreover, there are some arts whose products
are not judged of solely, or best, by the artists themselves, namely,
those arts whose products are recognized even by those who do not
possess the art; for example, the knowledge of the house is not
limited to the builder only; the user, or, in other words, the master,
of the house will even be a better judge than the builder, just as the
pilot will judge better of a rudder than the carpenter, and the guest
will judge better of a feast than the cook.

This difficulty seems now to be sufficiently answered, but there is another akin to it. That inferior persons should have authority in greater matters than the good would appear to be a strange thing, yet the election and calling to account of the magistrates is the greatest of all. And these, as I was saying, are functions which in some states are assigned to the people, for the assembly is supreme in all such matters. Yet persons of any age, and having but a small property qualification, sit in the assembly and deliberate and judge, although for the great officers of state, such as treasurers and generals, a high qualification is required. This difficulty may be solved in the same manner as the preceding, and the present practice of democracies may be really defensible. For the power does not reside in the dicast, or senator, or ecclesiast, but in the court, and the senate, and the assembly, of which individual senators, or ecclesiasts,[1] or dicasts,[2] are only parts or members. And for this reason the many may claim to have a higher authority than the few; for the people, and the senate, and the courts consist of many persons, and their property collectively is greater than the property of one or of a few individuals holding great offices. But enough of this.

There is a sense in which this passage may be truly described as a "defense of democracy," but the description requires some important qualifications if it is not to be misleading. In the first place, the "many" of whom Aristotle speaks include only the citizens. They would themselves be a minority of the total inhabitants of their city.

Secondly, if democracy means "government by the people," it is not democracy which is defended here. Nothing that Aristotle says here suggests that the people are fitted to govern. The capacity of collective wisdom which he attributes to them qualifies them to judge the merits of their governors; but that does not necessarily involve a capacity to perform the task of government themselves, any more than a discriminating taste in the judgment of food qualifies the diner to undertake the work of the cook. What "the many" may claim on the strength of this faculty of judgment is the right of electing — but not from among themselves — those who are to rule them,

[1] Members of the general assembly of the people.
[2] Members of the judicial courts.

and of submitting their conduct to a judicial scrutiny when their term of office is over.

Nor would it be correct to say that Aristotle is arguing in favor of the sovereignty of the people. The Greek word which is translated as "supreme" in the first line of the passage quoted is sometimes translated "sovereign"; and it is true that there is no other word in the Greek language which comes so near to meaning "sovereign" as this. Nevertheless, this translation is misleading. The Greeks did not possess the conception which is expressed in that crucial modern word, and there is justice in the claim of the sixteenth-century philosopher, Bodin, that he was the first writer to grasp it fully. But, discussion on this point will be better deferred to the section immediately following.

Nor, finally, must it be assumed that Aristotle would without qualification adopt as his own the position which he is here defending. He is pursuing the method which he most frequently employs in the moral and political parts of his philosophy. He examines in turn the various and conflicting opinions which have been adopted upon a given topic, with a view to discovering how much truth there is in each, but without necessarily committing himself to the unconditional acceptance of any.

With the doctrine of collective judgment contained in this passage, compare a saying of Macaulay: "Canning used to say that the House [of Commons] had better taste than the man of best taste in it, and I am very much inclined to think that Canning was right." [1]

Something very like the principle of Aristotle's doctrine is implied in the commonly accepted admission that in the appreciation of works of literature no pronouncement by an individual critic, however brilliant, is to be accorded the same authority as what is called "the judgment of posterity." For the "judgment of posterity" is a collective judgment of many men, each of whom by himself is a worse critic than the supposed brilliant individual. (Of course, in this instance the individual opinions of which the collective judgment is constituted are not expressed contemporaneously with one another, but are successive in time, so that the collective judgment develops gradually out of them. But this difference does not destroy the resemblance.)

Perhaps a simpler example is the familiar one of a committee. It would be useless to appoint a committee to recommend a course of

[1] G. O. TREVELYAN, THE LIFE AND LETTERS OF LORD MACAULAY (1876), chap. IV.

action unless it was assumed that the collective judgment of its members would be wiser than that of the wisest individual among them. Otherwise it would always pay to refer the question to the judgment of the wisest individual.

Supremacy of Law [1]

ॐ (a) There is also a doubt as to what is to be the supreme power in the state: — Is it the multitude? Or the wealthy? Or the good? Or the one best man? Or a tyrant? Any of these alternatives seems to involve disagreeable consequences. If the poor, for example, because they are more in number, divide among themselves the property of the rich, — is not this unjust? No, by heaven (will be the reply), for the supreme authority justly willed it. But if this is not injustice, pray what is? Again, when in the first division all has been taken, and the majority divide anew the property of the minority, is it not evident, if this goes on, that they will ruin the state? Yet surely, virtue is not the ruin of those who possess her, nor is justice destructive of a state; and therefore this law of confiscation clearly cannot be just. If it were, all the acts of a tyrant must of necessity be just; for he only coerces other men by superior power, just as the multitude coerce the rich. But is it just then that the few and the wealthy should be the rulers? And what if they, in like manner, rob and plunder the people, — is this just? If so, the other case will likewise be just. But there can be no doubt that all these things are wrong and unjust.

Then ought the good to rule and have supreme power? But in that case everybody else, being excluded from power, will be dishonoured. For the offices of a state are posts of honour; and if one set of men always hold them, the rest must be deprived of them. Then will it be well that the one best man should rule? Nay, that is still more oligarchical, for the number of those who are dishonoured is thereby increased. Some one may say that it is bad in any case for a man, subject as he is to all the accidents of human passion, to have the supreme power, rather than the law. But

---

[1] (a) POLITICS, Book III, chap. 10; (b) *ibid.*, Book III, chap. 11; (c) *ibid.*, Book III, chap. 16; (d) *ibid.*, Book IV, chap. 4.

what if the law itself is democratical and oligarchical, how will that help us out of our difficulties? Not at all; the same consequences will follow.

.   .   .   .

(b) The discussion of the first question shows nothing so clearly as that laws, when good, should be supreme; and that the ruler or rulers should regulate those matters only on which the laws are unable to speak with precision owing to the difficulty of any general principle embracing all particulars.

.   .   .   .

(c) At this place in the discussion there impends the inquiry respecting the king who acts solely according to his own will; he has now to be considered. The so-called limited monarchy, or kingship according to law, as I have already remarked, is not a distinct form of government, for under all governments, as, for example, in a democracy or aristocracy, there may be a general holding office for life, and one person is often made supreme over the administration of a state. A magistracy of this kind exists at Epidamnus, and also at Opus, but in the latter city has a more limited power. Now absolute monarchy, or the arbitrary rule of a sovereign [1] over all the citizens, in a city which consists of equals, is thought by some to be quite contrary to nature; it is argued that those who are by nature equals must have the same natural right and worth, and that for unequals to have an equal share, or for equals to have an unequal share, in the offices of state, is as bad as for different bodily constitutions to have the same food and clothing. Wherefore it is thought to be just that among equals every one be ruled as well as rule, and therefore that all should have their turn.

We thus arrive at law; for an order of succession implies law. And the rule of the law, it is argued, is preferable to that of any individual. On the same principle, even if it be better for certain individuals to govern, they should be made only guardians and ministers of the law. For magistrates there must be, — this is admitted; but then men say that to give authority to any one man

---

[1] A misleading translation. See p. 160, *infra.* Translate rather "the supremacy of a single arbitrary ruler."

when all are equal is unjust. Nay, there may indeed be cases which the law seems unable to determine, but in such cases can a man? Nay, it will be replied, the law trains officers for this express purpose, and appoints them to determine matters which are left undecided by it, to the best of their judgement. Further, it permits them to make any amendment of the existing laws which experience suggests. Therefore he who bids the law rule may be deemed to bid God and Reason alone rule, but he who bids man rule adds an element of the beast; for desire is a wild beast, and passion perverts the minds of rulers, even when they are the best of men. The law is reason unaffected by desire.

. . . .

(d) Of forms of democracy first comes that which is said to be based strictly on equality. In such a democracy the law says that it is just for the poor to have no more advantage than the rich; and that neither should be masters, but both equal. For if liberty and equality, as is thought by some, are chiefly to be found in democracy, they will be best attained when all persons alike share in the government to the utmost. And since the people are the majority, and the opinion of the majority is decisive, such a government must necessarily be a democracy. Here then is one sort of democracy. There is another, in which the magistrates are elected according to a certain property qualification, but a low one; he who has the required amount of property has a share in the government, but he who loses his property loses his rights. Another kind is that in which all the citizens who are under no disqualification share in the government, but still the law is supreme. In another, everybody, if he be only a citizen, is admitted to the government, but the law is supreme as before. A fifth form of democracy, in other respects the same, is that in which, not the law, but the multitude, have the supreme power, and supersede the law by their decrees. This is a state of affairs brought about by the demagogues. For in democracies which are subject to the law the best citizens hold the first place, and there are no demagogues; but where the laws are not supreme, there demagogues spring up. For the people becomes a monarch, and is many in one; and the many have the power in their hands, not as individuals, but collectively. Homer says that "it is not

good to have a rule of many," but whether he means by this corporate rule, or the rule of many individuals, is uncertain.

At all events this sort of democracy, which is now a monarch, and
no longer under the control of law, seeks to exercise monarchical
sway, and grows into a despot; the flatterer is held in honour; this
sort of democracy being relatively to other democracies what
tyranny is ᵗo other forms of monarchy.   The spirit of both is the
same, and they alike exercise a despotic rule over the better citizens.
The decrees of the demos correspond to the edicts of the tyrant; and
the demagogue is to the one what the flatterer is to the other.   Both
have great power; — the flatterer with the tyrant, the demagogue
with democracies of the kind which we are describing.   The demagogues make the decrees of the people override the laws, by referring
all things to the popular assembly.   And therefore they grow great,
because the people have all things in their hands, and they hold in
their hands the votes of the people, who are too ready to listen to
them.   Further, those who have any complaint to bring against the
magistrates say, "let the people be judges"; the people are too
happy to accept the invitation; and so the authority of every office
is undermined.   Such a democracy is fairly open to the objection
that it is not a constitution at all; for where the laws have no
authority, there is no constitution.   The law ought to be supreme
over all, and the rulers should judge of particulars, and only this
should be considered a constitution.   So that if democracy be a real
form of government, the sort of system in which all things are regulated by decrees is clearly not even a democracy in the true sense
of the word, for decrees relate only to particulars.

The doctrine which these four passages express is fundamental to
Aristotle's theory.   States differ from one another according as the
supreme power within them is vested in one man, in several, or in
many.   But there is one condition to which all these different kinds of
state must conform.   In all of them the supreme body must exercise
its power according to a law.   It must not exercise power arbitrarily
and without respect to any law.   If it does so, the result is not that a
different, or an inferior, form of state comes into existence.   What
then comes into existence is something which cannot properly be called

a state at all. "Such a democracy," says Aristotle (and his words would apply equally to a tyrant or an oligarchy who ruled entirely by arbitrary decree), "is fairly open to the objection that it is not a constitution at all; for where the laws have no authority, there is no constitution. The law ought to be supreme over all, and the rulers should judge of particulars, and only this should be considered a constitution." [1]

The position here ascribed to the ruling body in a state may be compared to that of a doctor in relation to his patient. In treating his patient the doctor is always applying certain rules, the rules of the art of medicine. He may apply them well or badly, and will be a better or a worse doctor according as he does the one or the other. But, if he were to cease to apply any rules at all, if his treatment were to become entirely arbitrary, and he were to handle his patient with no other guidance than the capricious whim of the moment, then he would not have become a bad doctor, he would have ceased to be a doctor at all. The relation of doctor and patient would have disappeared. The parties to the transaction would no more be doctor and patient than a lunatic who sticks pins into another becomes thereby his doctor, or he who suffers pins to be stuck into him the patient of the former.

The only question, then, which can arise about the forms of state is the question: Which part of the state is to bear supremacy over the others *under the law*? There can be no question of any power in the state being supreme over the law, because such supremacy is incompatible with the nature of a state.

Now, the definition of sovereignty is: supremacy over the law. Thus the existence of a sovereign body, or a sovereign will, is ruled out by Aristotle's conception of the state. To allow a will or power above law is to abrogate the law, and law is essential to political society. We may express the same thing by saying that in Aristotle's conception *the law itself* is sovereign. But this is only to say that there is no power supreme over the law; i.e., no sovereign.

In this matter of sovereignty, as in many other things, it is Plato rather than Aristotle who contains the germ of the modern idea. It is Plato who declared [2] that scientific knowledge makes a man

[1] P. 160, *supra.*
[2] See p. 108, *supra.*

superior to rules; so that if a man fully understood the principles underlying legislation, he would be superior to the written laws in which those principles were embodied.[1] In one of the most important passages of the *Republic* Plato asserts that it is necessary to the existence of the state that it should contain within it a body of men possessing this scientific understanding of the principles of legislation. "It will be necessary that there shall always be present in the city a class possessing that insight into the principles of the constitution, in the light of which you, Glaucon, the lawgiver, laid down its laws."[2] In other words, there must always be in the state a body superior to the laws of the state; a body which shall not merely execute laws (as a government does), but originate them; a body which shall not derive its authority from the laws, but confer their authority on them.

It would not be wrong to say that Plato in this passage is making his rulers into sovereigns. Nevertheless, this notion of sovereignty is not identical with that which is characteristic of modern political theory. Plato's rulers are set above the laws of their state, but they are not conceived as creating these laws. Their superiority depends upon their knowledge, by which they grasp the eternal principles to which laws ought to conform. They are superior to the laws only in so far as they are themselves subject in their turn to these principles. The authority of the laws which they lay down is derived in strictness not from them, the legislators, but from principles which exist eternally, and independently of them.

There is no place in the political theories of classical Greece for sovereignty in the modern sense of the term. A sovereign in this sense is one who creates law by willing it: he is supposed invested with an authority which confers the force of law upon whatever he wills. This is the authority which is ascribed by Hobbes to the sovereign prince (or assembly) of a commonwealth, and by Rousseau to the sovereign people.

[1] There is one place (in POLITICS, Book III, chap. 13) in which Aristotle seems to propound a similar doctrine. I have ignored it, as an isolated passage which is unsupported by his general doctrine.

[2] REPUBLIC, VI, 497, quoted p. 86, *supra*.

To What Extent Warlike Aggrandisement Should be the End of Statesmanship[1]

∾ Others, again, are of opinion that arbitrary and tyrannical rule alone consists with happiness; indeed, in some states the entire aim both of the laws and of the constitution is to give men despotic power over their neighbours. And, therefore, although in most cities the laws may be said generally to be in a chaotic state, still, if they aim at anything, they aim at the maintenance of power: thus in Lacedaemon and Crete the system of education and the greater part of the laws are framed with a view to war. And in all nations which are able to gratify their ambition military power is held in esteem, for example among the Scythians and Persians and Thracians and Celts. In some nations there are even laws tending to stimulate the warlike virtues, as at Carthage, where we are told that men obtain the honour of wearing as many armlets as they have served campaigns. There was once a law in Macedonia that he who had not killed an enemy should wear a halter, and among the Scythians no one who had not slain his man was allowed to drink out of the cup which was handed round at a certain feast. Among the Iberians, a warlike nation, the number of enemies whom a man has slain is indicated by the number of obelisks[2] which are fixed in the earth round his tomb; and there are numerous practices among other nations of a like kind, some of them established by law and others by custom.

Yet to a reflecting mind it must appear very strange that the statesman should be always considering how he can dominate and tyrannize over others, whether they will or not. How can that which is not even lawful be the business of the statesman or the legislator? Unlawful it certainly is to rule without regard to justice, for there may be might where there is no right. The other arts and sciences offer no parallel; a physician is not expected to persuade or coerce his patients, nor a pilot the passengers in his ship. Yet most men appear to think that the art of despotic government is statesmanship, and what men affirm to be unjust and inexpedient in their own case they are not ashamed of practising towards others:

[1] POLITICS, Book VII, chaps. 2 and 14. [2] Or "spits."

they demand just rule for themselves, but where other men are concerned they care nothing about it. Such behaviour is irrational; unless the one party is, and the other is not, born to serve, in which case men have a right to command, not indeed all their fellows, but only those who are intended to be subjects; just as we ought not to hunt mankind, whether for food or sacrifice, but only the animals which may be hunted for food or sacrifice, that is to say, such wild animals as are eatable. And surely there may be a city happy in isolation, which we will assume to be well-governed (for it is quite possible that a city thus isolated might be well-administered and have good laws); but such a city would not be constituted with any view to war or the conquest of enemies, — all that sort of thing must be excluded. Hence we see very plainly that warlike pursuits, although generally to be deemed honourable, are not the supreme end of all things, but only means. And the good lawgiver should inquire how states and races of men and communities may participate in a good life, and in the happiness which is attainable by them.

  •   •   •   •   •   •   •   •   •   •   •

The whole of life is further divided into two parts, business and leisure, war and peace, and of actions some aim at what is necessary and useful, and some at what is honourable. And the preference given to one or the other class of actions must necessarily be like the preference given to one or other part of the soul and its actions over the other; there must be war for the sake of peace, business for the sake of leisure, things useful and necessary for the sake of things honourable. All these points the statesman should keep in view when he frames his laws; he should consider the parts of the soul and their functions, and above all the better and the end; he should also remember the diversities of human lives and actions. For men must be able to engage in business and go to war, but leisure and peace are better; they must do what is necessary and indeed what is useful, but what is honourable is better. On such principles children and persons of every age which requires education should be trained. Whereas even the Hellenes of the present day, who are reputed to be best governed, and the legislators, who gave them their constitutions, do not appear to have framed their governments with a regard to the best end, or to have given them laws and education with a view to all the virtues, but in a vulgar spirit have fallen back on those which promised to be more useful and profitable.

Many modern writers have taken a similar view: they commend the Lacedaemonian constitution, and praise the legislator for making conquest and war his sole aim, a doctrine which may be refuted by argument and has long ago been refuted by facts. For most men desire empire in the hope of accumulating the goods of fortune; and on this ground Thibron and all those who have written about the Lacedaemonian constitution have praised their legislator, because the Lacedaemonians, by being trained to meet dangers, gained great power. But surely they are not a happy people now that their empire has passed away, nor was their legislator right. How ridiculous is the result, if, while they are continuing in the observance of his laws and no one interferes with them, they have lost the better part of life! These writers further err about the sort of government which the legislator should approve, for the government of freemen is nobler and implies more virtue than despotic government. Neither is a city to be deemed happy or a legislator to be praised because he trains his citizens to conquer and obtain dominion over their neighbours, for there is great evil in this. On a similar principle any citizen who could, should obviously try to obtain the power in his own state, — the crime which the Lacedaemonians accuse king Pausanias of attempting, although he had so great honour already.

No such principle and no law having this object is either statesmanlike or useful or right. For the same things are best both for individuals and for states, and these are the things which the legislator ought to implant in the minds of his citizens. Neither should men study war with a view to the enslavement of those who do not deserve to be enslaved; but first of all they should provide against their own enslavement, and in the second place obtain empire for the good of the governed, and not for the sake of exercising a general despotism, and in the third place they should seek to be masters only over those who deserve to be slaves. Facts, as well as arguments, prove that the legislator should direct all his military and other measures to the provision of leisure and the establishment of peace. For most of these military states are safe only while they are at war, but fall when they have acquired their empire; like un-

used iron they lose their temper in time of peace. And for this
the legislator is to blame, he never having taught them how to lead
the life of peace.

Material Conditions of the Best City: the Best Size [1]

In what has preceded I have discussed other forms of government; in what remains the first point to be considered is what
should be the conditions of the ideal or perfect state; for the perfect
state cannot exist without a due supply of the means of life. And
therefore we must presuppose many purely imaginary conditions,
but nothing impossible. There will be a certain number of citizens,
a country in which to place them, and the like. As the weaver or
shipbuilder or any other artisan must have the material proper for
his work (and in proportion as this is better prepared, so will the
result of his art be nobler), so the statesman or legislator must also
have the materials suited to him.

First among the materials required by the statesman is population: he will consider what should be the number and character of
the citizens, and then what should be the size and character of the
country. Most persons think that a state in order to be happy
ought to be large; but even if they are right, they have no idea
what is a large and what a small state. For they judge of the size
of the city by the number of the inhabitants; whereas they ought
to regard, not their number, but their power. A city too, like an
individual, has a work to do; and that city which is best adapted
to the fulfilment of its work is to be deemed greatest, in the same
sense of the word great in which Hippocrates might be called greater,
not as a man, but as a physician, than some one else who was taller.
And even if we reckon greatness by numbers, we ought not to include everybody, for there must always be in cities a multitude of
slaves and sojourners [2] and foreigners; but we should include those
only who are members of the state, and who form an essential part
of it. The number of the latter is a proof of the greatness of a city;
but a city which produces numerous artisans and comparatively

[1] POLITICS, Book VII, chap. 4.
[2] Or "resident aliens."

few soldiers cannot be great, for a great city is not to be confounded with a populous one.

Moreover, experience shows that a very populous city can rarely, if ever, be well governed; since all cities which have a reputation for good government have a limit of population. We may argue on grounds of reason, and the same result will follow. For law is order, and good law is good order; but a very great multitude cannot be orderly: to introduce order into the unlimited is the work of a divine power — of such a power as holds together the universe. Beauty is realized in number and magnitude, and the state which combines magnitude with good order must necessarily be the most beautiful. To the size of states there is a limit, as there is to other things, plants, animals, implements; for none of these retain their natural power when they are too large or too small, but they either wholly lose their nature, or are spoiled. For example, a ship which is only a span long will not be a ship at all, nor a ship a quarter of a mile long; yet there may be a ship of a certain size, either too large or too small, which will still be a ship, but bad for sailing. In like manner a state when composed of too few is not, as a state ought to be, self-sufficing; when of too many, though self-sufficing in all mere necessaries, as a nation may be, it is not a state,[1] being almost incapable of constitutional government. For who can be the general of such a vast multitude, or who the herald, unless he have the voice of a Stentor?

A state, then, only begins to exist when it has attained a population sufficient for a good life in the political community: it may indeed, if it somewhat exceed this number, be a greater state. But, as I was saying, there must be a limit. What should be the limit will be easily ascertained by experience. For both governors and governed have duties to perform; the special functions of a governor are to command and to judge. But if the citizens of a state are to judge and to distribute offices according to merit, then they must know each other's characters; where they do not possess this knowledge, both the election to offices and the decision of lawsuits will go wrong. When the population is very large they are manifestly settled at haphazard, which clearly ought not to be. Besides, in

---

[1] Notice this explicit statement of Aristotle's conviction that a nation cannot be a state. Cf. p. 17, *supra*.

an over-populous state foreigners and metics [1] will readily acquire the rights of citizens, for who will find them out? Clearly then the best limit of the population of a state is the largest number which suffices for the purposes of life, and can be taken in at a single view. Enough concerning the size of a state.

A similar discussion follows concerning the best extent of territory, best geographical situation, and the natural qualities desirable in the people.

Leisure [2]

(*a*) Men in general think that magistrates should be chosen not only for their merit, but for their wealth: a man, they say, who is poor cannot rule well — he has not the leisure.

(*b*) That in a well-ordered state the citizens should have leisure and not have to provide for their daily wants is generally acknowledged.

(*c*) No man can practise virtue who is living the life of a mechanic or labourer.

(*d*) The legislator should direct all his military and other measures to the provision of leisure and the establishment of peace.

(*e*) Since the end of individuals and of states is the same, the end of the best man and of the best constitution must also be the same; it is therefore evident that there ought to exist in both of them the virtues of leisure; for peace, as has been often repeated, is the end of war, and leisure of toil. But leisure and cultivation may be promoted, not only by those virtues which are practised in leisure, but also by some of those which are useful to business. For many

---

[1] Resident aliens.

[2] (*a*) POLITICS, Book II, chap. 11; (*b*) *ibid.*, Book II, chap. 9; (*c*) *ibid.*, Book III, chap. 5 (quoted on p. 145, *supra*); (*d*) *ibid.*, Book VII, chap. 14; (*e*) *ibid.*, Book VII, chap. 15; (*f*) *ibid.*, Book VIII, chap. 3; (*g*) NICOMACHEAN ETHICS, Book X, chap. 6.

necessaries of life have to be supplied before we can have leisure. Therefore a city must be temperate and brave, and able to endure: for truly, as the proverb says, "There is no leisure for slaves," and those who cannot face danger like men are the slaves of any invader. Courage and endurance are required for business and philosophy for leisure, temperance and justice for both, and more especially in times of peace and leisure, for war compels men to be just and temperate, whereas the enjoyment of good fortune and the leisure which comes with peace tend to make them insolent.

(*f*) Concerning music [1] a doubt may be raised — in our own day most men cultivate it for the sake of pleasure, but originally it was included in education, because nature herself, as has been often said, requires that we should be able, not only to work well, but to use leisure well; for, as I must repeat once again, the first principle of all action is leisure. Both are required, but leisure is better than work and is its end; and therefore the question must be asked, what ought we to do when at leisure? Clearly we ought not to be amusing ourselves, for then amusement would be the end of life. But if this is inconceivable, and amusement is needed more amid toilsome occupations than at other times (for he who is hard at work has need of relaxation, and amusement gives relaxation, whereas toil is always accompanied with exertion and effort), we should introduce amusements only at suitable times, and they should be our medicines, for the emotion which they create in the soul is a relaxation, and from the pleasure we obtain rest. But leisure of itself gives pleasure and happiness and enjoyment of life, which are experienced, not by the man at work, but by those who have leisure. For he who is engaged in toil has in view some end which he has not attained; but happiness is an end, since all men deem it to be accompanied with pleasure and not with pain. This pleasure, however, is regarded differently by different persons, and varies according to the habit of individuals; the pleasure of the best man is the best, and springs from the noblest sources.

It is clear, then, that there are branches of learning and education which we must study merely with a view to leisure spent in liberal pursuits, and these are to be valued for their own sake; whereas

[1] "Music" is used in the same wide sense in which Plato used it. See p. 53, *supra.*

those kinds of knowledge which are useful in work are to be deemed necessary, and exist for the sake of other things.[1] And therefore our fathers admitted music into education, not on the ground either of its necessity or utility, for it is not necessary, nor indeed useful in the same manner as reading and writing, which are useful in money-making, in the management of a household, in the acquisition of knowledge, and in political life, nor like drawing, useful for a more correct judgement of the works of artists, nor again like gymnastic, which gives health and strength; for neither of these is to be gained from music. There remains, then, the use of music for the life of leisure; which is in fact evidently the reason of its introduction, this being one of the ways in which it is thought that a freeman should pass his leisure.

Now that we have spoken of the virtues, the forms of friendship, and the varieties of pleasure, what remains is to discuss in outline the nature of happiness, since this is what we state the end of human nature to be. Our discussion will be the more concise if we first sum up what we have said already. We said, then, that it is not a disposition; for, if it were, it might belong to some one who was asleep throughout his life, living the life of a plant, or again, to some one who was suffering the greatest misfortunes. If these implications are unacceptable, and we must rather class happiness as an activity, as we have said before, and if some activities are necessary, and desirable for the sake of something else, while others are so in themselves, evidently happiness must be placed among those desirable in themselves, not among those desirable for the sake of something else; for happiness does not lack anything, but is self-sufficient. Now, those activities are desirable in themselves from which nothing is sought beyond the activity. And of this nature virtuous actions are thought to be; for to do noble and good deeds is a thing desirable for its own sake.

Pleasant amusements also are thought to be of this nature; we choose them not for the sake of other things; for we are injured rather than benefited by them, since we are led to neglect our bodies and our property. But most of the people who are deemed happy take refuge in such pastimes, which is the reason why those who

[1] This is the basis of the distinction, which the modern world has inherited, between liberal and technical education.

are ready-witted at them are highly esteemed at the courts of tyrants; they make themselves pleasant companions in the tyrants' favourite pursuits, and that is the sort of man they want. Now these things are thought to be of the nature of happiness because people in despotic positions spend their leisure in them, but perhaps such people prove nothing; for virtue and reason, from which good activities flow, do not depend on despotic position; nor, if these people, who have never tasted pure and generous pleasure, take refuge in the bodily pleasures, should these for that reason be thought more desirable; for boys, too, think the things that are valued among themselves are the best. It is to be expected, then, that, as different things seem valuable to boys and to men, so they should to bad men and to good. Now, as we have often maintained, those things are both valuable and pleasant which are such to the good man; and to each man the activity in accordance with his own disposition is most desirable, and, therefore, to the good man that which is in accordance with virtue. Happiness, therefore, does not lie in amusement; it would, indeed, be strange if the end were amusement, and one were to take trouble and suffer hardship all one's life in order to amuse oneself. For, in a word, everything that we choose we choose for the sake of something else — except happiness, which is an end. Now, to exert oneself and work for the sake of amusement seems silly and utterly childish. But to amuse oneself in order that one may exert oneself, as Anacharsis puts it, seems right; for amusement is a sort of relaxation, and we need relaxation because we cannot work continuously. Relaxation, then, is not an end; for it is taken for the sake of activity.

The happy life is thought to be virtuous; now, a virtuous life requires exertion, and does not consist in amusement. And we say that serious things are better than laughable things and those connected with amusement, and that the activity of the better of any two things — whether it be two elements of our being or two men — is the more serious; but the activity of the better is *ipso facto* superior and more of the nature of happiness. And any chance person — even a slave — can enjoy the bodily pleasures no less than the best man; but no one assigns to a slave a share in happiness — unless he assigns to him also a share in human life. For happiness does not lie in such occupations, but, as we have said before, in virtuous activities.

Nothing is more important for an understanding of Aristotle than to avoid misapprehension of what he means by "leisure." It is hardly too much to say that this conception is the key to his entire political theory.

Waking life is made up of three parts, according to Aristotle; there is labor or toil, rest or recreation, and leisure. With the first two of these we are familiar enough. We are accustomed to the notion that a man's life is composed of hours of work and hours of recreation. But, if we were to use the word "leisure," we should probably use it as a synonym for "recreation." "A leisure hour" means for us the same as an hour of recreation; "a life of leisure" means simply a life in which no work is done.

Aristotle does not mean this by "leisure." He thinks it an important part of the justification of slavery that the labor of the slave provides leisure for the master; this does not mean that he thinks it just that some men should work in order that others may be idle. He says that the legislator should direct his measures to the provision of leisure; this does not mean that the aim of statesmanship is to secure that the people have as little as possible to do. He thinks it indispensable that citizenship should be confined to a leisured class; this does not mean a class which can afford to play while other men work.

Leisure, for Aristotle, is not relaxation, but a form of activity. How, then, does it differ from the activity of work? In this: work includes all activities which are performed because they are a means to certain necessary or desirable results, but *which would not be performed for their own sake*. No one would dig a field for the sake of digging it, but only because it is necessary in order to produce crops; no one would mine metals if metals could be had without mining, nor tend cattle if cattle could tend themselves. These, therefore, are forms of work or of what Aristotle calls "necessary" or "useful" activity. But there are other activities which are worth performing for their own sake, because in them man realizes and exercises his human virtue. These are the activities for which man is destined by his nature, and it is these which are designated by the term "leisure."

What activities are these? Practically all activities beyond those to which man is driven by the necessity of supplying his economic and material needs; first and foremost, the political activity of ruling, the performance of public services, the activity of warfare, in which the virtue of courage is actualized; the conduct of social relations with fellow-citizens, which calls forth the virtues of temperance, generosity, magnanimity, and goodfellowship; participation in athletic contests, in dramatic performances, and in the services of religion; and finally the pursuit of science and philosophy. The hours which the ordinary Athenian citizen spent in the public assembly, in the law courts, in the theater, in the temples, on campaign, in the gymnasia, or, later, in the philosophical schools — these were his hours of intensest activity; but they were all included under his leisure. The activities of leisure are thus identical with the activities of "the good life," for the sake of which the state exists.[1]

The change which our conceptions have undergone since Aristotle's time is forcibly illustrated by the meaning which the adjective "leisurely" has come to bear. "Leisurely" is the opposite of "intense," and it is characteristic of us in general that we are more intensely active in our work than in our leisure. We take our work seriously, but our leisure not. Aristotle's attitude is the reverse of this in two respects. Not only does he regard leisure as something more serious than we do, but he also regards work as something less serious than we do. I have already touched upon the former point; to be at leisure is for Aristotle to be active in doing the things which are best worth doing, and such an activity should be the reverse of leisurely. But it is worth noticing also that Aristotle lacked the conception which is prevalent in the modern world of the seriousness of work. This conception has not always existed. It is a legacy of the Puritans, who brought to work a religious devotion. In the ancient world we may suspect that "leisureliness" in our sense of the word characterized the proceedings of the slave and the menial worker rather than those of the free man and the citizen.

The Highest Life for Man: Contemplation [2]

🖜 If happiness is activity in accordance with virtue, it is reasonable that it should be in accordance with the highest virtue; and this will be that of the best thing in us. Whether it be reason or something

[1] See pp. 124–25, *supra.*

[2] NICOMACHEAN ETHICS, Book x, chap. 7.

else that is this element which is thought to be our natural ruler and guide and to take thought of things noble and divine, whether it be itself also divine or only the most divine element in us, the activity of this in accordance with its proper virtue will be perfect happiness. That this activity is contemplative we have already said.

Now this would seem to be in agreement both with what we said before and with the truth. For, firstly, this activity is the best (since not only is reason the best thing in us, but the objects of reason are the best of knowable objects); and, secondly, it is the most continuous, since we can contemplate truth more continuously than we can *do* anything. And we think happiness has pleasure mingled with it, but the activity of philosophic wisdom is admittedly the pleasantest of virtuous activities; at all events the pursuit of it is thought to offer pleasures marvellous for their purity and their enduringness, and it is to be expected that those who know will pass their time more pleasantly than those who inquire. And the self-sufficiency that is spoken of must belong most to the contemplative activity. For while a philosopher, as well as a just man or one possessing any other virtue, needs the necessaries of life, when they are sufficiently equipped with things of that sort the just man needs people towards whom and with whom he shall act justly, and the temperate man, the brave man, and each of the others is in the same case, but the philosopher, even when by himself, can contemplate truth, and the better the wiser he is; he can perhaps do so better if he has fellow-workers, but still he is the most self-sufficient. And this activity alone would seem to be loved for its own sake; for nothing arises from it apart from the contemplating, while from practical activities we gain more or less apart from the action. And happiness is thought to depend on leisure; for we are busy that we may have leisure, and make war that we may live in peace.

Now the activity of the practical virtues is exhibited in political or military affairs, but the actions concerned with these seem to be unleisurely. Warlike actions are completely so (for no one chooses to be at war, or provokes war, for the sake of being at war; any one would seem absolutely murderous if he were to make enemies of his friends in order to bring about battle and slaughter); but the action of the statesman is also unleisurely, and — apart from the political action itself — aims at despotic power and honours, or at all events happiness, for him and his fellow citizens — a happiness different from political action, and evidently sought as being different. So, if among virtuous actions political and military actions are distinguished by nobility and greatness, and these are unleisurely and aim at an end and are not desirable for their own sake, but the activity of reason, which is contemplative, seems both to be superior in serious worth and to aim at no end beyond itself, and to have its pleasure proper to itself (and this augments the activity), and the self-sufficiency, leisureliness, unweariedness (so far as this is possible for man), and all the other attributes ascribed to the supremely happy man are evidently those connected with this activity, it follows that this will be the complete happiness of man, if it be allowed a complete term of life (for none of the attributes of happiness is *in*complete).

But such a life would be too high for man; for it is not in so far as he is man that he will live so, but in so far as something divine is present in him; and by so much as this is superior to our composite nature is its activity superior to that which is the exercise of the other kind of virtue. If reason is divine, then, in comparison with man, the life according to it is divine in comparison with human life. But we must not follow those who advise us, being men, to think of human things, and, being mortal, of mortal things, but must, so far as we can, make ourselves immortal, and strain every nerve to live in accordance with the best thing in us; for even if it be small in bulk, much more does it in power and worth surpass everything. This would seem, too, to be each man himself, since it is the authoritative and better part of him. It would be strange, then, if he were to choose not the life of his self, but that of something else. And what we said before will apply now; that which is proper to each thing is by nature best and most pleasant for each thing; for man, therefore, the life according to reason is best and pleasantest, since reason more than anything else *is* man. This life therefore is also the happiest.

Much in this passage contradicts what I have said of Aristotle's political doctrine; but it contradicts also what Aristotle has said. He gave us in the *Politics* the theory implicit in the life of the Greek city-state; he gives us here the theory which sapped the life of the city-state, or at least arose from its decay. That theory identified the "good life" for man with political activity (in the wide sense which we have seen this term must bear);[1] this theory identifies the best life with an activity which is not political at all, for the highest enjoyment of contemplation is possible to a solitary man. This profoundly affects the individual's relation to the state. According to that theory, the individual was, it is true, bound to the state by necessity; "the state comes into existence for the sake of life," and a man must belong to it or starve. *But* (so that theory proceeded) the state exists for the sake of the good life; i.e., man's spiritual nature receives its fullest exercise and development in that same social organization which his material wants necessitate. He is bound to society by economic necessity, but this is no bondage to him because his necessity and his highest good draw him in the same direction. But the case is quite altered when his highest good is made to reside in a non-social activity. He is still bound to society by material necessity, because a philosopher's soul must still inhabit an animal body, but necessity will draw him from his good, not to it. He will reduce the extent of his participation to that minimum which his bodily needs make unavoidable. He will belong to society as a member in an economic partnership for the reciprocal supply of material wants; but he will not devote his leisure to a partnership in those common activities which transform economic into political society. These are now themselves degraded to the status of "work" in contrast with the true leisure of contemplation, and are to be shunned as hindrances to the pursuit of the highest good.

Hegel said that the ancient Greek world was destroyed by the emergence in human consciousness of a new principle, the "principle of individual self-determination," discovered by Socrates, propounded by the Stoics, and adopted by Christianity as the cornerstone of its system. We need not raise the question here whether this movement of thought was a cause or only a symptom of the decay of the Greek world, nor discuss the adequacy of Hegel's phrase to describe it (no phrase can pretend to do more than *designate* something infinitely subtle and complex, and Hegel's serves this purpose as well as another). But when all reservations have been made, there is something both

[1] P. 125, *supra.*

true and important in what Hegel maintains. We shall find the philosophies which we have yet to consider developing the implications of a new set of ideas which are inconsistent with the theory of Greek political life. What we have now to remark is that the germs of these new, revolutionary ideas are to be found within the classical Greek philosophies themselves.

They are introduced in the character of "the philosopher"; and this explains the otherwise unaccountable importance ascribed in those philosophies to this character. Take away all that is said about "the philosopher," and the philosophies of Plato and Aristotle are the theory of Greek practice; the theory of "the philosopher" is the new wine destined to burst the old bottles.

But the new idea takes different forms in Plato and in Aristotle. For Plato, philosophy extends to the sphere of practice. It qualifies the statesman to make constitutions, and it gives the private individual a standard of conduct.[1] But for Aristotle all matters of practice are insusceptible of scientific treatment. Only the inevitable and eternal principles of the universe are proper objects of philosophical understanding. Hence the sole activity of the philosopher is contemplation, and his concern with the world of practical affairs is neither to reform it nor to conduct his life within it, but to retire from it as completely as possible.

For Further Reading

Translation of the POLITICS by B. Jowett, revised by W. D. Ross. Oxford: Clarendon Press, 1921.

Commentaries and General Works

BARKER, ERNEST, THE POLITICAL THOUGHT OF PLATO AND ARISTOTLE. New York: G. P. Putnam's Sons, 1906.

BRADLEY, A. C., "ARISTOTLE'S CONCEPTION OF THE STATE."
> *An essay published in the volume of essays by various hands entitled* HELLENICA (Evelyn Abbott, editor; second edition; New York: Longmans, Green and Company, 1898). BRADLEY'S *essay is one of the best things written on Aristotle's political theory.*

---

[1] See pp. 109 *et seq.*, *supra.*

NEWMAN, W. L., Introductory essays in vol. I of his four-volume edition of
ARISTOTLE'S POLITICS.   New York: Oxford University Press, 1887–1902.
> *Contains some Greek, but most of the book can be read with profit by a
> Greek-less reader.*

STOCKS, JOHN L., ARISTOTELIANISM.   New York: Longmans, Green and Company, 1925.
> *A short introduction to the philosophy of Aristotle as a whole.*

Social and Political Background of Plato and Aristotle

FOWLER, W. WARDE, THE CITY-STATE OF THE GREEKS AND ROMANS.   New York:
The Macmillan Company, 1893.

GLOTZ, GUSTAVE, LE TRAVAIL DANS LA GRÈCE ANCIENNE.   Translated by M. R.
DOBIE, ANCIENT GREECE AT WORK.   New York: Alfred A. Knopf, 1925.

THUCYDIDES' HISTORY.   Several English translations.

ZIMMERN, SIR A. E., THE GREEK COMMONWEALTH.   Fourth edition; New York:
Oxford University Press, 1925.

CHAPTER FOUR

Cicero

The Life of Cicero

Cicero was born in 106 B.C. and died in 43 B.C. His career coincided with the last years of the Roman Republic, and he lived to see the rise of Caesar to supreme power, but not the final establishment of the Empire by Augustus. He was the greatest of all Roman orators, and won fame early as a pleader in the Roman courts. His public career was brilliant in its beginnings, but unfortunate in its end, for he sought to preserve the old forms of the constitution against the encroachments of autocracy, but lacked the decisiveness and judgment which might have enabled him to succeed. He opposed the rise of Caesar, who was magnanimous enough to bear no malice. But, after Caesar's murder, he denounced Mark Antony in the series of speeches known as the *Philippics*, and his temerity cost him his life.

Besides his speeches, Cicero was the author of various literary works. Two of these deal with political theory, the dialogues called the *Republic* and the *Laws*, which were written in the period between 54 and 44 when Caesar's supremacy in the state both curtailed Cicero's employments and secured his leisure.

Political Philosophy

In passing directly from Aristotle to Cicero we pass over an interval of nearly three centuries. During this interval there had come into being two great sources of new ideas in political theory. One of these was the philosophy which developed in the Greek world after Aristotle in the schools of the Epicureans, the Skeptics, and especially the Stoics. The other was the political experience and the legal system of Rome. The importance of Cicero for our purpose does not lie in the originality of his own contribution to political theory. He was not a great philosopher, and the ideas which he presents are derived either from philosophers who had gone before him or from notions generally current in his time. For this reason his works are well suited to indicate the development which had taken place in political theory since the classical philosophy of Greece. Cicero was catholic in his selection, and much that he writes is directly inspired by Plato and Aristotle themselves. I have on the whole neglected these points of agreement, and have chosen the passages which follow mainly with a view to illustrating what in him is new since Aristotle.

There follow illustrations of this new point of view from Cicero's two principal political works, the *Republic* and the *Laws*, both of them cast in dialogue form in imitation of Plato.

Definition of a State [1]

🙋 SCIPIO.[2]   Well, then, a commonwealth is the property of a people. But a people is not any collection of human beings brought together in any sort of way, but an assemblage of people in large numbers associated in an agreement with respect to justice and a partnership for the common good.   The first cause of such an association is not so much the weakness of the individual as a certain social spirit which nature has implanted in man.   For man is not a solitary or unsocial creature, but born with such a nature that not even under conditions of great prosperity of every sort [is he willing to be isolated from his fellow men]. . . .

There is an Eternal Law Which is Prior to All Positive Laws [3]

(a) MARCUS.[4]   Once more, then, before we come to the individual laws, let us look at the character and nature of Law, for fear that, though it must be the standard to which we refer everything,

---

[1] REPUBLIC, I, XXV, 39.

[2] Scipio is one of the persons of the dialogue.

[3] (a) LAWS, II, IV, 8–11, VI, 15; (b) *ibid.*, I, VI, 18–1, VII, 23; (c) *ibid.*, I, X, 28–1, XIII, 35; (d) REPUBLIC, III, XXII, 33.

[4] The persons of the dialogue are Marcus Tullius Cicero himself; Quintus Tullius Cicero, his brother; and Titus Pomponius Atticus, his friend.

we may now and then be led astray by an incorrect use of terms, and forget the rational principles on which our laws must be based.

QUINTUS. Quite so, that is the correct method of exposition.

MARCUS. Well, then, I find that it has been the opinion of the wisest men that Law is not a product of human thought, nor is it any enactment of peoples, but something eternal which rules the whole universe by its wisdom in command and prohibition. Thus they have been accustomed to say that Law is the primal and ultimate mind of God, whose reason directs all things either by compulsion or restraint. Wherefore that Law which the gods have given to the human race has been justly praised; for it is the reason and mind of a wise lawgiver applied to command and prohibition.

QUINTUS. You have touched upon this subject several times before. But before you come to the laws of peoples, please make the character of this heavenly Law clear to us, so that the waves of habit may not carry us away and sweep us into the common mode of speech on such subjects.

MARCUS. Ever since we were children, Quintus, we have learned to call, "If one summon another to court," [1] and other rules of the same kind, laws. But we must come to the true understanding of the matter, which is as follows: this and other commands and prohibitions of nations have the power to summon to righteousness and away from wrongdoing; but this power is not merely older than the existence of nations and States, it is coeval with that God who guards and rules heaven and earth. For the divine mind cannot exist without reason, and divine reason cannot but have this power to establish right and wrong. No written law commanded that a man should take his stand on a bridge alone, against the full force of the enemy, and order the bridge broken down behind him; yet we shall not for that reason suppose that the heroic Cocles [2] was not obeying the law of bravery and following its decrees in doing so noble a deed. Even if there was no written law against rape at Rome in the reign of Lucius Tarquinius, we cannot say on that account that Sextus Tarquinius did not break that eternal Law by

---

[1] A quotation from the Laws of the Twelve Tables, the earliest written laws of Rome.

[2] Horatius Cocles, who with two companions held the bridge over the Tiber against the Etruscan army. See MACAULAY, LAYS OF ANCIENT ROME.

✥ violating Lucretia, the daughter of Tricipitinus. For reason did exist, derived from the Nature of the universe, urging men to right conduct and diverting them from wrongdoing, and this reason did not first become Law when it was written down, but when it first came into existence; and it came into existence simultaneously with the divine mind. Wherefore the true and primal Law, applied to command and prohibition, is the right reason of supreme Jupiter.

QUINTUS. I agree with you, brother, that what is right and true is also eternal, and does not begin or end with written statutes.

MARCUS. Therefore, just as that divine mind is the supreme Law, so, when [reason] is perfected in man, [that also is Law; and this perfected reason exists] in the mind of the wise man; but those rules which, in varying forms and for the need of the moment, have been formulated for the guidance of nations, bear the title of laws rather by favour than because they are really such. For every law which really deserves that name is truly praiseworthy, as they prove by approximately the following arguments. It is agreed, of course, that laws were invented for the safety of citizens, the preservation of States, and the tranquillity and happiness of human life, and that those who first put statutes of this kind in force convinced their people that it was their intention to write down and put into effect such rules as, once accepted and adopted, would make possible for them an honourable and happy life; and when such rules were drawn up and put in force, it is clear that men called them "laws." From this point of view it can be readily understood that those who formulated wicked and unjust statutes for nations, thereby breaking their promises and agreements, put into effect anything but "laws." It may thus be clear that in the very definition of the term "law" there inheres the idea and principle of choosing what is just and true. I ask you then, Quintus, according to the custom of the philosophers: if there is a certain thing, the lack of which in a State compels us to consider it no State at all, must we consider this thing a good?

QUINTUS. One of the greatest goods, certainly.

MARCUS. And if a State lacks Law, must it for that reason be considered no State at all?

QUINTUS. It cannot be denied.

MARCUS. Then Law must necessarily be considered one of the greatest goods.

❧ QUINTUS. I agree with you entirely.

MARCUS. What of the many deadly, the many pestilential statutes which nations put in force? These no more deserve to be called laws than the rules a band of robbers might pass in their assembly. For if ignorant and unskilful men have prescribed deadly poisons instead of healing drugs, these cannot possibly be called physicians' prescriptions; neither in a nation can a statute of any sort be called a law, even though the nation, in spite of its being a ruinous regulation, has accepted it. Therefore Law is the distinction between things just and unjust, made in agreement with that primal and most ancient of all things, Nature; and in conformity to Nature's standard are framed those human laws which inflict punishment upon the wicked but defend and protect the good.

QUINTUS. I understand you completely, and believe that from now on we must not consider or even call anything else a law.

MARCUS. Then you do not think the Titian [1] or Apuleian [1] Laws were really laws at all?

QUINTUS. No; nor the Livian [1] Laws either.

MARCUS. And you are right, especially as the Senate repealed them in one sentence and in a single moment. But the Law whose nature I have explained can neither be repealed nor abrogated.

(b) Now, let us investigate the origins of Justice.

Well then, the most learned men have determined to begin with Law, and it would seem that they are right, if, according to their definition, Law is the highest reason, implanted in Nature, which commands what ought to be done and forbids the opposite. This reason, when firmly fixed and fully developed in the human mind, is Law. And so they believe that Law is intelligence, whose natural function it is to command right conduct and forbid wrongdoing. They think that this quality has derived its name in Greek from the idea of granting to every man his own, and in our language I believe it has been named from the idea of choosing. For as they have

---

[1] Examples of laws passed at Rome at various dates in her history. It is not, of course, implied by the speakers that they were bad laws. The defect imputed to them is that which they have in common with all positive laws, namely, that they have been brought into force at one point of time, and may consequently go out of force at another. The laws of nature, by contrast, being eternally in force, "can neither be repealed nor abrogated."

attributed the idea of fairness to the word law, so we have given it that of selection, though both ideas properly belong to Law. Now if this is correct, as I think it to be in general, then the origin of Justice is to be found in Law, for Law is a natural force; it is the mind and reason of the intelligent man, the standard by which Justice and Injustice are measured. But, since our whole discussion has to do with the reasoning of the populace, it will sometimes be necessary to speak in the popular manner, and give the name of law to that which in written form decrees whatever it wishes, either by command or prohibition. For such is the crowd's definition of law. But, in determining what Justice is, let us begin with that supreme Law which had its origin ages before any written law existed or any State had been established.

QUINTUS. Indeed that will be preferable and more suitable to the character of the conversation we have begun.

MARCUS. Well, then, shall we seek the origin of Justice itself at its fountain-head? For, when that is discovered, we shall undoubtedly have a standard by which the things we are seeking may be tested.

QUINTUS. I think that is certainly what we must do.

ATTICUS. Put me down also as agreeing with your brother's opinion.

MARCUS. Since, then, we must retain and preserve that constitution of the State which Scipio proved to be the best in the six books devoted to the subject, and all our laws must be fitted to that type of State, and since we must also inculcate good morals, and not prescribe everything in writing, I shall seek the root of Justice in Nature, under whose guidance our whole discussion must be conducted.

ATTICUS. Quite right. Surely with her as our guide, it will be impossible for us to go astray.

MARCUS. Do you grant us, then, Pomponius (for I am aware of what Quintus thinks), that it is by the might of the immortal gods, or by their nature, reason, power, mind, will, or any other term which may make my meaning clearer, that all Nature is governed? For if you do not admit it, we must begin our argument with this problem before taking up anything else.

ATTICUS. Surely I will grant it, if you insist upon it, for the singing of the birds about us and the babbling of the streams relieve me from all fear that I may be overheard by any of my comrades in the school.

MARCUS. Yet you must be careful; for it is their way to become very angry at times, as virtuous men will; and they will not tolerate your treason, if they hear of it, to the opening passage of that excellent book, in which the author has written, "God troubles himself about nothing, neither his own concerns nor those of others."

ATTICUS. Continue, if you please, for I am eager to learn what my admission will lead to.

MARCUS. I will not make the argument long. Your admission leads us to this: that animal which we call man, endowed with foresight and quick intelligence, complex, keen, possessing memory, full of reason and prudence, has been given a certain distinguished status by the supreme God who created him; for he is the only one among so many different kinds and varieties of living beings who has a share in reason and thought, while all the rest are deprived of it. But what is more divine, I will not say in man only, but in all heaven and earth, than reason? And reason, when it is full grown and perfected, is rightly called wisdom. Therefore, since there is nothing better than reason, and since it exists both in man and God, the first common possession of man and God is reason. But those who have reason in common must also have right reason in common. And since right reason is Law, we must believe that men have Law also in common with the gods. Further, those who share Law must also share Justice; and those who share these are to be regarded as members of the same commonwealth. If, indeed, they obey the same authorities and powers, this is true in a far greater degree; but as a matter of fact they do obey this celestial system, the divine mind, and the God of transcendent power. Hence we must now conceive of this whole universe as one commonwealth of which both gods and men are members.

(c) MARCUS. The points which are now being briefly touched upon are certainly important; but out of all the material of the philosophers' discussions, surely there comes nothing more valuable than the full realization that we are born for Justice, and that right is based, not upon men's opinions, but upon Nature. This fact will immediately be plain if you once get a clear conception of man's fellowship and union with his fellow-men. For no single thing is so like another, so exactly its counterpart, as all of us are to one another. Nay, if bad habits and false beliefs did not twist the weaker minds and turn them in whatever direction they are inclined, no one would be so like his own self as all men would be like all others. And so, however we may define man, a single definition will apply to all. This is a sufficient proof that there is no difference in kind between man and man; for if there were, one definition could not be applicable to all men; and indeed reason, which alone raises us above the level of the beasts and enables us to draw inferences, to prove and disprove, to discuss and solve problems, and to come to conclusions, is certainly common to us all, and, though varying in what it learns, at least in the capacity to learn it is invariable. For the same things are invariably perceived by the senses, and those things which stimulate the senses, stimulate them in the same way in all men; and those rudimentary beginnings of intelligence to which I have referred, which are imprinted on our minds, are imprinted on all minds alike; and speech, the mind's interpreter, though differing in the choice of words, agrees in the sentiments expressed. In fact, there is no human being of any race who, if he finds a guide, cannot attain to virtue.

The similarity of the human race is clearly marked in its evil tendencies as well as in its goodness, for pleasure also attracts all men; and even though it is an enticement to vice, yet it has some likeness to what is naturally good. For it delights us by its lightness and agreeableness; and for this reason, by an error of thought, it is embraced as something wholesome. It is through a similar misconception that we shun death as though it were a dissolution of nature, and cling to life because it keeps us in the sphere in which we were born; and that we look upon pain as one of the greatest of evils, not only because of its cruelty, but also because it seems to lead to the destruction of nature. In the same way, on account of the similarity between moral worth and renown, those who are publicly honoured are considered happy, while those who do not attain fame are thought miserable. Troubles, joys, desires, and fears haunt the minds of all men without distinction, and even if different men have different beliefs, that does not prove, for example, that it is not the same quality of superstition that besets those races which worship dogs and cats as gods, as that which torments other races. But what nation does not love courtesy, kindliness, gratitude, and remembrance of favours bestowed? What people does not hate and despise the haughty, the wicked, the cruel, and the ungrateful? Inasmuch as these considerations prove to us that the whole human race is bound together in unity, it follows, finally, that knowledge of the principles of right living is what makes men better.

If you approve of what has been said, I will go on to what follows. But if there is anything that you care to have explained, we will take that up first.

ATTICUS. We have no questions, if I may speak for both of us.

MARCUS. The next point, then, is that we are so constituted by Nature as to share the sense of Justice with one another and to pass it on to all men. And in this whole discussion I want it understood that what I shall call Nature is [that which is implanted in us by Nature]; that, however, the corruption caused by bad habits is so great that the sparks of fire, so to speak, which Nature has kindled in us are extinguished by this corruption, and the vices which are their opposites spring up and are established. But, if the judgments of men were in agreement with Nature, so that, as the poet says, they considered "nothing alien to them which concerns mankind," then Justice would be equally observed by all. For those creatures who have received the gift of reason from Nature have also received right reason, and therefore they have also received the gift of Law, which is right reason applied to command and prohibition. And if they have received Law, they have received Justice also. Now, all men have received reason; therefore, all men have received Justice. Consequently, Socrates was right when he cursed, as he often did, the man who first separated utility from Justice; for this separation, he complained, is the source of all mischief. For what gave rise to Pythagoras' famous words about friendship? ... From this it is clear that, when a wise man shows toward another endowed with equal virtue the kind of benevolence which is so widely diffused among men, that will then have come to pass which, unbelievable as it seems to some, is after all the inevitable result — namely, that he loves himself no whit more than he loves another. For what difference can there be among things which are all equal? But, if the

❧ least distinction should be made in friendship, then the very name of friendship would perish forthwith; for its essence is such that, as soon as either friend prefers anything for himself, friendship ceases to exist.

Now, all this is really a preface to what remains to be said in our discussion, and its purpose is to make it more easily understood that Justice is inherent in Nature. After I have said a few words more on this topic, I shall go on to the civil law, the subject which gives rise to all this discourse.

QUINTUS. You certainly need to say very little more on that head, for from what you have already said, Atticus is convinced, and certainly I am, that Nature is the source of Justice.

ATTICUS. How can I help being convinced, when it has just been proved to us, first, that we have been provided and equipped with what we may call the gifts of the gods; next, that there is only one principle by which men may live with one another, and that this is the same for all, and possessed equally by all; and, finally, that all men are bound together by a certain natural feeling of kindliness and good-will, and also by a partnership in Justice? Now that we have admitted the truth of these conclusions, and rightly, I think, how can we separate Law and Justice from Nature?

(d) ... True law is right reason in agreement with nature; it is of universal application, unchanging and everlasting; it summons to duty by its commands, and averts from wrongdoing by its prohibitions. And it does not lay its commands or prohibitions upon good men in vain, though neither have any effect on the wicked. It is a sin to try to alter this law, nor is it allowable to attempt to repeal any part of it, and it is impossible to abolish it entirely. We cannot be freed from its obligations by senate or people, and we need not look outside ourselves for an expounder or interpreter of it. And there will not be different laws at Rome and at Athens, or different laws now and in the future, but one eternal and unchangeable law will be valid for all nations and all times, and there will be one master and ruler, that is, God, over us all, for he is the author of this law, its promulgator, and its enforcing judge. Whoever is disobedient is fleeing from himself and denying his human nature, and by reason of this very fact he will suffer the worst penalties, even if he escapes what is commonly considered punishment. ...

The new notion which is expressed in these passages is that of natural law, or Law of Nature. This is the notion that there is a single law or system of laws governing the entire universe, to which all natural things have an obligation to conform. Inanimate things are bound to obedience to it by natural necessity; animals have instincts by which they conform blindly; man is obliged only by his reason. His reason is capable of discovering this law to him, and of directing his conduct in conformity with it. Thus it is clear that this "law" is something different from what modern science means by a natural law. A natural law in the modern scientific sense is something which may be binding upon reasonable creatures equally with inanimate matter. Men are no less subject than stones to the law of gravity. But though such laws are discoverable by man's reason, they are not laws which he is obliged only by his reason to obey. The law of gravity does not have to wait until I have recognized and accepted it in order that my bodily movements may become subject to it. Nor is this law of the kind which it is open to me, when I have discovered it, to disobey; for it is imposed upon my body by a natural necessity without the coöperation of my reason.

The Law of Nature which Cicero speaks of is not thus automatically compulsory upon rational creatures. It can order their conduct only in so far as they apprehend it by their reason and themselves impose it on their conduct by their will. We shall be nearer to Cicero's meaning if we speak not of a Law of Nature, but of a law of God: a description which Cicero himself uses as synonymous with the other. "Law is the primal and ultimate mind of God"; "the true and primal law, applied to command and prohibition, is the right reason of supreme Jupiter." No man need obey it, but every man can and all ought to.

The laws of particular states also claim obedience from the citizens of those states; but the conception of the Law of Nature carries with it the momentous consequence that the allegiance which the citizen owes to the laws of his state is conditional and not absolute. If these laws do not conform to the laws of Nature, then, though he may be compelled by superior force to obey them, he is under no moral obligation to do so. They then "no more deserve to be called laws than the rules a band of robbers might pass in their assembly." If they conform to the Law of Nature then the citizen ought to obey them, but only because of this conformity, not because they are the laws of his state.

It will be remembered that Plato, in the most boldly original of all his doctrines, had claimed a similar liberty for the philosopher to sit in judgment on the laws of his state.[1]   But Plato had thought that those who were fitted by nature to attain philosophical knowledge were very few; perhaps one or two, perhaps none in any state.   Cicero thinks that every man is endowed with the capacity of discerning the natural law.

Thus, in Cicero the doctrine of the law of Nature is combined with another of perhaps still greater importance: the doctrine of the natural equality of men.   "No single thing is so like another . . . as all of us are to one another. . . . And so, however we may define man, a single defini-tion will apply to all.   This is a sufficient proof that there is no differ-ence in kind between man and man; for if there were, one definition could not be applicable to all men; and indeed reason, which alone raises us above the level of the beasts . . . is certainly common to us all and, though varying in what it learns, at least in the capacity to learn it is invariable."

One corollary of the doctrine of the Law of Nature may be mentioned here.   Men are constituted fellow-citizens with one another of a political society by being subject to an identical law.   Roman citizens are made fellow-citizens with one another not by bonds of race or geo-graphical situation, but by their common partnership in the Roman law; the bond which unites Athenian citizens is the law of Athens, and similarly with all other states.   If, then, there is a law which extends equally to all men whatever, it follows that all men are by this very fact made fellow-members with one another in a society coextensive with humanity and transcending the differences of particular states.   "Those who share Law must also share Justice; and those who share these are to be regarded as members of the same commonwealth.   If, indeed, they obey the same authorities and powers, this is true in a far greater degree; but as a matter of fact they do obey this celestial system, the divine mind and the God of transcendent power.   Hence we must now conceive of this whole universe as one commonwealth of which both gods and men are members."

Men, however they may be divided from one another by the differ-ences of particular states, are still "by nature" members of a universal commonwealth, in which all men (besides gods) are included.   Notice how significantly this differs from the Aristotelian doctrine that man is

[1] See p. 108, *supra*.

"by nature" a member of a state. As a member of a state, he is in society only with that limited number of individuals who are his fellow-members in the same state, but out of society with the rest of mankind.

Membership of the larger society does not of course exclude membership of a particular state as well. On the contrary, it is in accordance with the Law of Nature itself that man should belong to a state (the mind "realizes that it is born to take part in the life of a state"), and that he should (like Cocles) sacrifice his life, if necessary, in performing his duties to it. But this obligation to the "closed" society will be derivative only from his membership of the "open"; [1] it will be obligatory on him to perform what his state demands never simply because his state demands it, but only because the Law of Nature commands its performance.

The reader may have been struck by the modernity of Cicero's thought and language in these passages. I do not mean by this that they read as though they might have been written in the twentieth century. But the idiom of the thought is familiar. We have not here, as we have with Plato and Aristotle, to be continually discounting subtle differences in what seem familiar expressions.

The reason is that Cicero's thought is based upon the two doctrines, new since Aristotle's time, of natural law and the equality of man, and that we in our thought about political matters habitually assume these very doctrines. We presuppose their truth not only in most of our political theories, but in most of our political practice. Until a very few years ago it would have been possible to say that these two principles formed part of the universally accepted groundwork of modern political thought. Now, it is possible to say only that they are two of the fundamental principles of what is called "democracy," in opposition to the new totalitarian and communist régimes.

There is not only an affinity but an actual historical connection between our thought and Cicero's upon these matters. The sources from which Cicero's ideas are derived are the sources from which we have derived our own. They have come to us through two main channels. The first is Christianity, which incorporated much of the Hellenistic philosophy within itself, and which has been the most powerful agent in the formation of men's ideas that the world has ever

[1] I adopt these expressive terms from HENRI BERGSON'S TWO SOURCES OF MORALITY AND RELIGION (1932).

known.   The second is the system of Roman law,[1] from which most of
the legal systems of western civilization have been derived, and by
which all have been profoundly influenced.   All men whose ideas have
been formed in the school of Christianity (their number included until
recently all participants in western civilization), and whose conduct
has been conformed to the standards of Roman law, necessarily have
their minds imoued with the principles which are fundamental to these
disciplines.   Two principles which are common to both are those of
natural law and human equality.   It is no wonder, therefore, that we
are conscious of familiarity with them when we find them expressed in
Cicero.

Since I have described the theory of natural law as something new
since Aristotle, it is necessary to notice here that there is one passage in
Aristotle's own writings in which a doctrine of natural law is propounded.

The passage is as follows:[2]

〜 The rule of just conduct for the citizen of a state may be derived
either from nature or from convention.   Natural justice has the
same force everywhere, and its force does not depend upon being
adopted or not.   Just by convention is that which was originally
indifferent, but ceases to be so once the rule has been laid down; for
example, that the amount of a ransom shall be a mina or that a goat
shall be sacrificed, and not two sheep.   Laws, also, which prescribe
for a single occasion are conventional, such as the law commanding
a sacrifice to Brasidas, and laws which take the form of decrees.
Some hold that all laws are of this kind, on the ground that what is
natural is unchangeable and has the same force everywhere (as fire
burns identically here and in Persia), whereas they see that the rules
of justice vary.   But the truth is not as they hold, but rather as follows: Among men at least (perhaps not among gods), though some
things are by nature, all are liable to variation; and yet in spite of
their variability we may distinguish between what is natural and

---

[1] I do not wish to suggest that the Roman law exercised an influence independent of
Christianity, or parallel to it.   The Roman law itself was adopted into the Christian
system, and owed a large part of its power to influence the modern world to the circumstance of its adoption.   But it is of sufficient importance to merit being mentioned separately.

[2] NICOMACHEAN ETHICS, Book v, chap. 7.

what is not. How, then, are we to distinguish between what is by nature, and what is by convention and agreement only, if both alike are liable to change and variation? In the same way as the distinction is drawn in other spheres. Thus, the right hand is naturally the stronger, yet any man may be ambidextrous. Those parts of justice which depend upon agreement and expediency are like weights and measures; for the measures of wine and corn are not everywhere identical, but are larger where these commodities are bought, and smaller where they are sold. Similarly, the rules of justice which are not natural, but human, are not everywhere identical, for neither are the constitutions of states identical everywhere, but everywhere there is one constitution only marked out by nature as the best.

This is an isolated passage in Aristotle, but it clearly contains an anticipation of the later doctrine, and makes it necessary to modify the sharpness of the distinction between him and his successors. Thus Aquinas, when he propounds his fully developed doctrine of natural law, appeals to this passage of Aristotle in support.[1]

Nevertheless, when all this has been admitted, there remains an important difference between the significance which this doctrine bears in Aristotle and that which it came to bear later.

Aristotle is thinking of states in the same way as he thinks of biological specimens. For each biological type there is a certain structure or constitution of bones, muscles, nerves, and so on, laid down by Nature. The different individual specimens of the type will vary to some extent in the degree to which they conform to Nature's plan. The finest specimens will be those which conform to it most nearly, but less perfect organisms will exhibit deviations, defects, and anomalies. If we inspect any specimen with the ideal structures of the species in our mind, we can, by the application of this norm, distinguish those features within it which are in conformity with nature's plan from those which are deviations from it; i.e., we can distinguish what is according to Nature from what is not.

Similarly with states. These are a type of organism, exhibiting a structure of laws and institutions, as animal organisms exhibit a structure of bones and muscles. For states also there is a norm prescribed

[1] See p. 260, *infra*.

by Nature, and by the application of it we are able within individual states to distinguish the respects in which a given constitution agrees to this norm from those in which it deviates from it; i.e., to distinguish that in them which is "by nature" from that which is only conventional. By the same method we are enabled to judge some states to be better and others worse, according as they approach more or less nearly to the natural plan.

"We" are able to pass these judgments. But who are "we"? We are the scientist (or, as Aristotle would say, the philosopher) who has passed in review the various specimens of states which history presents, and by a comparative study of them has discovered the universal norm implicit in varying degrees in them all. Knowledge of this norm enables him to judge them as better or worse, and to distinguish within each imperfect specimen what is according to nature and what is not. But the fact that the philosopher can make this distinction has no practical consequence for men who are citizens of imperfect states. For, in the first place, this knowledge is confined to philosophers, who are necessarily few, and who must have withdrawn themselves from practical interests in order to pursue philosophy. And, secondly, even if we could suppose the philosophic insight to be universally diffused, it could not practically influence the conduct of its possessors. The law of his state as it is — that is an imperative to the citizen, and a determining influence on his conduct. But the philosophic conception of what his state ought to be — this would supply him with a ground upon which he might criticize the actual laws, it might inspire him with regret at the discrepancy between what Nature has designed and what man has effected, but it would not supply him with a rule of conduct alternative to that of the actual laws. It would provide him with a standard of speculative judgment, not with another imperative. It might serve, no doubt, as a model for reform, if a man with the necessary insight should find himself in the position of a lawgiver; but this would be in any case an exceptional occurrence, and Aristotle himself never hints even at this practical application.

Far different is Cicero's theory. In the first place, he lays it down that all men are equal in respect of their capacity to discern the natural law; and, more important, what they so discern is not a model of what law ought to be, and of what it might be if a wise enough legislator were to arise in their community. What they discern is an actual law, the law of a society which now exists, namely, the society of the universe, of which they are at present members, presenting them not with the ideal of a law which might one day exist, but with an imperative claiming their immediate obedience.   The citizen of Cicero's theory is an actual member of two societies, and is thus subject (as the citizen of Aristotle's is not) to two systems of law, one positive and one eternal. When they conflict, he has the duty of rejecting the former.   And since the latter is always perfect, he bears the responsibility for all imperfections of his own conduct.

FOR FURTHER READING

Translation

CICERO's political writings, DE RE PUBLICA, DE LEGIBUS, are translated by G. W. Keyes, in the Loeb Classical Library.   New York: G. P. Putnam's Sons, 1928.   This is the translation which has been quoted in this chapter.

Commentaries and General Works

BEVAN, EDWYN R., STOICS AND SCEPTICS.   New York: Oxford University Press, 1913.

CARLYLE, R. W. and A. J., HISTORY OF MEDIAEVAL POLITICAL THEORY IN THE WEST.   Edinburgh: William Blackwood and Sons, Ltd., 1903–36.   6 vols. Vols. 1–5, New York: G. P. Putnam's Sons, 1912–28.   The first volume is introductory, and covers the Hellenistic and Roman periods.   It brings out well the importance of the great new principles which emerged at this time, those of human equality, natural law, and the universal society.

CHAPTER FIVE

Augustine

ST. AUGUSTINE was born in A.D. 354 at Tagaste, a town in northern Africa. At the time of his birth, the Roman Empire still covered the civilized world, but it was becoming harder to resist the pressure on its frontiers of the barbarian peoples from the north. The Emperor Constantine (323–337) had transferred the principal seat of government to Byzantium, which he renamed Constantinople, and the so-called "Byzantine Empire," comprising the eastern part of the Roman Empire, remained in existence until the capture of Constantinople by the Turks in 1453. But the western portions of the Empire were soon to succumb to the barbarian invasions. The city of Rome was sacked by Alaric and the Goths in 410.

Christianity had spread rapidly within the Roman Empire in the centuries which had elapsed since its foundation. The last persecutions had taken place under Diocletian (284–305), and under Constantine Christianity had become the official religion of the Empire.

Augustine was a pagan in his youth. He studied at Carthage, and gave promise of a brilliant career. In his *Confessions* he has written the story of his own life, and described the experiences which led ultimately to his conversion to Christianity: the excesses of his youth, his subsequent search for truth wherever it might be found, his adhesion first to the Manichaeans, then to the Neo-Platonists, and his final adoption of the Christian faith in 387 at the age of thirty-three. In 391 he was ordained a priest, and in 395 became Bishop of Hippo in North Africa, where he remained until his death. In 429 the Vandals invaded Africa, in 430 they besieged Hippo, and Augustine died during the siege.

POLITICAL PHILOSOPHY

Throughout his life Augustine wrote, and the volume of his written work is enormous. It comprises sermons and letters, theological and controversial writings, commentaries on the Scriptures, defences of Christianity; besides the *Confessions*, which are in a category of their own. The greatest of his works is the *City of God* (*Civitas Dei*). He undertook the writing of this in 413, three years after the sack of Rome by Alaric, as a defence of the Christian religion against those who charged it with the responsibility for Rome's fall. Christianity, they said, was to blame for the neglect of the old Roman gods, and of the old Roman virtues, which had kept Rome safe and made her great in the past.

The earlier books of Augustine's work consist, hence, mainly in an attack upon the pagan deities of Rome. The weaknesses and inconsistencies of the pagan beliefs are exposed, and it is argued that such deities can never have been responsible for the former greatness and prosperity of Rome. This greatness was not a gift of the Roman gods, who never had the power to confer it, but was granted to Rome by the providence of the one God of all the earth, as a reward for the Roman virtues.

But the *City of God* took thirteen years to write. It did not appear all together, but was published in parts year by year as it was written, and its theme soon outgrew its author's original intention. It embraces a vast multiplicity of topics; it discusses the resurrection of the body, the future life, the duties of the Christian in his relations with the civil power; and it offers an interpretation of the whole past history of the world in the light of the Christian revelation. Nor is this multiplicity reduced to the order of a coherent philosophical system. Augustine was not primarily concerned with constructing a system, nor was his interest in the problems which he discusses primarily a philosophical one. The problems were urgent, not merely interesting, and men were waiting for the answers.

It follows from this that it is not easy to give a succinct account of Augustine's philosophy; it is not always easy even to reduce different passages into consistency with one another.

In the realm with which we are concerned, namely, in that of political theory, the most important ideas of Augustine are those which center round his doctrine of the "two cities," the earthly city and the City of God. (*Civitas terrena* and *Civitas Dei* are the Latin terms, and they are difficult to render exactly into English. A more exact translation of *civitas* would be "state." It is probably best, however, to adopt the traditional rendering of "city," but to remember that it is used figuratively and to gather its precise significance from the doctrine itself.)

The City of God [1]

◆ (a) We give the name of the city of God unto that society whereof that Scripture bears witness, which has got the most excellent authority and pre-eminence of all other works whatsoever, by the disposing of the divine providence, not the affectation of men's judgments. For there it is said: "Glorious things are spoken of thee, thou city of God:" and in another place, "Great is the Lord and greatly to be praised, in the city of our God, even upon His holy mountain, increasing the joy of all the earth." And by and by in the same psalm: "As we have heard, so have we seen in the city of the Lord of Hosts, in the city of our God: God hath established it for ever." And in another: "The rivers' streams shall make glad the city of God, the most high has sanctified His tabernacle, God is in the midst of it unmoved."

These testimonies, and thousands more, teach us that there is a city of God, whereof His inspired love makes us desire to be members. The earthly citizens prefer their gods before this heavenly city's holy founder, knowing not that He is the God of gods, not of those false, wicked, and proud ones [2] (which wanting His light so universal and unchangeable, and being thereby cast into an extreme needy power, each one follows his own state, as it were, and begs peculiar honours of his servants), but of the godly and holy ones, who select their own submission to Him, rather than the world's to them, and love rather to worship Him, their God, than to be worshipped for gods themselves. The foes of this holy city, our former nine books (by the help of our Lord and King), I hope have fully

---

[1] (a) CIVITAS DEI, XI, 1; (b) *ibid.*, XIV, 1; (c) *ibid.*, XV, 1; (d) *ibid.*, XVIII, 49.
[2] *Sc.*, the deities of the pagan world.

ᵃᵇaffronted. And now, knowing what is next expected of me, as my promise — viz., to dispute (as my poor talent stretches) of the original, progress, and consummation of the two cities that in this world lie confusedly together: by the assistance of the same God, and King of ours, I set pen to paper, intending first to show the beginning of these two, arising from the difference between the angelical powers.

(b) We said in our precedent books that it was God's pleasure to propagate all men from one, both for the keeping of human nature in one social similitude, and also to make their unity of original be the means of their concord in heart. Nor would any of this kind have died had not the first two [1] (the one whereof was made from the other, and the other from nothing) incurred this punishment by their disobedience: in committing so great a sin, that their whole nature, being hereby depraved, was so transfused through all their offspring in the same degree of corruption, and necessity of death; whose kingdom hereupon became so great in man, that all would have been cast headlong in the second death, that has no end, by this due punishment, had not the undue grace of God acquitted some from it: whereby it comes to pass, that whereas mankind is divided into so many nations, distinct in language, discipline, habit, and fashion: yet are there but two sorts of men that do properly make the two cities we speak of: the one is, of men that live according to the flesh, and the other of those that live according to the spirit, either in his kind: and when they have attained their desire, either do live in their peculiar peace.

(c) I think we have sufficiently discussed the doubts concerning the beginning of the world, the soul, and mankind: which last is divided into two sorts: such as live according to man, and such as live according to God. These we mystically call "two cities" or societies, the one predestinated to reign eternally with God: the other condemned to perpetual torment with the devil. This is their end: of which hereafter. Now seeing we have said sufficient concerning their original, both in the angels whose number we know not, and in the two first parents of mankind: I think it fit to pass on to their career, from man's first offspring until he cease to beget any

[1] Adam and Eve.

more.   Between which two points all the time included, wherein the
livers ever succeed the diers, is the career of these "two cities."

Cain, therefore, was the first begotten of those two that were mankind's parents: and he belongs to the city of man: Abel was the
later, and he belongs to the city of God.   For as we see that in that
one man (as the apostle says) that which is spiritual was not first, but
that which is natural first, and then the spiritual (whereupon all that
comes from Adam's corrupted nature must needs be evil and carnal
at first, and then if he be regenerate by Christ, becomes good and
spiritual afterward): so in the first propagation of man, and course
of the "two cities" of which we dispute, the carnal citizen was born
first, and the pilgrim on earth, or heavenly citizen, afterwards, being
by grace predestinated, and by grace elected, by grace a pilgrim upon
earth, and by grace a citizen in heaven.   For, as for his birth, it was
out of the same corrupted mass that was condemned from the beginning: but God like a potter (for this simile the apostle himself uses)
out of the same lump made "one vessel to honour and another to
reproach."   The vessel of reproach was made first, and the vessel of
honour afterwards.   For in that one man, as I said, first was repro-
bation, whence we must needs begin (and wherein we need not
remain), and afterwards, goodness, to which we come by profiting,
and coming thither, therein making our abode.

Whereupon it follows that no one can be good that has not first
been evil, though all that be evil become not good: but the sooner a
man betters himself the quicker does this name follow him, abolish-
ing the memory of the other.   Therefore it is recorded of Cain that
he built a city, but Abel was a pilgrim, and built none.   For the city
of the saints is above, though it have citizens here upon earth,
wherein it lives as a pilgrim until the time of the kingdom come, and
then it gathers all the citizens together in the resurrection of the
body and gives them a kingdom to reign in with their King, for ever
and ever.

(d) Therefore, in these mischievous days, wherein the Church
works for His future glory in present humility, in fears, in sorrows,
in labours, and in temptations, joying only in hope when she joys
as she should, many reprobate live amongst the elect: both come
into the Gospel's net, and both swim at random in the sea of mortal-

ity, until the fishers draw them to shore, and then the bad are thrown
from the good, in whom as in His temple, God is all in all. We
acknowledge therefore His words in the Psalm, "I would declare and
speak of them, but they are more than I am able to express, to be
truly fulfilled." This multiplication began at that instant when
first John His messenger, and then Himself in person began to say,
"Repent ye, for the kingdom of God is at hand." He chose Him disciples, and named the apostles: poor, ignoble, unlearned men, that
what great work soever was done He might be seen to do it in them.
He had one, who abused His goodness, yet used He this wicked man
to a good end, to the fulfilling of His passion, and presenting His
Church an example of patience in tribulation. And, having sown
sufficiently the seed of salvation, He suffered, was buried, and rose
again; shewing by His suffering what we ought to endure for the
truth, and by His resurrection what we ought to hope for from eternity, besides the ineffable sacrament of His blood, shed for the
remission of sins. He was forty days on earth with His disciples
afterwards, and in their sight ascended to heaven, ten days later
sending down His promised Spirit upon them: which in the coming,
gave that manifest and necessary sign of the knowledge in languages
of all nations, to signify that it was but one catholic Church, that in
all those nations should use all those tongues.

The doctrine of the City of God is derived on the one hand, as Augustine himself declares, from the Christian revelation. On the other
hand it incorporates and develops the notion, which we have found
already growing up in the Hellenistic philosophers and in Cicero, of a
society coterminous with the universe, which transcends all the limited
associations of state, race, or class, and of which all men are qualified to
be members simply in virtue of their common humanity.

It is true that there is an important distinction between, say, Cicero's
conception of this society and Augustine's. According to the former,
men are members of it by nature, and hence all men are members of it;
according to the latter, although it was God's plan in the creation of the
human race that all men should be members of it, this plan has been
defeated by the fall of man. Since the fall, men can become members
of the Kingdom only by grace, and since grace is not given to all, not all
men are members of it. But this difference is not important for our

present purpose, for, although some men are excluded from the City of God, they are not excluded on the ground of their not belonging to a given race, class, or state. Any man whatever may receive the grace of God, and hence Augustine's city, though it does not include all men, is not the less completely indifferent to the boundaries and distinctions of human societies.

The question may be raised: In what sense can the members of the Kingdom be said to form a society at all? The one thing which they all have in common is that all love and worship the one God; but it is not immediately obvious that this must constitute a bond of society among the worshippers. Thus, for example, all the admirers of Homer have a common admiration for the same poet; but they are not by this fact made into a society. They may, it is true, come together and found a Homer society, and their common admiration for Homer will be the reason for their doing so. But the formation of the society is a subsequent act, which may or may not take place; the common admiration of Homer does not in itself constitute them members of a society with one another.

The common love and worship of God, on the other hand, has of necessity this consequence, according to Augustine, that the very act of worship (not any subsequent foundation) constitutes the worshippers members of one community. The members of the heavenly City, in a. phrase which recurs many times, "enjoy community with God *and with one another* in God." The latter is conceived by Augustine as an inseparable consequence of the former.

M. Gilson [1] has illustrated the connection between these two things by a simile.

To understand the origin of social life, let us observe it in the process of its formation, in a public spectacle, such, for example, as a play in a theatre. When the spectators assemble to attend the performance, they do not know one another and do not form a society. But if one of the actors performs with skill, those to whom his acting appeals, enjoy it with a keen delight; they may experience therein the keenest pleasure which the art of the theatre can provide. But they are not satisfied with loving the actor who provides them with this enjoyment; a sort of reciprocal sympathy is soon established between

[1] É. GILSON, INTRODUCTION À L'ÉTUDE DE ST. AUGUSTIN (Paris: 1931), p. 220.

all those who love him. If the spectators come then to love one another, this is clearly not for one another's sake, but for the sake of that individual for whom all have a common love. This is proved by the fact that the more an actor delights us, the more we multiply our applause, in order to induce the other spectators to admire him. We should like to increase the numbers of his admirers, we stimulate those who are tepid, and if any one has a mind to oppose us, we detest in him the disdain which he feels for the object of our affection. Thus love for an object gives rise spontaneously to a society formed of those whose affections are centred on it, and exclusive of all those who despise it. This conclusion, which has a universal application, applies especially to the love of God. He who loves God finds himself in virtue of this very fact in a social relation with all those who love Him.

It would, of course, be far-fetched to use M. Gilson's analogy as anything more than an illustration. Common admiration of a human artist does not necessarily constitute the bond of a society among his admirers. That the love of God necessarily gives rise to a community among those who love him — this is not something which the love of God has in common with the love of finite persons or objects. It is something peculiar to the love of God, and distinguishing it from the love of other objects (though, as we have seen, it may be illustrated by means of the latter). *Why* it is that the love of God has this necessary consequence, I do not know whether Augustine anywhere explains. His theory bears some affinity to the fundamental Christian doctrine that a man's love of God issues inevitably in love of his neighbor; but seems not to be identical with it, since members of the "earthly city" would be included among his neighbors.

The Catholic Church

Augustine occasionally uses language which suggests that the City of God is identical with the catholic Christian Church, but the passages just quoted make it clear that they must be distinguished. The City has a wider membership than the Church, since it includes both the good angels and the elect who have departed this life; and the Church contains in its ranks some who are not members of the City. Nevertheless, the two are closely connected. Man can attain membership of the City only by the gift of grace, and the normal means of the conferment of grace are the sacraments of the Church. Thus (apart from the good angels, and those upon whom God may by a special exercise of power have conferred grace without the sacraments) the City is composed exclusively of those who either are or have been members of the Church. The Church is both one section of the City, comprising those members who are still on their pilgrimage through the world, and the avenue through which all (or almost all) who are members of the City must have passed.

The society which is the City of God realizes in an eminent degree the two values, justice and peace (*Justitia* and *Pax*).

I. *Justitia*

Justice is conformity to order, and every society involves a certain order. Thus the family, the smallest and first society to which an individual belongs, imposes an order upon its members, and would be dissolved if they utterly rejected the duties which this order involves. An individual who accepts and fulfils these duties may be said to be relatively just; i.e., he is just in relation to the order of the family. But the family is itself included within a wider society, the state, and its order is therefore subordinate to the order of the state. It is conceivable that a family which commanded the devoted loyalty of its members might itself rebel against the order of the state. In this case the family itself would be unjust, and the conduct of its members, though just in relation to the order of the family, would be found unjust in relation to the more universal order of the state; and, therefore, not just in any absolute sense of the word.

But the state itself is not the widest society, nor the order of the state the universal order. The widest society is the society of all men under the kingship of God, and the universal order is that prescribed by the will of God for all men. A state may violate this order and will then be unjust, and in that case the obedience of its citizens to it, though "just" relatively to its order, will be in actual truth not just.

Thus, there is no justice in an absolute sense in the state as such.

A state exists by imposing an order upon its members, and its strength and vigor depend upon the willingness and devotion with which they accept it. But its justice is not necessarily in proportion to its strength. Its justice depends upon its conformity to the universal order, and it may well use its strength to infringe and violate this order. In such a case, it will be no less a state, no less strong, and its citizens no less devoted in obedience to its order. But in this case it will not possess justice, and the obedience of its citizens will not be just.

Thus, absolute justice belongs only to the universal order, or to a narrower order only in so far as it conforms to this. To conform to the universal order is to obey the will of God.

No Justice in Earthly Kingdoms and Pagan States [1]

✌ (a) Now it is time to perform a promise which I passed in the second book of this work: and that was, to shew that Rome never had a true commonwealth as Scipio defines one in Tully's [2] book *De Republica*. His definition was: a commonwealth is the estate of the people, *Respublica est res populi*. If this be true, Rome never had any, for it never had an estate of the people, which he defines the commonwealth by: for he defines the people to be a multitude, united in one consent of law and profit: what he means by a consent of law, he shews himself: and shews thereby that a state cannot stand without justice: so that where true justice is wanting, there can be no law. For what law does, justice does, and what is done unjustly, is done unlawfully. For we may not imagine men's unjust decrees to be laws: all men defining law to arise out of the fountain of justice; and that that same unjust assertion of some, is utterly false: "That is law which is profitable unto the greatest." So then, where justice is not, there can be no society united in one consent of law, therefore no people, according to Scipio's definitions in Tully. If no people, then no estate of the people, but rather of a confused multitude, unworthy of a people's name. If then the commonwealth be an estate of the people, and that they be no people that are not united in one consent of law: nor that a law, which is not grounded upon

---

[1] (a) CIVITAS DEI, XIX, 21; (b) *ibid.*, IV, 3, 4, 6.
[2] I.e., Cicero's, see p. 180, *supra*.

justice: then it must needs follow, that where no justice is, there no commonwealth is.

Now, then, *ad propositum:* justice is a virtue distributing unto everyone his due. What justice is that, then, that takes man from the true God, and gives him unto the condemned fiends? Is this distribution of due? Is he that takes away thy possessions, and gives them to one that has no claim to them, guilty of injustice; and is not he so likewise, that takes himself away from his Lord God, and gives himself to the service of the devil? There are wise and powerful disputations in those books, *De Republica*, for justice against injustice. Wherein, it having first been argued for injustice, against justice, and averred that a state could not stand without injustice; and this brought as a principal confirmation hereof, that it is injustice for man to rule over man, and yet if the city whose dominion is so large should not observe this form of injustice, she could never keep the provinces under. Unto this it was answered on the behalf of justice, that this was a just course, it being profitable for such to serve, and for their good to wit, when the power to do hurt is taken from the wicked; they will carry themselves better being curbed, because they carried themselves so badly before they were curbed. To confirm this answer this notable example was alleged, as being fetched from nature itself: "If it were unjust to rule, why does God rule over man, the soul over the body, reason over lust, and all the mind's other vicious affections?"

This example teaches plain that it is good for some to serve in particular, and it is good for all to serve God in general. And the mind serving God is lawful Lord over the body: so is reason being subject unto God, over the lusts and other vices. Wherefore if man serve not God, what justice can be thought to be in him? seeing that if he serve not Him the soul has neither lawful sovereignty over the body, nor the reason over the affections: now if this justice cannot be found in one man, no more can it then in a whole multitude of such like men. Therefore, amongst such there is not that consent of law which makes a multitude a people, whose estate makes a commonwealth: what need I speak of the profit, that is named in the definition of a people? For although none live profitably that live wickedly, that serve not God but the devils [1] (who are so much the

[1] The pagan deities.

more wicked in that they, being most filthy creatures, dare exact sacrifices as if they were gods): yet I think that what I have said of the consent of law may serve to shew that they were no people whose estate might make a weal-public, having no justice amongst them. If they say they did not serve devils, but holy gods, what need we rehearse that here which we said so often before? Who is he that has read over this work unto this chapter, and yet doubts whether they were devils that the Romans worshipped or no? Unless he be either senselessly thick-headed, or shamelessly contentious? But, to leave the powers that they offered unto, take this place of holy writ for all: "He that sacrificeth unto gods, shall be rooted out, save unto one God alone." He that taught this in such threatening manner will have no gods sacrificed unto, be they good or be they bad.

(b) Now then, let us examine the nature of this spaciousness, and continuance of empire, which these men give their gods such great thanks for; to whom also they say they exhibited those plays [1] (that were so filthy both in actors and the action) without any offence of honesty. But, first, I would make a little inquiry, seeing you cannot show such estates to be anyway happy as are in continual wars, being still in terror, trouble, and guilt of shedding human blood, though it be their foes; what reason, then, or what wisdom shall any man show in glorying in the largeness of empire, all their joy being but as a glass, bright and brittle, and evermore in fear and danger of breaking? To dive the deeper into this matter, let us not give the sails of our souls to every air of human breath, nor suffer our understanding's eye to be smoked up with the fumes of vain words, concerning kingdoms, provinces, nations, or so. No, let us take two men (for every particular man is a part of the greatest city and kingdom of the world, as a letter is a part of a word), and of these two men, let us imagine the one to be poor, or but of a mean estate, the other potent and wealthy; but withal, let my wealthy man take with him fears, sorrows, covetousness, suspicion, disquiet, contentions, let these be the hooks for him to hale in the augmentation of his estate, and with all the increase of

[1] The reference is to the games which were connected with the worship of the ancient gods.

*those cares, together with his estate; and let my poor man take with him sufficiency with little, love of kindred, neighbours, friends, joyous peace, peaceful religion, soundness of body, sincereness of heart, abstinence of diet, chastity of carriage, and security of conscience. Where should a man find anyone so sottish, as would make a doubt which of these to prefer in his choice?

Well then, even as we have done with these two men, so let us do with two families, two nations, or two kingdoms. Lay them both to the line of equity; which done, and duly considered, when it is done, here doth vanity lie bare to the view, and there shines felicity. Wherefore it is more convenient, that such as fear and follow the law of the true God, should have the swaying of such empires, not so much for themselves, as for those over whom they are emperors. For themselves, their piety, and their honesty (God's admired gifts) will suffice them, both to the enjoying of true felicity in this life, and the attaining of that eternal and true felicity in the next. So that here upon earth, the rule and regality that is given to the good man, does not return him so much good, as it does to those that are under this his rule and regality. But contrariwise, the government of the wicked harms themselves far more than their subjects, for it gives themselves the greater liberty to exercise their lusts; but for their subjects, they have none but their own iniquities to answer for; for what injury soever the unrighteous master does to the righteous servant, it is no scourge for his guilt, but a trial of his virtue. And therefore he that is good is free, though he be a slave, and he that is evil, a slave though he be a king. Nor is he slave to one man, but that which is worst of all, unto as many masters as he affects vices; according to the Scripture, speaking thus hereof: "Of whatsoever a man is overcome, to that he is in bondage."

Set justice aside, then, and what are kingdoms but great robberies? because what are robberies but little kingdoms? for in thefts, the hands of the underlings are directed by the commander, the confederacy of them is sworn together, and the pillage is shared by the law amongst them. And if those raggamuffins grow but up to be able enough to keep forts, build habitations, possess cities, and conquer adjoining nations, then their government is no more called thievish, but graced with the eminent name of a kingdom, given and gotten, not because they have left their practices, but because that now they may use them without danger of law: for elegant and excellent was that pirate's answer to the great Macedonian Alexander, who had taken him: the king asking him how he durst molest the seas so, he replied with a free spirit, "How darest thou molest the whole world? But, because I do it with a little ship only, I am called a thief: thou, doing it with a great navy, art called an emperor."

Now, to war against one's neighbours, and to proceed to the hurt of such as hurts not you, for greedy desire of rule and sovereignty, what is this but flat thievery in a greater excess and quantity than ordinary?

Augustine's conception of a single universal order has made clear to him a distinction which was never clear to Plato:[1] the distinction between the strength of a state and its justice. Plato saw clearly that the strength of a state depends upon the submission of its members to its "order." The preservation of this "order" Plato calls the justice of the state, and hence he regards it as self-evident that to make a state just is to make it strong, and vice versa. Because he had not the conception of a universal order transcending that of the state, he was not confronted with the problem that a state might command the utmost devotion of its citizens, and so be strong, and yet transgress the rules of a more universal order, and so be unjust. He is hardly aware of the conflict between what is right and what is expedient for a state, and it is consequently vain to look to him for any light upon the problems of international morality.

Nor, of course, is Augustine concerned with such problems in the form in which they have arisen since his time. The society which transcends the state is for him not a society of states, but a society of individuals. He is not concerned to impose upon states the rules of an international morality; his appeal is to individuals to transfer their ultimate allegiance from the state to the universal society.

The step from Plato's to Augustine's ideas about justice is a step into a more familiar world of thought. We can translate Augustine's *justitia* as "justice" without the use of mental inverted commas to remind us that we are dealing with a notion subtly different from our

[1] See p. 51, *supra*.

own nearest equivalent to it. What is the root of this difference between Plato and Augustine?

For both, justice implies law; and law, society. But, whereas for Plato man belongs to no society wider than the state, and is therefore subject to no law transcending the state-law,[1] for Augustine every man is member of a universal and eternal society, and hence subject to its universal and eternal law. The justice of Plato's citizen is thus relative to a social order limited both in space and time; it is binding only on him and his fellow-citizens, and it will change or pass away. But the law which is the standard of the Augustinian justice is the same for all times and for all men. Hence is derived the notion, still inherent in our own use of the term, that what is just at all must be just by an absolute standard.

Because Augustine has the conception of a universal law, he can apply the standard of justice to the judgment of states, in a sense which was not possible to Plato. In the same way as a man can be unjust by transgressing the order of his state, so also can a state be unjust by transgression of the universal order appointed by God. But, when he speaks of the injustice of a state, the transgression which Augustine has in mind is not solely its infringement of the rights of other states; it is also, as the passages last quoted make clear, its infringement of the rights of God. It infringes these rights when it claims for itself the service and worship which men owe only to God, or when it seeks to divert this service (as the persecuting Roman emperors endeavored to do) from the true God to false gods. "What justice is that, then, which takes man from the true God, and gives him unto the condemned fiends?"

This lays down the principle — unknown to the ancient world in its classical period, but fundamental to the medieval and still to the modern — of the distinction between a secular and a religious sphere of life, and the exclusion of the state from the latter.

II. Pax

The word "peace" has come for us to have little more than a negative meaning; it is the negative of "war." It signifies no positive

---

[1] This is not true of the *philosopher* in Plato's state — an exception, of course, of great importance. See pp. 109–113, *supra*, and pp. 224–226, *infra*.

relation, but merely the absence of a hostile one. But peace for Augustine means a positive relation, embracing partners in concord. It no more occurs to him that you can be at peace without a partner than that you can be at war without an enemy.

Peace, in this positive sense of the word, is the end to which all men and all creatures strive by the natural law of their being.[1]

Who will not confess this with me, who marks man's affairs, and the general form of nature? For joy and peace are desired alike of all men. The warrior would but conquer: war's aim is nothing but glorious peace: what is victory but a suppression of resistants, which being done, peace follows? So that peace is war's purpose, the scope of all military discipline, and the limit at which all just contentions level. All men seek peace by war, but none seek war by peace. For they that perturb the peace they live in, do it not for hate of it, but to shew their power in alteration of it. They would not disannul it, but they would have it as they like; and though they break into seditions from the rest, yet must they hold a peaceful force with their fellows that are engaged with them, or else they shall never effect what they intend. Even the thieves themselves that molest all the world besides them, are at peace amongst themselves. Admit one be so strong, or subtle that he will have no fellow, but plays all his parts of roguery alone, yet such as he can neither cut off, nor care to make known his deeds unto, with those he must needs hold a kind of peace. And at home, with his wife and family, there must he needs observe quietness, and questionless delights in their obedience unto him, which if they fail in, he chases, and chides and strikes, setting all in order by force if need be, or by cruelty: which he sees he cannot do, unless all the rest be subjected under one head, which is himself. And might he have the sway of a city, or province in such sort as he has that of his house, he would put off his thievish nature, and put on a king's, albeit his covetousness and malice remained unchanged. Thus then you see that all men desire to have peace with such as they would have live according to their liking. For those against whom they wage war, they would make their own if they could, and if they conquer them they give them such laws as they like. . . .

[1] CIVITAS DEI, XIX, 12 and 13.

The very wild beasts ... do preserve a peace with other in their kind, begetting, breeding, and living together amongst themselves, being otherwise the insociable births of the deserts: I speak not here of sheep, deer, pigeons, starling, or bees, but of lions, foxes, eagles, and owls. For what tiger is there that does not purr over her young ones, and fawn upon them in their tenderness? What kite is there, though he fly solitarily about for his prey, but will seek his female, build his nest, sit his eggs, feed his young, and assist his mate in her motherly duty, all that in him lies? Far stronger are the bands that bind man unto society, and peace with all that are peaceable: the worst men of all do fight for their fellows' quietness, and would (if it lay in their power) reduce all into a distinct form of state, drawn by themselves, whereof they would be the heads, which could never be, but by a coherence either through fear or love. For herein is perverse pride an imitator of the goodness of God, having equality of others with itself under Him, and laying a yoke of obedience upon its fellows, under itself, instead of Him: thus hates it the just peace of God, and builds an unjust one for itself. Yet can it not but love peace, for no vice, however unnatural, can pull nature up by the roots. But he that can discern between good and bad, and between order and confusion, may soon distinguish the godly peace from the wicked.

Now that perverse confusion must be reformed by the better disposing of the thing wherein it is, if it be at all, as, for example: hang a man up with his head downwards, all his posture is confounded, that which should be lowest, having the highest place, and so contrary this confusion disturbs the flesh, and is troublesome to it. But it is the soul's peace with the body that causes the feeling of that disturbance. Now, if the soul leave the body by the means of those troubles, yet as long as the body's form remains it has a certain peace with itself, and in the very manner of hanging, shews that it desires to be placed in the peace of nature, the very weight, seeming to demand a place for rest, and though life be gone, yet very nature sways it unto that order wherein she placed it. For if the dead body be preserved from putrefaction by unguents, and embalmings, yet the peace of nature is kept, for the body's weight is applied thereby to an earthly sympathising site, and convenient place for it to rest in. But, if it be not embalmed, but left to nature's dissolving, it is so long altered by ill-tasting vapours, until each part be wholly reduced to the particular natures of the elements, yet is not a tittle of the Creator's all-disposing law controlled: for, if there grow out of this carcase a many more living creatures, each body of these serves the quantity of life that is in it, according to the same law of creation. And, if that be devoured up, by other ravenous beasts or birds, it shall follow the ordinance of the same law, disposing all things congruently, into what form of nature soever it be changed.

The body's peace, therefore, is an orderly disposal of the parts thereof: the unreasonable soul's,[1] a good temperature of the appetites thereof: the reasonable soul's, a true harmony between the knowledge and the performance. That of body and soul alike, a temperate and undiseased habit of nature in the whole creature. The peace of mortal man with immortal God is an orderly obedience unto His eternal law, performed in faith. Peace of man and man is a mutual concord: peace of a family, an orderly rule and subjunction amongst the parts thereof: peace of a city, an orderly command, and obedience amongst the citizens: peace of God's City a most orderly coherence in God, and fruition of God: peace of all things, is a well disposed order. For order is a good disposition of discrepant parts, each in the fittest place, and therefore the miserable (as they are miserable) are out of order, wanting that peaceable and unperturbed state which order exacts. But because their own merits have incurred this misery, therefore even herein they are imposed in a certain set order howsoever. Being not conjoined with the blessed, but severed from them by the law of order, and being exposed to miseries, yet these are adapted unto the places wherein they are resident, and so are digested into some kind of methodical form, and consequently into some peaceful order. But this is their misery, that although that some little security wherein they live may exempt them from present sorrows, yet are they not in that state which secludes sorrow for ever, and affords eternal security. And their misery is far greater if they want the peace of nature: and, when they are offended, the part that grieves is the first disturber of their peace: for that which is neither offended, nor dissolved, preserves the peace of nature still. So, then, as one may possibly live without

[1] "The unreasonable soul"; the emotions, appetites, passions, etc.

grief, but cannot possibly grieve unless he live: so may there be peace without any war or contention: but contention cannot be without some peace (not as it is contention, but), because the contenders do suffer and perform diverse things herein according to nature's prescript, which things could not consist, had they not some peaceful order amongst them.

The End at Which All Societies Aim [1]

(a) Every society, earthly and heavenly alike, aims at peace. The two societies differ only in the kind of peace at which they aim. The former aims only at a concord of men in ordered relations with one another; but the end of the latter is the peace of God, "the most orderly and concordant partnership in the fruition of God and of one another in God."

All temporal things are referred unto the benefit of the peace which is resident in the terrestrial city, by the members thereof: and unto the use of the eternal peace, by the citizens of the Heavenly society. Wherefore, if we wanted reason, we should desire only an orderly state of body, and a good temperature of desires: nothing but fleshly ease, and fulness of pleasure. For the peace of the body augments the quiet of the soul: and if it be awanting, it procures a disturbance even in brute beasts, because the emotions have not their true temperature.

Now, both these combined add unto the peace of soul and body both, that is, unto the healthful order of life. For as all creatures shew how they desire their bodies' peace, in avoiding the causes of their hurt: and their souls', in following their appetites when need requires: so in flying of death, they make it as apparent how much they set by their peace of soul and body. But man, having a reasonable soul, subjects all his actions common to animals, unto the peace of that, to work so both in his contemplation and action, that there may be a true consonance between them both, and this we call the peace of the reasonable soul. To this end he is to avoid molestation by grief, disturbance by desire, and dissolution by death, and to aim at profitable knowledge, whereunto his actions may be

[1] (a) CIVITAS DEI, XIX, 14; (b) ibid., XIX, 11.

conformable. But lest his own infirmity, through the much desire to know, should draw him into any pestilent inconvenience of error, he must have a divine instruction, to whose directions and assistance, he is to assent with firm and free obedience. And because that during this life "He is absent from the Lord, he walketh by faith, and not by sight," and therefore he refers all his peace of body, of soul, and of both unto that peace which mortal man has with immortal God: to live in an orderly obedience under His eternal law, by faith.

Now God, our good Master, teaching us in the two great commandments the love of Him, and the love of our neighbour, to love three things, God, our neighbour, and ourselves, and seeing he that loves God, offends not in loving himself: it follows that he ought to counsel his neighbour to love God, and to provide for him in the love of God, sure he is commanded to love him, as his own self. So must he do for his wife, children, family, and all men besides: and wish likewise that his neighbour would do as much for him, in his need: thus shall he be settled in peace and orderly concord with all the world. The order whereof is, first, to do no man hurt, and secondly, to help all that he can. So that his own have the first place in his care, and thus, his place and order in human society affords him more conveniency to benefit. Whereupon St. Paul says, "He that provideth not for his own, and, namely, for them that be of his household, denieth the faith, and is worse than an infidel." For this is the foundation of domestic peace, which is, an orderly rule, and subjection in the parts of the family, wherein the provisors are the commanders, as the husband over his wife; parents over their children, and masters over their servants: and they that are provided for, obey, as the wives do their husbands, children their parents, and servants their masters. But in the family of the faithful man, the heavenly pilgrim, there the commanders are indeed the servants of those they seem to command: ruling not in ambition, but being bound by careful duty: not in proud sovereignty, but in nourishing pity.

(*b*) We may therefore say that peace is our final good, as we said of life eternal: because the psalm says unto that city whereof we write this laborious work: "Praise the Lord, O Jerusalem, praise thy Lord, O Sion: for He hath made fast the bars of thy gates, and blessed thy children within thee; He giveth peace in thy borders." When the bars of the gates are fast, as none can come in, so none can go out. And therefore this peace which we call final, is the borders and bounds of this city: for the mystical name hereof, Jerusalem, signifies, "a vision of peace": but, because the name of peace is ordinary in this world where eternity is not resident, therefore we choose rather to call the bound wherein the chief good of this city lies, "life eternal," rather than "peace." Of which end the apostle says, "Now being freed from sin, and made servants to God, ye have your fruit in holiness, and the end, everlasting life." But on the other side, because such as are ignorant in the Scriptures may take this "everlasting life" in an ill sense, for the life of the wicked, which is eternally evil, either, as some philosophers held, because the soul cannot die, or, as our faith teaches, because torments cannot cease: yet would not the wicked feel them eternally, unless they have also their eternal life: therefore the main end of this city's aim is either to be called Eternity in peace, or Peace in eternity, and thus it is plain to all. For the good of peace is generally the greatest wish of the world, and the most welcome when it comes. Whereof I think we may take leave of our reader, to have a word or two more, both because of the city's end, whereof we now speak, and of the sweetness of peace, which all men do love.

Universal Peace

Of the philosophers whom we have hitherto considered, Augustine is the first to propound the ideal of universal peace, which ever since his time has haunted the imagination of the West, and has not been without an effect on the conduct of men.

This does not mean that Augustine's predecessors had glorified war, or regarded war as an end desirable in itself. Plato in the *Republic* had come the nearest to doing this, for it is war which calls into existence the guardian class,[1] which forms an essential part of the state, and without which the highest excellences of men would never be developed. But in spite of the fact that the virtues of the guardians are nurtured

[1] REPUBLIC, II, 372–373; pp. 49–50, *supra*.

in the environment of a camp, it is in peace and not in war that they find their proper exercise and highest development: [1] in contemplation, educating, and ruling, not in fighting. War between states may be necessary, but is not in itself good, and it arises only from that vice or degeneration of states which swells their needs beyond what their own land can supply.

In a world of perfect states there would be, therefore, according to Plato, no war. But such a condition would be very different from that which Augustine conceives as the condition of universal peace. The peace between Platonic states is merely negative. There is no collision only because there is no contact between them. Within each state there reigns a peace of quite a different kind, consisting not in the isolation of the members from one another, but in *concord* beneath a common order.

For Augustine there is a universal order to which all men are subject (because all men are subject to one God), and the ideal of universal peace depends upon this universal order. It is the extension to the whole world of that positive peace which Plato could conceive to be possible only within the single state. "Since [a man] is commanded to love [his neighbour] as his own self, so must he do for his wife, children, family, *and all men besides*: then shall he be settled *in peace and orderly concord with all the world*." [2]

Such a world-order is not, of course, a system of states; it is a system of individuals transcending the divisions of states. Nor had Augustine's inspiration solely a religious source. He saw before him in the Pax Romana an actual approximation to such an ideal. The Roman Empire upheld an order, seemingly almost world-wide, in which all men were organized in peaceful relations with one another under the system of Roman law.

This secular order is called by Augustine the "peace of the earthly city," and he does not undervalue it. But this is not for him an end in itself. A system of legal relationships is one thing, but the highest

---

[1] In his latest work, the LAWS, Plato says (1, 628): "No man is a true statesman whose aim is directed solely or principally to war. The genuine legislator regulates war with a view to peace, not peace with a view to war." Cf. Aristotle: "Peace . . . is the end of war, and leisure of toil. But . . ., as the proverb says, 'There is no leisure for slaves,' and those who cannot face danger like men, are the slaves of any invader." POLITICS, Book VII, chap. 15; quoted, pp. 168–169, *supra*.

[2] Quoted, p. 215, *supra*. My italics.

kind of peace is concord, a system united by the bond of love. Such
love, extending beyond family and state to all men, is possible only to
those who have the love of God. A system in which all men are
actively united with one another by the love of one another in God —
this is what Augustine means by universal peace; not the mere absence
of war, or the mere stabilization of relationships by the enforcement
of legal rules.

The Peace of an Earthly Society is a Good, Though Not the Highest Good

The peace which it is the end of earthly (or secular) society to preserve is not the highest good, but it is a good.[1]

❧ But the temporal, earthly city (temporal, for when it is condemned
to perpetual pains it shall be no more a city) has all the good here
upon earth, and therein takes that joy that such an object can
afford. But because it is not a good that acquits the possessors of
all troubles, therefore this city is divided in itself into wars, alterca-
tions, and appetites of bloody and deadly victories. For any part
of it that wars against another, desires to be the world's conqueror,
whereas indeed it is vice's slave. And if it conquer, it extols itself
and so becomes its own destruction: but if we consider the condition
of worldly affairs, and grieve at man's openness to adversity, rather
than delight in the events of prosperity, thus is the victory deadly:
for it cannot keep a sovereignty for ever where it got a victory for
once. Nor can we call the objects of this city's desires, good, it itself
in its own human nature, far surmounting them. It desires an
earthly peace, for very low ambitions, and seeks it by war, where if it
subdue all resistance, it attains peace: which notwithstanding the
other side, that fought so unfortunately for the same reasons, lack.
This peace they seek by laborious war, and obtain (they think) by
a glorious victory. And when they conquer that had the right
cause, who will not congratulate their victory, and be glad of their
peace? Doubtless those are good, and God's good gifts. But if the
things appertaining to that celestial and supernal city where the

[1] CIVITAS DEI, XV, 4.

victory shall be everlasting, be neglected for those goods, and those goods desired as the only goods, or loved as if they were better than the other, misery must needs follow and increase that which is inherent before.

The Christian's Relation to the Secular Power

The peace which the earthly society secures is a good not only to the man who knows no higher peace, but also to the members of the City of God themselves, so long as they are pilgrims on earth. They need the security and order which it provides in order to be free from disturbance and molestation in the performance of their religious duties. They must, therefore, respect the laws by which this security is maintained and render obedience to the power by whom the laws are enforced. In respect of their willingness to obey they will not be distinguished from those who are citizens of the earthly society alone; they will differ from them only in the spirit with which their obedience is rendered. For the others the attainment of the earthly peace is an end in itself, but they will use the earthly peace as a means to the attainment of heavenly peace.[1]

(a) Wherefore, as the soul is the flesh's life, so is God the beatitude of man, as the Hebrew's holy writ affirms: "Blessed is the people whose God is the Lord"; wretched then are they that are strangers to that God, and yet have those a kind of allowable peace, but that they shall not have for ever, because they used it not well when they had it. But that they should have it in this life is for our good also; because that during our commixture with Babylon, we ourselves make use of her peace, and faith does free the people of God at length out of her, yet so, as in the meantime we live as pilgrims in her. And therefore the apostle admonished the Church, to pray for the kings and potentates of that earthly city, adding this reason, "That we may lead a quiet life in all godliness and charity." And the prophet Jeremiah, foretelling the captivity of God's ancient people, commanding them (from the Lord) to go peaceably and patiently to Babylon, advised them also to pray, saying, "For in

[1] (a) CIVITAS DEI, XIX, 26; (b) ibid., XIX, 17.

her peace shall be your peace," meaning that temporal peace which is common both to good and bad.

(*b*) But they that live not according to faith angle for all their peace in the sea of temporal profits: whereas the righteous live in full expectation of the glories to come, using the occurrences of this world, but as pilgrims, not to abandon their course towards God for mortal respects, but thereby to assist the infirmity of the corruptible flesh, and make it more able to encounter with toil and trouble. Wherefore the necessaries of this life are common, both to the faithful and the infidel, and to both their families: but the ends of their two usages thereof are far different.

The faithless, "worldly city" aims at earthly peace, and settles the self therein, only to have an uniformity of the citizens' wills in matters only pertaining to mortality.   And the "Heavenly City," or rather that part thereof, which is as yet a pilgrim on earth and lives by faith, uses this peace also: as it should, it leaves this mortal life, wherein such a peace is requisite, and therefore lives (while it is here on earth) as if it were in captivity, and having received the promise of redemption, and divers spiritual gifts as seals thereof, it willingly obeys such laws of the "temporal city" as order the things pertaining to the sustenance of this mortal life, to the end that both the cities might observe a peace in such things as are pertinent hereunto.

Limits of Secular Authority

But the Christian will render this obedience to the secular authority only within the limits of secular affairs.   The same consideration for his soul's supreme good which makes him obedient to the power of the state so long as it is confined to the securing of earthly peace, compels him to renounce his obedience so soon as the state seeks to enforce laws of religion.

❧ But because that the "earthly city" has some members whom the Holy Scriptures utterly disallow, and who standing either too well affected to the devils, or being deluded by them, believed that each thing had a peculiar deity over it, and belonged to the charge of a several god: as the body to one, the soul to another, and in the body itself the head to one, the neck to another, and so of every member: as likewise of the soul, one had the wit, another the learning, a third the wrath, a fourth the desire: as also in other necessaries or accidents belonging to man's life, the cattle, the corn, the wine, the oil, the woods, the monies, the navigation, the wars, the marriages, the generations, each being a several charge unto a particular power, whereas the citizens of the "Heavenly State" acknowledged but the only God, to whom that worship, which is called λατρεία was peculiarly and solely due; hence came it that the "two hierarchies" could not be combined in one religion, but must needs dissent herein, so that the good part was fain to bear the pride and persecution of the bad, had not their own multitude sometimes, and the providence of God continually stood for their protection.

This "celestial society" while it is here on earth, increases itself out of all languages, never respecting the temporal laws that are made against so good and religious a practice: yet not breaking, but observing their diversity in divers nations, all which do tend unto the preservation of earthly peace, if they oppose not the adoration of one only God. So that you see, the "Heavenly City" observes and respects this temporal peace here on earth, and the coherence of men's wills in honest morality, as far as it may with a safe conscience; yea, and so far desires it, making use of it for the attainment of the peace eternal: which is so truly worthy of that name, as that the orderly and uniform combination of men in the fruition of God, and of one another in God, is to be accounted the reasonable creature's only peace, which being once attained, mortality is banished, and life then is the true life indeed, nor is the carnal body any more an encumbrance to the soul, by corruptibility, but is now become spiritual, perfected and entirely subject unto the sovereignty of the will.

This peace is that unto which the pilgrim in faith refers the other which he has here in his pilgrimage, and then lives he according to faith, when all that he does for the obtaining hereof is by himself referred unto God, and his neighbour withal, because being a citizen, he must not be all for himself, but sociable in his life and actions.[1]

[1] CIVITAS DEI, XIX, 17.

Slavery [1]

ᔰ Thus has nature's order prescribed, and man by God was thus
created. "Let them rule," saith He, "over the fishes of the sea,
and the fowls of the air, and over every thing that creepeth upon the
earth." He made him reasonable, and lord only over the unreasonable, not over man, but over beasts. Whereupon the first holy men
were rather shepherds than kings, God shewing herein what both
the order of the creation desired, and what the merit of sin exacted.
For justly was the burden of servitude laid upon the back of transgression. And, therefore, in all the Scriptures we never read the
word servant, until such time as that just man Noah laid it as a
curse upon his offending son. So that it was guilt, and not nature
that gave original unto that name. The Latin word *servus*, had the
first derivation from hence: those that were taken in the wars, being
in the hands of the conquerors to massacre or to preserve, if they
saved them, then were they called *servi*, of *servo*, "to save." Nor
was this effected beyond the desert of sin. For in the justest war,
the sin upon one side causes it; and if the victory fall to the wicked
(as sometimes it may) it is God's decree to humble the conquered,
either reforming their sins herein, or punishing them. Witness that
holy man of God, Daniel, who, being in captivity, confessed unto
his Creator that his sins, and the sins of the people were the real
causes of that captivity.

Sin, therefore, is the mother of servitude, and first cause of man's
subjection to man: which notwithstanding comes not to pass but by
the direction of the highest, in whom is no injustice, and who alone
knows best how to proportionate his punishment unto man's of-
fences: and he himself says: "Whosoever committeth sin is the servant of sin," and therefore many religious Christians are servants
unto wicked masters, yet not unto freemen, for that which a man is
addicted unto, the same is he slave unto. And it is a happier servitude to serve man than lust: for lust (to omit all the other passions)
practises extreme tyranny upon the hearts of those that serve it, be
it lust after sovereignty or fleshly lust. But in the peaceful orders

[1] CIVITAS DEI, XIX, 15 and 16.

of states, wherein one man is under another, as humility does benefit the servant, so does pride endamage the superior. But take a man as God created him at first, and so he is neither slave to man nor to sin. But penal servitude had the institution from that law which commands the conservation, and forbids the disturbance of nature's order: for if that law had not first been transgressed, penal servitude had never been enjoined.

Therefore the apostle warns servants to obey their masters and to serve them with cheerfulness, and good will: to the end that if they cannot be made free by their masters, they make their servitude a freedom to themselves, by serving them, not in deceitful fear, but in faithful love, until iniquity be overpassed, and all man's power and principality disannulled, and God only be all in all.

Wherefore although our righteous forefathers had servants in their families, and according to their temporal estates, made a distinction between their servants and their children, yet in matter of religion (the fountain whence all eternal good flows), they provided for all their household with an equal respect unto each member thereof.

Augustine's theory of slavery is difficult and unsatisfactory. The whole basis of the theory by which Aristotle had justified slavery is denied when Augustine denies that any man is a slave by nature. One who justifies slavery on the lines of Aristotle must maintain that, on the whole and in spite of individual exceptions, those in the position of masters are better men than those who are their slaves. But for Augustine, since the grace of God was bestowed freely without distinction of class or race, any slave was as likely to be among the elect as his master.

In spite of this, Augustine does not condemn slavery. He regards it as divinely ordained for the retribution of sin. God would not have ordained it if men had not sinned; but the Fall has disqualified men for the enjoyment of the equality which God intended.

This might be a tenable theory, if it were possible to hold that slaves on the whole were more sinful than their masters. But Augustine is very far from this; nor does he in fact ever suggest that the condition of any particular slave is a retribution for his individual sin. His theory is that the institution of slavery as a whole is, as it were, a coi-

lective retribution upon the human race for the fall of humanity in
Adam. Such a theory might be employed to explain the reduction of
the whole human race to slavery, but it seems powerless to account for
a condition of things in which some particular individuals are condemned to serve, while others are elevated to mastery at their
expense.

But it would be a mistake to ignore the importance of the Augustinian theory just because Augustine himself did not proceed to the
practical application of its consequences. His theory swept away the
whole theoretical basis by which slavery had been justified in the ancient world; and if not Augustine himself, some of Augustine's successors drew the consequence that slavery was not justifiable at all.

What is the important and fundamental thing in Augustine's political theory? It lies, I think, in his doctrine that no man owes an absolute allegiance to any earthly society. The word "absolute" must
be underlined. A man's membership of the heavenly kingdom does
not release him from the duties which he owes to the limited or
"closed" [1] societies of which he is necessarily a member; to his family,
in the first place, and in particular to the political society, or state, to
which he belongs. On the contrary, for the most part it sanctions and
reinforces these obligations. But this very fact places him in a different position from the man for whom the political society itself is
the ultimate authority. He obeys the civil laws; but because they
have the sanction of an authority higher than the civil. And in cases
where the civil authority oversteps its bounds and interferes with matters of religion, he must resist the civil power in the name of the same
superior authority which in general commands him to submit to it.

The doctrine has thus a twofold consequence; it involves a distinction between the secular and the religious spheres, and it places the
secular authority even within its own sphere under the sanction of a
higher authority.

This central idea of Augustine was not of course entirely new to the
world. It is contained already in the command of Christ in the Gospels, to "render unto Caesar those things which are Caesar's and unto
God those things which are God's," and it had inspired the teaching of
Saint Paul.

[1] See p. 191, *supra*, n. 1.

Nor was it entirely original to Christianity. It was foreign indeed to classical Greek practice and to the classical Greek political philosophy. These had recognized no distinction between the secular and religious spheres. The gods which the Greek worshipped were the gods of his city; his duties to his city were his duties to his city's gods, and vice versa. Nor did he in general conceive of any authority wider than his city, to which he owed an ultimate allegiance.

But in both the great classical philosophers of Greece, especially in Plato, we find more than what I have called the classical philosophy of Greece. The whole of that part of Plato's teaching which is concerned with the life, duties, and destiny of the *philosopher* represents the irruption of a new idea, and contains the germs of the doctrine which is developed in Augustine. Philosophy, according to Plato,[1] enables a man to escape from the limits of his city, and to become the inhabitant of a wider sphere, in which he lives "a life better than the political."[2] Here already is a distinction analogous to that between the religious and the secular spheres of life. Plato adds that the philosopher who has attained the higher sphere will not wish to dwell in it continuously, but will recognize the obligation to return to the performance of political duties in his state. The philosopher's position in respect to these duties will then be precisely analogous to that of the Christian who performs his civil obligations out of obedience to a higher than the civil authority.

This doctrine of the influence of philosophy in liberating its practitioner from a restricted allegiance reappears, though with a limited scope, in Aristotle; and it runs through the whole development of later Greek philosophy.

This idea was adopted by Christianity, and it is needless to say that it was profoundly modified in the process of its adoption. Of the modifications which it underwent, I will mention only that which seems most important from our present point of view. Christianity ascribed to religion the liberating influence which had previously been ascribed to philosophy; and whereas Plato and Aristotle, at least, had held that the capacity for philosophy was confined to a few exceptional natures, it was a fundamental principle of Christianity that the path of religion was open to all men equally. Thus Christianity placed all men in that

[1] See especially Plato's simile of the Cave, quoted, pp. 92–99, *supra.*
[2] P. 98, *supra.*

position vis à vis the civil power which had been occupied previously by the philosopher alone.[1]

But we may better estimate the importance of the doctrine by looking forward to the fruits which it produced than by looking back to the antecedents from which it was derived. It is not too much to say that this doctrine in one form or another has dominated the subsequent develop.ment of western political thought and practice from Augustine's time until quite recent years. "In one form or another," the doctrine has developed in a striking variety of forms, which make it not easy at first sight to recognize the identity of principle underlying them; though it has become easier to do so since there have arisen in our days political philosophies in which the entire principle is repudiated.

Thus there seems, and is, a great and striking difference between the Roman Catholic and the Protestant theories on this subject: but it is a difference in the interpretation of an identical principle. Both hold that there is an authority superior to the state, or political authority, for the direction of men's conduct, and that the authority of the state itself is derived from the sanction of this higher power. They differ as to the seat in which this higher authority resides, in that Catholicism attributes to the Church *on earth* some part at least of that authority which Protestantism denies to any institution upon earth, and reserves wholly to the eternal.[2] Both agree in distinguishing between the realms of religious and secular duties; but they tend to differ in the place at which they draw the line. Catholicism distinguishes among actions between those which have a religious significance and those which are merely of secular importance. Protestantism tends more to the be-

---

[1] Cf. E. R. BEVAN, CHRISTIANITY (Home University Library, 1932), p. 56, for an illustration of the same truth in the sphere of Morals: "When S. Augustine wants to set forth the special thing which distinguishes Christianity on the moral side from the old Paganism, he does not claim that Christianity has a wholly new standard, he claims that the ideal once considered attainable by only a few philosophers is now attained by innumerable ordinary men (Aug., DE VERA RELIGIONE, III, 5)."

Doctor Bevan also quotes the following passage from Galen (second century A.D.): "We have seen in our own time those people who are called Christian draw their faith from fables. Yet these people sometimes act in the same way as genuine philosophers do. Their contempt of death we can all see plain enough; also how through a certain kind of modesty they abstain from sexual pleasure; ... there are some of them who, in ruling and mastering their impulses, and in their zeal for virtue, are not a whit behind real philosophers."

[2] Both interpretations can find some support in Augustine's writings.

lief that actions as such, being external, are relatively indifferent from the religious point of view. It therefore submits to the regulation of outward actions by the secular power, and draws the line not between some actions and others, but between actions on the one hand and the "interior life" of belief, conviction, and feeling on the other. It allows the secular power to regulate the former; but the life of Protestantism depends on its resisting any encroachment of this power upon the latter.

It is perhaps harder, but it is not less important, to see that the same principle is fundamental to that form of polity which was once coextensive with western civilization, but which is now confined to those states which have what is called a "democratic," as opposed to an "authoritarian," constitution. The point really at issue between these two different theories of politics is not well expressed by the use of those terms, for the issue is not simply the old issue between democracy and absolutism, whether the will of the people or the will of a single ruler shall be supreme. The true issue is better suggested by the term "totalitarian" applied to one of the contrasted sides.[1] The theory of totalitarianism involves the repudiation of any authority above the state, and the denial of a sphere in the life of its citizens upon which the state may not encroach. Thus, we see the state ceasing to be, what it has been ever since Christianity first dominated the West, a merely secular institution, and transforming itself into a religious one. The totalitarian state, in other words, is founded upon the rejection of the principle which we have found in Augustine.

The so-called "democratic" state, on the other hand, depends upon the maintenance of this principle — a principle, be it noted, inherited by the modern world directly from Christianity. The essence of what is now called "democracy" consists in the restriction of the state to the secular sphere,[2] and in the refusal, even in the act of assenting to the commands of the state, to concede an absolute allegiance to it.

The continuity which exists between the democratic and the Chris-

[1] I am thinking primarily, in what follows, of the contrast between democratic and Fascist states. But most of what I say will, I think, apply equally to the contrast between democracy and communism, as represented in Russia. This communism is a form of "totalitarianism."

[2] "Perhaps the main pillar in the edifice of democracy is freedom of worship." The United States Ambassador to Great Britain, in a speech reported in THE TIMES (London), September 3, 1938.

tian principle escapes recognition mainly for the following reason. When the Christian theory relegates the state to an inferior position, it is clear what authority it sets above it: the authority of God, whether mediated by the Church or communicated immediately to the conscience of the individual. When the Christian theory restricts the activity of the state to a "secular" sphere, it is clear what is to fill the sphere from which the state is excluded: the practice of the Christian religion. But "democratic" theory (although it still owes far more than it recognizes to its Christian origin) is no longer overtly Christian. When, therefore, the question is asked of it, by what superior authority the claims of the state are to be sanctioned, it must reply: the authority of the private judgment, or the individual conscience. But it cannot specify by what higher authority that judgment is to be guided or that conscience enlightened. When it is asked what activity is to fill the sphere from which the state is excluded in being restricted to the temporal, it must leave the filling of it (or the leaving it unfilled) to the choice of the individual.

The future of "democracy" depends upon whether these answers are sufficient. It may be thought that their sufficiency has already been proved by the successful working of democracy during the last hundred years, for it is at least as long as this since Christianity ceased to be universally professed by the citizens of western "democratic" states. But that period has not been a fair test, because individuals or nations may continue to regulate their conduct by principles derived from a religion long after they have abandoned the practice of the religion itself. In matters of morals and conduct, Dean Inge has well said, the nineteenth century was "living on Christian capital." When the capital has been exhausted, the twofold question will be decided: Whether the individual can bear the responsibility of a private judgment which is really private, in the sense that it is destitute of guidance by an authority higher than himself, and: Whether the "earthly city" can be excluded permanently from encroaching on a sphere which is filled by nothing else.

FOR FURTHER READING

Translations

That used in the text is John Healey's (1610), a fine specimen of Elizabethan English. There is a convenient abridged edition of this translation published by Dent (London, 1931), with an introduction by Ernest Barker.

There is a more modern translation by Marcus Dods (Edinburgh; T. & T. Clark, 1872–1934, 15 vols.), but it has not the quality of the earlier one.

Commentaries

BAYNES, N. II., THE POLITICAL IDEAS OF ST. AUGUSTINE'S "DE CIVITATE DEI."
    Historical Association Leaflet no. 104. London: George Bell & Sons, 1936.

CARLYLE, R. W. and A. J., HISTORY OF MEDIAEVAL POLITICAL THEORY IN THE WEST.

> Gives a very useful account of the whole course of political theory from the Roman Empire to the Renaissance.

GILSON, É., INTRODUCTION À L'ÉTUDE DE LA PHILOSOPHIE DE ST. AUGUSTIN, Paris, 1931.

> The following books (which are among the finest productions of modern times in political philosophy) are not about Augustine, but they will serve to show that the issues which he dealt with are not dead today:

BARTH, K., A LETTER TO GREAT BRITAIN FROM SWITZERLAND. London: Shildon Press, 1941.

ELIOT, T. S., THE IDEA OF A CHRISTIAN SOCIETY. New York: Harcourt, Brace and Company, 1940.

CHAPTER SIX

The Interval before Aquinas[1]

BETWEEN Augustine and Aquinas there intervene eight centuries which contain no political philosopher of the first magnitude. This does not mean that thought on political matters was stagnant during the whole of that period, or that no new ideas were being formed within it. On the contrary, the civil lawyers continued to produce works of jurisprudence on the basis of the Roman law; the ecclesiastical lawyers founded the whole system of canon law; the controversies of the times produced an abundance of polemical literature, especially on the crucial issue of the relations between the Pope and the temporal rulers. All this contained a political philosophy in embryo, but it was not reduced to the unity of a philosophical system until the time of the great scholastics of the thirteenth century, of whom the chief was Thomas Aquinas.

Nevertheless it is possible to detect certain leading ideas which dominate the work of the intervening centuries.

I. NATURAL LAW

The first of these is the notion of natural law, inherited from those sources in which we previously discovered it, the Roman law and the Stoic philosophy, and developed under the influence of Christian doctrines.

There is a certain eternal order of what is right or fitting (*aequum*), which has not its source in any will, not even in God's will. This order is the Law of Nature, and justice consists in the conformity of will to this law. God's will, being always just, always conforms to it.[2]   Man

---

[1] Almost all my knowledge of this intervening period is derived from R. W. and A. J. CARLYLE, MEDIAEVAL POLITICAL THEORY IN THE WEST (6 vols., 1903–1936).

[2] This does not mean that God is subject to a law external to himself, for the eternal principle of order is God's own nature.   ("'Aequitas' is a name of God ... 'aequitas' is nothing other than God himself," is the expression of a jurist early in the Middle

is capable of injustice, and his will may therefore deviate from it, but, being endowed with reason, he is always capable of knowing it.

There is another kind of law which has its source in will, and is thus essentially a command. This law is not natural, but positive.

Positive Law:

(a) Divine

There is a divine positive law, derived from the commands of God in matters which natural law does not regulate. Thus the commandment to keep holy the Sabbath day is a law binding upon man because it is the will of God. But it is not necessitated by natural law, and God might therefore rescind it by a subsequent command. What is now wrong (namely to neglect the Sabbath) would then become right. But other commandments of God (e.g., Thou shalt do no murder) are governed by natural law. To commit murder is a violation of the eternal order, not merely disobedience to a command. No subsequent command of God, therefore, can ever make such acts right.

(b) Human

There is also a human positive law which is the command of the duly constituted ruler in a state, and includes also the customs which are binding upon its inhabitants. In matters not determined by natural law, what the positive law commands is obligatory upon the subject simply for the reason that it is the positive law. For example, if it is the law of my land to perform certain services, or pay certain taxes to the government, that fact in itself suffices to make it wrong for me to do otherwise. But in matters which are determined by natural law, positive law has authority only so far as it conforms to natural. Thus a canonist of the twelfth century writes:[1] "Whatever customary or constitutional rules, whether commands or prohibitions, are contrary

Ages. "PRAGUE FRAGMENT": quoted in CARLYLE, *op. cit.*, vol. II, p. 8.) But it is unalterable by any act of God's *will*.

[1] Rufinus, quoted in CARLYLE, *op. cit.*, vol. II, p. 107.

to natural law, are judged null and void.   For the Lord said, 'I am truth,' not 'I am custom, or constitution.'   Such rules the subject not only has no duty to obey.   He, with all other reasonable creatures, is subject to a higher law, which may impose on him the duty of disobeying them."

Contents of the Natural Law

One of the fundamental principles of the natural law is the equality of men.   "All men are by nature equal."   Others are given in a definition of Saint Isidore of Seville as follows: [1] "The law of nature is common to all nations, being founded not upon any legal constitution, but upon a universal instinct of nature; for example, the union of man and woman, the begetting and nurture of children, common possession of all things, equal freedom of all men, appropriation of the fruits of the earth and the beasts of the earth, sea and air.   Again, it is the law of nature to restore deposits, or money entrusted, and to repel violence by force.   For these and similar things are never held to be unjust, but are always natural and right (aequum)."

Status of Political Institutions

A difficulty arises in that some social institutions, which appear to be both necessary and universal, are yet contrary to the Law of Nature. The institution of slavery is clearly contrary to the law of "equal liberty"; and not slavery only, but the distinction of ruler and subject, which appears essential to political society, is incompatible with the equality of men.   Nor can the institution of private property be reconciled with the "possession of all things in common."   Are these things, then, to be repudiated as positive laws which infringe the Law of Nature?

To repudiate them would be to deny the rightfulness of civil society, and the writers of our period were very far from doing that.   They held, on the contrary, that civil society was divinely ordained, and that

---

[1] Beginning of the seventh century.   His definition is quoted by Gratian in the twelfth century.   CARLYLE, op. cit., vol. II, p. 102.

temporal rulers, in so far as they ruled justly, derived their authority from God. They were enabled to hold this without surrendering their belief in the authority of natural law by the application of a device which Augustine had used to justify slavery.[1] Private property and political subjection, like slavery, are not natural to man in his perfect state. But man, since the Fall, has been in a state of sin, and these institutions have been ordained by God as a result and as a remedy of sin.

II. DISTINCTION OF SPIRITUAL AND SECULAR SPHERES

The second also of the great principles by which men's thoughts were governed in this period we have met already. It is the principle of the separate spheres of secular and spiritual authority. Each is legitimate (though of course either may be abused) and therefore each ought to be obeyed; but each must be restricted from encroaching upon the proper domain of the other.[2]

The principle goes back to the command of Christ in the Gospels: "Render unto Caesar the things which are Caesar's, and unto God the things that are God's."[3] It informs the teaching of Saint Paul and Saint Peter in their epistles. "Let every soul be subject unto the higher powers. For there is no power but of God. The powers that be are ordained of God."[4] "Obey God and honour the king."[5] It is the principle of Augustine's doctrine that the Christian on his pilgrimage in the world makes use of the peace of the "earthly city."[6] It was indeed the *modus vivendi* of the early church in the Roman world, that its members held themselves bound to pay absolute obedience to the civil magistrate, save only when he sought to control their worship and religious beliefs.

Gelasius, a pope in the fifth century, laid down the principle in a form to which later writers constantly recur.[7]

[1] See pp. 222–224, *supra.*

[2] The two spheres are regulated by two laws, the human and the divine law, respectively (see p. 231, *supra*). Thus the separation of spheres involves a theory of the relation of human law (not now to the natural, but) to the divine law. Cf. further pp. 255 *et seq., infra.*

[3] MATT. XXII, 21.　　　　[4] ROM. XIII, 1.

[5] I PETER II, 17.　　　　[6] P. 219, *supra.*

[7] TRACTATUS, IV, 11; quoted by Carlyle, *op. cit.*, vol. I, p. 190.

ᔰ They [i.e., the civil authorities] shrink from interference with religious matters, and recognize that these do not fall within the measure of their authority, which has been allotted to them for the judgment of human things, not also for the controlling of divine things; how then can they claim jurisdiction over those men who are ministers of the divine things?   It may be true that before the coming of Christ certain persons . . . existed who were at the same time priests and kings, as the holy scripture tells us Melchisedech was. And the devil did likewise among his own peoples . . . bringing it about that the pagan emperors bore also the title of Chief Priests. But, after the coming of Christ (who was Himself both the true king and the true priest), no emperor thereafter has assumed the title of priest, and no priest has seized a regal throne. . . . For Christ, being mindful of human frailty, provided by a grand dispensation for the salvation of his people.   He separated the kingly duties and powers from the priestly, according to the different functions and dignity proper to each, wishing that his people should be preserved by a saving humility, and not again ensnared by human pride. Henceforth Christian Emperors should stand in need of priests for their eternal life, and priests for their part should employ the aid of the imperial government for the direction of temporal matters; to the end that spiritual employment might be removed from carnal diversions, and that the soldier of the Lord might be as little as possible entangled in secular business, and that one involved in secular affairs might not be seen occupying the leadership of the church. Thus it was sought to secure that both the orders might be humble since no man could combine eminence in both of them, and that the profession of each might be suited to the special aptitudes of those who follow it.

It is a profound observation of Gelasius that the separation of powers dates only from the coming of Christ.   In the classical polities of Greece and Rome, duties to God were not distinguished from duties to the state, for the gods were the gods of the state.   Similarly for the Jews of the Old Testament, Jehovah was the God of Israel, and it was impossible to distinguish the service of Jehovah from the service of Israel.

Gelasius writes to the Roman Emperor in a similar sense.[1]

[1] EP., XII, 2; quoted by CARLYLE, *op. cit.*, vol. I, p. 191.

❧ There are two chief powers by which this world is governed, August Emperor: the sacred authority of the prelates and the kingly power. Wherein the burden laid upon the priests is the heavier, in that they will have to render an account at the divine judgement even for the kings of men. You know, most clement son, that although you are placed in rank above all the race of men, nevertheless you bow your neck in devoted submission to those who are set in charge of matters of religion. You look to them for the means of your own salvation. . . . So far as concerns the rule of public order, the leaders of religion themselves obey your laws, recognizing that the imperial authority has been conferred upon you from on high. . . . With how much greater zeal, then, ought you to obey those who are set in charge of the sacred mysteries?

Nearly seven centuries after Gelasius the same teaching is summed up by Stephen of Tournai, a canonist of the twelfth century, in the following words: "Within one commonwealth and under one king are two peoples; as there are two peoples, there are two ways of life; as there are two lives, there are two authorities; as there are two authorities, there is a twofold order of jurisdiction. The commonwealth is the church; the king of the commonwealth is Christ; the two peoples are the two orders in the church, clerics and laymen; the two ways of life are the spiritual and the carnal; the two authorities are the priesthood and the kingship; the twofold jurisdiction is the divine law and the human. Give to each its due, and all will be in harmony." [1]

(Notice an important development which the principle has undergone, in consequence of the extension of the Christian Church. The "two powers" began by being the Christian Church on the one hand and the pagan Empire of Rome on the other. But by the twelfth century — and, of course, much earlier — not only the civil rulers themselves, but all their subjects, had accepted Christianity, and were thus themselves members of the Church. The distinction between the two powers has thus become a distinction between two orders, the lay and the clerical, within the Church itself.)

The greatest disputes of the Middle Ages centered round this principle; but the principle itself was never disputed. It was never doubted that the spiritual and secular spheres ought to be separated, and that

[1] SUMMA DECRETORUM, Introduction, quoted by CARLYLE, *op. cit.*, vol. II, p. 198.

the powers of each, the Church and the civil rulers, the Pope and the Emperor, should be supreme each in his own sphere. The disputes concerned the application of the principle, for it is not easy to sever the secular and religious spheres so clearly that there is no overlapping. Thus in the eleventh and twelfth centuries the intellectual energies of Europe were engaged for a long period in what is known as the "investiture controversy." This was a dispute between successive popes on the one hand, and successive kings of France and emperors of Germany on the other, as to the share rightfully belonging to each in the appointment of bishops. Neither party denied the principle of the separation of powers, but no simple application of the principle could solve this question. For the bishop in medieval society was on the one hand an officer of the Church, and as such his appointment belonged to the Church. But he was on the other hand a feudal tenant, a member of the King's Council, holder of estates upon condition of supplying military forces to the king. The king could claim with reason that the bishop was an officer in the administration and defense of the realm, and that therefore the civil power, by the very principle of separation, should not be excluded from a share in his appointment.

The same difficulty is seen in the whole course of the great controversy between the Papacy and the Empire which dominates medieval history. The Empire was the Holy Roman Empire, which was established by Charlemagne, and which claimed to be the legal successor of the ancient Roman Empire. The Emperor was elected from among the German princes, and the actual power of the Empire was never in fact commensurate with its legal claims. Nevertheless the Emperor was universally accorded a pre-eminent status among secular rulers, so that the struggle between emperors and popes was a struggle between the secular and spiritual powers in the persons of the highest representatives of each.

There is no doubt that the claims of the Papacy grew on the whole progressively greater in course of the centuries which we are considering. This was inevitable for two reasons. (1) The Church in the ancient Roman Empire had been faced with a civilized pagan state. The authorities of the state were supported by all the prestige of the ancient civilization which they represented. But after the collapse of the Roman Empire the secular power was borne by the barbarian kings of the Teutonic nations, while it was the Church which preserved, so far as it was preserved, the tradition of ancient culture. Thus the prestige of learning and civilization now reinforced instead of counter-balancing the authority of the Church. (2) The spread of Christianity among the peoples of Europe inevitably operated towards the same result.[1] The kings and their peoples were now themselves Christians, that is to say, were themselves now members of the Church. The opposition was thus now no longer between the Church and the completely independent state, but between clergy and laymen within the same church. Kings were now themselves members of the Pope's flock, and subject to his spiritual jurisdiction.

There is no doubt that some of the claims of some of the popes involved, if they had been carried to their logical conclusion, the destruction of the system of separate powers, and the subordination of the temporal to the spiritual authority. But it would be a mistake to infer that the principle of separation was abandoned during this period. Encroachments on the part of the papal authority were opposed by clerics themselves on the very ground that they infringed this principle. Thus the German churchman, Gerhoh Reichersberg (early twelfth century), who had supported the papal cause in the investiture controversy, writes: [2]

〜 Nay, more: just as the emperors sometimes arrogated to themselves functions belonging to the priesthood and the church; so they [3] on the other hand imagine that their priesthood confers on them also an imperial, or more than imperial, power. In declaring in pictures, speech and writing that the emperors owe them homage, in commanding that the imperial train may advance thus far, but no further, in laying down which states the emperor may attack, and which he must spare, even when they are in revolt against the empire — in all this are they not setting themselves up as emperors and over-lords of the Emperors, nay, are they not making the Emperors their vassals? Is not this to destroy an authority set up by God, and to resist what God has ordained? Or is it not a destruction of the Empire, if some state which lays waste other

---

[1] Cf. p. 235, *supra*.
[2] COMMENTARY ON PSALM LXIV. Quoted by CARLYLE, *op. cit.*, vol. IV, p. 371.
[3] *Sc.*, the papal party.

states and revolts against justice and the Empire shall escape the vengeance of the Emperor and all satisfaction of justice by the protection of our lord the Pope and (it is most likely) by the aid of papal gold?   What then will have become of those two swords of the Gospel,[1] if the apostle of Christ shall be all, or if the Emperor shall be all?   If either the Empire or the priesthood shall be robbed of its strength and dignity, it will be as though you were to take one of the two great luminaries from the sky.

Nor did the defenders of the papal claims repudiate the principle to which their opponents appealed.   Here, as always, the problem lay in its application.   Thus, for example, the Pope, as head of the Church, possessed the undisputed right for sufficient cause to excommunicate any of its members, and therefore to excommunicate emperors and kings.   But to excommunicate the king was tantamount to absolving his Christian subjects from their oaths of allegiance to him, and was therefore equivalent to a claim to depose the king.   Thus an almost unlimited authority might be ascribed to the Pope over the secular powers; and yet it might be argued that this was no encroachment, but a legitimate exercise of his purely spiritual jurisdiction.

III. Feudalism

The King as Representative of the People

We have been concerned so far with elements of political theory which the Middle Ages had inherited from the past.   We have now to notice something new, namely the theory implicit in the native constitutional practices of the Teutonic peoples, the Franks and other Germanic folk who had overrun the ancient Roman Empire and who now formed at least the ruling class of the population over the greater part of western Europe.

Each people was ruled by its king, but the king was not absolute. The nobles, by whom his power was supported, were not his ministers,

---

[1] Peter says to Christ in the Gospel: "Lo, here are two swords" (LUKE XXII, 38), and the two swords were regarded in the Middle Ages as the symbol of the two powers.

nor instruments of his will. They owed him certain well-defined duties and services, but it was not in his power to determine what these duties should be, and he was himself bound by reciprocal obligations to them.

The king was in no sense sovereign. He could not *make* law, but was himself bound by it. The source of law was the custom of the people. It was the function of the king to declare and formulate this custom, to apply it in judicial decisions, and to enforce it by executive power; but in no case to override it.[1] Thus Bracton, an English jurist of the thirteenth century, writes:[2] "The king himself ought to be under no man, but under God and under the law, because law makes the king. Let the king, therefore, give authority and rule to the law, seeing that these are conferred upon the king himself by the law. For there is no king where will rules and not law." And Manegold of Lautenbach writes in the eleventh century: "No man can make himself emperor or king. It is the people which raises an individual above itself, that he may rule and direct it according to the principles of just government, assigning to each his own, protecting the pious and destroying the impious, and rendering justice to all."[3]

This is no theory of the sovereignty of the people, and it would be the gravest error to find even the germ of, say, Rousseau's theory here. The *will* of the people is no more held to be the source of law than is the will of the king. Both king and people are subject to a law which neither makes, and which assigns to each rank and class within the state its functions, duties, and rights. Such a theory lacks the conception of sovereignty as completely as Aristotle's did.[4] All powers in the state are regarded as subject to a law which none of them is competent to revoke or to alter.

This new element of political theory was not wholly digested by medieval philosophy. The notion that the king is essentially subject to law agrees of course with the doctrines of natural law which we have

---

[1] [This illustrates the divergence between theory and fact. In England, the King's justices, overriding local custom, built up a law common to the whole country — the "common law" or judge-made law. The custom was the custom of the King's court. *Editor.*]

[2] DE LEGIBUS ET CONSUETUDINIBUS ANGLIAE; quoted by CARLYLE, *op. cit.*, vol. III, p. 38.

[3] MANEGOLD, AD GEBEHARDUM; quoted in CARLYLE, *op. cit.*, vol. III, p. 112.

[4] See p. 161, *supra*.

already considered. But whereas according to the natural law doctrine the law to which the king is subject is derived from God, it is derived according to the Teutonic theory from the custom of the king's people; according to the former doctrine it is absolutely universal in its validity, according to the latter its validity is presumably limited to the members of the people in question; according to the former the law is prescribed by a timeless reason, according to the latter it is rooted in history. The medieval philosophers, I believe, sometimes used such phrases as that "the king is subject to the law" without being conscious of the profound differences between the two views which such phrases might be used to express.[1] The germ which was present in the political institutions of the northern peoples did not achieve its full development until after the Middle Ages. We may recognize it as the remote source of the political philosophy of Burke, and therefore of the philosophy of English Conservatism. It is the germ which developed into the political theories of the German Romantics, according to whom the constitution of the state was the expression of the national soul, and important parts of Hegel's philosophy of the state bear marks of the same origin. But its greatest influence both in theory and in practice it owes to the following fact: it was a root from which the system of representative government was later developed.

[1] Cf. pp. 261–262, *infra*, for an example of this ambiguity in Aquinas.

CHAPTER SEVEN
Thomas Aquinas

LIFE OF AQUINAS

AQUINAS is one of the great systematic philosophers of the world. His was a work of synthesis, of putting together (which means, of course, thinking together) what had previously been apart, of imposing an architectonic design upon what had previously been more or less fragmentary. This does not mean that men's thought was chaotic in the centuries before Aquinas. We have seen, on the contrary, that it had certain clearly marked lines of direction. But it is true that in the previous centuries the different trends of thought had been to some extent distributed. Civil lawyers, canon lawyers, writers on Christian doctrine, commentators on the Scriptures, apologists for the Pope, apologists for the Emperor — each had his own starting point and represented his own point of view. The distinctive thing about Aquinas was that he assimilated these elements into the unity of a single system. He represents, as none of them singly does, the totality of medieval thought.

Aquinas was born near Naples about 1225 and died in 1274. He joined the Dominican Order at the age of nineteen, overcoming the determined opposition of his family, who wished a greater career for their son than membership of an order vowed to poverty. He went to Paris to study, and was a pupil there of Albert the Great, who was among the first to revive the study of Aristotle in western Europe. After four years spent with Albert in Cologne, he returned to Paris to lecture, and the rest of his life was spent, mostly in Paris, but partly also in Italy, in meditation, study, writing, lecturing, and disputing.

POLITICAL PHILOSOPHY

The biography of Aquinas throws little light for the understanding of his philosophical achievement: a study of the movement of thought in which he took his place throws more.   This is the movement known as medieval scholasticism.   Aquinas neither originated the movement, nor completed it.   Great scholastics before him were Anselm, Abelard, Peter Lombard, and Albertus Magnus, his own master; and after him were Duns Scotus and William of Ockham.   But Aquinas is by common consent the greatest.

Scholasticism, in its developed form, was a product of the university — that institution which is one of the most important achievements of the Middle Ages, and one of their greatest legacies to the modern world.   Universities began as guilds or corporations of masters and scholars.   The earliest universities were professional, and confined each to the cultivation of a single branch of knowledge.   Thus the earliest university, that of Salerno, was a school of medicine; the universities of Bologna and Padua were devoted exclusively to legal studies.   These professional universities were not very different in principle from the trade guilds, in which the practitioners of every skilled profession were organized in the Middle Ages, for the mutual protection of the members and for the instruction of the young in the secrets of the craft.   Corporations like those of Bologna were the trade guilds of the lawyers' profession.   They differed from other guilds mainly in this important respect, that they were not jealous of their learning, nor exclusive in their membership.   They did not seek to guard their legal knowledge as a trade secret of their own corporation, to be imparted only to those who had been initiated to its membership, but opened their doors to all comers, thereby implicitly recognizing that the subject of their instruction was of universal human interest, not an exclusively professional concern.

The secular schools of professional instruction were not the only source from which the universities grew.   The Church also was concerned with education, and from an early time had maintained cathedral schools; while the monasteries must always have provided for the instruction of their novices.   In a sense this also was a kind of professional instruction, since it was designed primarily to fit its recipients to be priests or monks.   But in this case the line was still harder to draw between what was of professional and what of generally human concern.   The prime qualification of the cleric was his knowledge of the Christian truth; but to possess this knowledge was also the primary interest of every man.   Poles apart as they are in other respects, the position of the medieval cleric is like that of the Platonic guardian in this: that his special qualification for his office consists only in his possession in a higher degree of the qualities which make a good man in general. It follows that the cleric's education, like the guardian's, is a general education disguised as a professional training.

The decisive step in the development of the university was taken when the various separate professional studies were combined as the faculties of a single institution. This happened in Paris, where, early in the thirteenth century, the university contained the four faculties of Law, Medicine, Arts, and Theology; and all later universities were modeled on Paris.

This was the ground on which scholasticism flourished. In such an institution the various branches of secular learning were brought in contact with one another, and secular learning as a whole was brought in contact with the Christian system of revealed truth. This gave stimulus to the effort which the Scholastics made, to think out the relation of the sciences to one another and of science to faith.[1]

It would be a mistake, nevertheless, to think of Aquinas merely as the systematizer of those elements of thought which we encountered in the last chapter. It would be wrong, in the first place, because it would suggest that his work was mainly one of arrangement or co-ordination of previously existing materials; whereas what Aquinas did was to rethink rather than to rearrange, and his work is better illustrated by the analogy of metabolism than by that of construction. But it is not necessary to dwell upon this point. Even when allowance has been made for this, it still remains true that the elements there enumerated do not exactly account for what is found in Aquinas. He contains both less and more.

He contains less, for he omits to do justice to what I have christened the "Teutonic" element: the doctrine, implicit in the ancient usages

[1] In this short description I have oversimplified many things, and one thing in particular. I have spoken as though the foundation of the universities preceded the scholastic conception of the unity of knowledge, and as though the latter was produced by the former as its result. But in such matters cause and effect are not to be so sharply distinguished from one another. It might have been said with equal truth that men's growing realization of the unity of knowledge and the reasonableness of faith was itself a cause of the foundation of universities. As a matter of historical fact, scholasticism and universities developed step by step together, each furthering the growth of the other.

of the European peoples, that the king, or other *de facto* ruler, is bound to rule according to the custom of his people. The ruler is the source of positive law, and the result of this doctrine is thus to set up a standard beyond the positive law, by which the legitimacy of any enactment of the ruler can be judged. When I say that Aquinas omits to do justice to this doctrine, I do not mean that he omits to mention it. But Aquinas has another doctrine of a law transcending the positive law — namely, the natural law.[1] This law is universal and unchanging, originating not in any local or national source, but in the eternal reason of God. When Aquinas introduces the doctrine that kings are limited in their power by the fact that they are bound to act as representatives of their people, he does so without recognizing that he is introducing something different from, indeed incompatible with, his predominant doctrine that they are limited by subjection to the natural law. I have therefore thought myself justified in the extracts which follow, in representing the natural law doctrine as the doctrine of Aquinas, and in giving an example of the other in a footnote only.[2] The latter is an alien element in Aquinas; it was developed by his successors, and its subsequent history made evident its inherent incompatibility with the main principles of his philosophy.

But Aquinas also contains more than has yet been mentioned. He introduces a great new ingredient into the medieval mixture: the philosophy of Aristotle, whose works had become known in western Europe at about the date of Aquinas's birth. The greatest of the tasks of reconciliation which Aquinas had to perform was to reconcile the philosophy of Aristotle with the truth of the Christian revelation. In order to do this, he did not demolish the Aristotelian system and use its fragments in the erection of a new structure. He adopts throughout the principle that Aristotelianism is true, but not the whole truth. It is the truth, so far as it can be discovered by the bare operation of human reason without the aid of faith. But the later revelation of faith has not annulled what was previously disclosed to reason, it has only completed it.

Thus in every department of philosophy, Aquinas sets, as it were, a Christian coping upon a Greek substructure. For example, he accepts the Aristotelian philosophy of nature; Aristotle is not erroneous in what he says about nature, but he is defective because he fails to recog-

---

[1] See pp. 251 *et seq.*, *infra.*　　　　　[2] Pp. 261–262, *infra.*

nize that the world of nature is not the whole world, but that there exists above it the realm of grace.[1]   Similarly in ethics, the Aristotelian theory is a true account of the way by which man can attain his natural end, namely, happiness.   Its defect springs from failure to recognize the Christian truth, that man has also a supernatural end, namely, salvation and future blessedness, to which the end of happiness in this life is itself subordinate.   Aquinas never denies that temporal happiness is a proper end of man; only it is subordinate to a higher end. The correction required of the Aristotelian ethics, therefore, is not that they should be rewritten, but that they should be incorporated within a larger whole.

We shall find the same principle at work in the political thought of Aquinas.   Aristotle sketches the framework of a society designed to supply the conditions of the good life for man; but he has in mind only man's life on earth.   For Aquinas, a good life on earth is indeed an end which society should secure, and Aristotle's theory of the means of securing it is the right one.   But man's eternal good in a future life is a higher end, and a further social organization (the Church) is needed in order to provide the conditions in which he can secure it.   Thus Aristotle's theory of society is to be adopted, but it is to be recognized for what it is, namely, a theory of *secular* society only.   The complete human society includes a secular and an ecclesiastical organization, and the former is subordinate to the latter.

In undertaking the task of an intellectual reconciliation of Greek thought with Christian faith, Aquinas was not embarking on a private venture of his own.   He was accomplishing in theory what medieval civilization accomplished in practice.   The civilization of the Middle Ages arose from the union of Christianity with the ancient culture of the Graeco-Roman world.[2]   In its early centuries the Christian Church had been hostile to "the world" (which meant the pagan world of classical antiquity).   It condemned the worship of the ancient gods as idolatrous, the disinterested study of nature as frivolous; and the Roman Empire, by which the whole ancient civilization was defended

---

[1] "Gratia perficit naturam, non tollit," said another Scholastic.   "Grace does not cancel nature, but perfects it."

[2] And all subsequent European civilization is an offspring of the same union.   This truth is harder to see, and does not belong to the present theme.   But it is important.

and maintained, stood once against the Church as an alien, if not hostile, power. The position was altered when the Roman emperors became Christian; this first bridged the gulf between the religious and the secular society, by the Christianization of the secular. And a greater change still was produced by the fall of the Roman Empire. Until that time, the secular power could claim to be the representative and defender of culture and civilization; the churchmen were the barbarians. But the kings of the northern nations, upon whom the secular power later devolved, were both Christian and uncultivated. The Church became the guardian not only of the Christian faith, but of the tradition of ancient civilization. Her monasteries preserved and copied the works of ancient literature, her theologians incorporated the teachings of Greek philosophy, her lawyers kept alive the principles of Roman law, and even the deities of the pagan world (so later critics alleged) crept into the worship of the Church disguised as Christian saints. Thus while "the world" had become Christian, the Church had become cultured; she ceased more and more to regard the leading of "a good life" in the Greek sense as inimical to the end of eternal salvation, but included it as a means toward that end. And by her inheritance of the ancient culture, she was qualified to school the European nations to the one end as well as to the other.

For Aquinas the Church is the crown of social organization, not a rival organization to the secular, but its completion. This is the significance of his adoption of Aristotle, for according to Aristotle the state is a good, not a necessary evil. The function which the Christian predecessors of Aquinas had ascribed to the state was that of maintaining order and securing peace, since these were conditions without which the Church could not perform its own task of saving men's souls. But Aquinas follows Aristotle in attributing an educative function to the state. It imposes a discipline which not only restrains men from committing injury, but makes them morally better men. Thus it does part of the Church's work for it; it does not merely secure the conditions in which the Church can do its own.

This change of attitude toward the state is illustrated by the following small but significant point, in which Aquinas departs from the tradition almost universal among his predecessors. They had held that the political subjection of ruled to ruler and the institution of property, like that of slavery, would not have existed among men but for the Fall, and that they have been ordained by God as a consequence and penalty of sin. According to Aquinas the first two of these (though not the third) are natural to man, and would have existed among mankind even if there had been no Fall.

The State is Natural

In the following passage Aquinas affirms his adhesion to the central principle of Aristotle's political philosophy; the principle, namely, that the state is natural to man, so that the restraint which political society necessarily imposes upon its members is not a hindrance but an indispensable means to their individual development.

Question XCVI, Art. iv:[1] *Whether man bore dominion over man in the state of innocence*

❧ Concerning the fourth Article there are the following arguments,
1. It appears that man in the state of innocence had no dominion over man. For Augustine says:[2] "God willed that man, a rational creature made after his own image, should have dominion only over irrational creatures; not over man, but over beasts."
2. Further, that which was introduced for the punishment of sin, cannot have existed in the state of innocence. But the subjection

[1] SUMMA THEOLOGICA, I, XCVI, iv.
The order of exposition adopted by Aquinas in the SUMMA THEOLOGICA is as follows: (i) The problem to be discussed in each Article is stated in its title. (ii) Arguments are enumerated in favor of a conclusion *opposite* to that which Aquinas will defend. (They are introduced by the formula: "Concerning the —— article, there are the following arguments: (1) ... (2) Further ... (3) Further...." Etc.) (iii) At the end of this list of opposite arguments there is *sometimes* inserted the citation of a fact or authority inconsistent with the conclusion to which they serve to point. This is introduced by the words: "But on the other hand ..." (iv) There follows an abbreviated abstract of Aquinas's own conclusion. These abstracts were not written by Aquinas himself, but by later editors. Their insertion at this point ruins the logical artistry of the Article as Aquinas wrote it, since the conclusion is made to precede the proof. But the abstracts are so clear and accurate that I have sacrificed artistry to convenience and retained them in square brackets. (v) Next comes the "body of the Article," in which Aquinas argues to his own conclusion. This is introduced by the words: "I reply that...." Finally (vi) each of the contrary arguments enumerated at the beginning is refuted in turn.
[2] CIVITAS DEI, XIX, 15.

of man to man was introduced for the punishment of sin. For, as the scripture says, it was said to Eve after the act of sin, "Thy husband shall rule over thee." [1] Therefore, man was not subject to man in the state of innocence.

3. Further, subjection is opposed to freedom. But freedom is one of the greatest goods, and could not therefore have been lacking in the state of innocence, since "nothing was lacking therein which a good will could desire," as Augustine says. [2] Therefore, man did not bear dominion over man in the state of nature.

But, on the other hand, the condition of men in the state of innocence was not superior to the condition of angels. But among angels some bear dominion over others; hence one of the angelic orders is called that of *Powers*. It is not, therefore, against the dignity of the state of innocence that man should bear dominion over man.

[CONCLUSION. Slavery must be the punishment of sin. In the state of innocence therefore man could not bear over man the dominion which a master has over his slave. But one who excelled in knowledge and justice might govern another for his good.]

I reply that there are two senses of dominion, or mastery. In one sense it is the correlative of slavery, and in this sense that man is called master to whom another is subjected as his slave, but in another sense it is applied generally to that which is subordinated in any way whatever; and in this sense he who has the office of governing and directing free men can be called their master. In the former sense, therefore, a man cannot have been master of another in the state of innocence; but in the second sense he could. For the slave differs from the free man in this, that the free man is an end in himself, but the slave a means to another's end. A man, therefore, has slave-mastery over another when he treats this other, as a means to his (the master's) advantage. And, since every man desires his own good, and it is hateful to him to yield only to another the good which should be his own, such mastery cannot exist save as punishment of those subject to it. Such dominion of man over man cannot, therefore, have existed in the state of nature. But a man has dominion over another as a free subject, when he directs

---

[1] GENESIS III, 16. [2] CIVITAS DEI, XIV, 10.

him to his (the subject's) good, or to the common good, and such
dominion of man over man would have existed in the state of innocence for two reasons: (i) Man is by nature a social animal.
Therefore, men must have lived in society in the state of innocence.
But there could not be a social life of many members unless there
were one at their head whose aim was the common good. For
many by themselves have diverse ends, and a single end requires
a single agent. Hence the Philosopher [1] says that, when many
particulars are ordered together to a single end, there is always
found a single centre in which the directive power resides. (ii)
If one man excelled others in knowledge and justice, it would be un-
fitting that he should not exercise these powers for the advantage of
others, according as it is said, "As every man hath received the gift,
even so minister the same one to another." [2] Hence also Augustine
says: "just men bear empire not from love of dominion, but from
duty to others' welfare," [3] and "this is prescribed by the natural
order, God willed it so when he made man." [4]

From this is clear the reply to all the objections, for they are all
based upon the former of the senses of dominion.

I shall not insert further quotations to illustrate Aquinas's version
of Aristotelianism. He does not follow Aristotle slavishly, and he
modifies the doctrine in certain points (e.g., in the theory of slavery),
but on the whole he accepts it as the truth. On the whole it is true,
but it is incomplete, requiring to be supplemented from other sources
of truth which were not accessible to Aristotle. Thus it is Aquinas's
task to incorporate the Aristotelian theory into the structure of a
larger system, and he believes that this incorporation is possible without essential modification of the theory itself.

The Eternal Law

The framework of the structure into which the Aristotelian theory
of the state is to be built is Aquinas's general theory of law. The
whole universe is governed by a hierarchy of law, within which the
law of the state has its own place as a subordinate system.

---

[1] Aristotle.   [2] I PETER IV, 10.   [3] CIVITAS DEI, XIX, 14.   [4] Ibid., 15.

Question XCI [1]

CONCERNING THE DIFFERENT KINDS OF LAW DIVIDED INTO
SIX ARTICLES

ART. I. *Whether there is an eternal law*

❧ Concerning the first article there are the following arguments.
1. It appears that there is no eternal law. For every law is imposed upon certain subjects. But subjects for the imposition of law have not existed from eternity; for God alone has existed from eternity. Therefore, no law is eternal.

2. Further, it belongs to the nature of law to be promulgated. But there cannot have been promulgation from eternity, because subjects have not existed from eternity to whom the promulgation could be made. Therefore, no law can be eternal.

3. Further, law signifies an order towards an end. But no means to an end is eternal, for only the ultimate end itself is eternal. Therefore, no law is eternal.

But on the other hand Augustine says: "The law which is called the supreme reason must be held by every thinking being to be unchangeable and eternal."

[CONCLUSION. There is an eternal law, namely, the reason existing in the mind of God by which the whole universe is governed.]

I reply that, as has been said earlier, law is nothing but a dictate of the practical reason in a ruler who governs a complete community. Now if, as we have held, the world is ruled by the divine providence, it is clear that the whole community of the universe is governed by the divine reason. And therefore the reason directing the government of things, existing in God as ruler of the universe, has itself the nature of law. And because the divine reason conceives no ideas in time, but its ideas are eternal, as is said in *Proverbs* viii, it follows that this sort of law must be called eternal.

The reply to the *first* argument, therefore, is that those things which do not exist in themselves, exist in the mind of God, insofar as they are known and foreordained by him; as is said in *Romans*

---

[1] SUMMA THEOLOGICA, Prima Secundae, Quaest. XCI. (For the order of exposition in the following argument, see note on p. 247, *supra*.)

ix. 17: "He calleth the things that are not, as though they were." In this way, therefore, the eternal conception of the divine law has the nature of an eternal law, in so far as it is ordained by God for the governance of the things foreknown by him.

The reply to the *second* is that promulgation may be either by word or by writing; and the eternal law has a promulgation of each kind with respect to God who is the promulgator, since both the divine Word and the writing of the book of life are eternal. With respect to the creature who is to hear or read it, the promulgation cannot be eternal.

The reply to the *third* is that law signifies an order towards an end in an active sense, that is, it signifies that the law orders things towards an end; not in a passive sense, that is, it is not meant that the law itself is ordered towards an end (except *per accidens* in the case of a governor whose end lies outside himself. In such a case his law also will be ordered towards the same end). But the end of the divine government is God himself; nor is his law anything other than himself; hence the eternal law is not ordered towards an end other than itself.

Natural Law

Art. II. *Whether there is a natural law in us*

Concerning the second Article there are the following arguments. 1. It appears that there is no natural law in us. For the eternal law suffices for the government of man. For Augustine says that "the eternal law is that by which it is right that all things should be most perfectly ordered." But, as nature does not fall short of what is necessary, so neither does it indulge in superfluities. Therefore, man has no natural law.

2. Further, the function of law is to order man's actions towards an end, as was held earlier. But human acts are not ordered by nature, as are those of the irrational creatures who act towards an end by natural appetite alone. Man acts towards an end by reason and will. Therefore, there is no law natural to man.

3. Further, the freer anyone is, the less he is subject to law. But man is freer than any of the other animals by reason of the freedom

✦of choice, by which he is distinguished from them.   Therefore, since other animals are not subject to natural law, neither can man be.

But on the other hand the commentary on the text in Romans ii — "the Gentiles, which have not the law, do by nature the things contained in the law" — says that, "if they have not the written law, they still have a natural law, by which every man understands in his own heart what is good and what bad."

[CONCLUSION.   There is in man a certain natural law, namely, his participation in the eternal law, by which he distinguishes good from bad.]

I reply that law is rule and measure, and that rule and measure, as was said above, can be present in two ways; the first as they are present in the person ruling and measuring, the second as they are present in the subject ruled and measured; for a thing may be said to participate in rule and measure in so far as rule and measure are imposed upon it.   Hence, since all things which are under the divine direction,[1] are subjected to rule and measure by the eternal law, as is clear from what has been said in the previous Article, it is manifest that all things participate in some manner in the eternal law, inasmuch, namely, as it impresses upon each a natural indication towards its proper actions and ends.   But rational creatures are subject to the divine direction in a manner superior to that of all other creatures, since they can direct themselves and others and thus become themselves sharers in the directive activity.   The rational creature has thus itself a share in the eternal reason and derives from this its natural inclination towards its proper action and end; and this manner of sharing in the eternal law, which is peculiar to the rational creature, is called the *natural law*.   Hence, the Psalmist says (Psalms iv. 5), "Offer the sacrifices of righteousness," and then, as though certain persons raised the question what the works of righteousness are, he adds: "There be many that say: Who will show us good things?"   And then, in answer to this question, he says: "The light of thy countenance, Lord, is lifted up upon us."[2]   By this he signifies that the light of natural reason, by

---

[1] The Latin word is *providentia* = providence.

[2] In these quotations I have departed slightly from the Authorized Version, in order to get a more exact translation of the Vulgate text, which Aquinas used.

which we distinguish what is good and what bad (a distinction pertaining to the natural law), is nothing other than the impression in us of the divine light. Hence it is clear that the natural law is nothing else than the share of a rational creature in the eternal law.

The reply to the *first* argument is, therefore, that that reasoning would hold if the natural law were something different from the eternal law; whereas it is nothing but a share of the eternal law, as has been said in the body of the Article.

The reply to the *second* is that every operation of reason and will is derived from our nature, as was said earlier. For all reasoning is derived from first principles which are known by nature, and all desire for those things which are means to an end is derived from a natural desire for the ultimate end. The ultimate direction of our acts towards an end ought therefore similarly to be effected by a natural law.

The reply to the *third* is that irrational animals also share in the eternal reason in their own way, as rational creatures do in theirs. But because the rational creature participates in the law by intellect and reason, his share of the eternal law is called law in the proper sense of the term; for law belongs to reason, as was said earlier. The irrational creature on the other hand does not participate in law through reason; hence its share can be termed law only by metaphor.

Human Law

ART. III. *Whether there is a human law*

Concerning the third Article there are the following arguments.

1. It appears that there is no human law. For the natural law is a share of the eternal law, as was said in the previous Article. But all things are most perfectly ordered by the eternal law, as Augustine says. Therefore, the natural law is sufficient for the ordering of all human matters. It is, therefore, not necessary that there should be a human law.

2. Further, it is the nature of law to be a measure, as has been said in the previous Question. But the human reason is not the measure of things; the converse of this is rather the truth, as has

ᴤᴥbeen said.[1]   Therefore, human reason cannot be the source of law.

3. Further, a measure ought to be most certain, as is said.[2]   But the dictates of the human reason concerning what is to be done are uncertain, according to the saying in the book of Wisdom, ix. 14. "The thoughts of mortals are timorous and our devices are prone to fail."   Therefore, human reason cannot be the source of law.

But on the other hand Augustine posits two laws, one eternal, the other temporal, and speaks of the second as human law.

[CONCLUSION.   There is besides the eternal and the natural law a law devised by men, for the particular and detailed regulation of what the natural law ordains.]

I reply that, as was said in the previous Question, law is a dictate of practical reason of a certain kind.   Now there is the same procedure in the practical as in the theoretical reason; both proceed from certain first principles to certain conclusions, as was held earlier. Thus, theoretical reasoning starts from indemonstrable principles which are known by nature, and produces from these the conclusions of the diverse sciences, which knowledge is not implanted in us by nature, but is acquired by the labour of reasoning.   Similarly, in the practical sphere, the human reason starts from the precepts of the natural law, which are universal and indemonstrable principles, but must proceed to a more specific deduction of particular rules. These particular rules deduced by the human reason are called *human laws*, provided that the other conditions pertaining to the nature of law have been observed.   Hence Cicero says in his *Rhetoric*: "The original source of law is in nature.   Then certain rules grow into custom by reason of their utility.   Finally, what has sprung from nature and has been proved by custom receives legal and religious sanction.

The reply to the *first* argument therefore is that the human reason is not able to share to the full in the dictates of the divine reason, but only according to the measure of its own imperfect nature.   And therefore, as in the sphere of theoretical reason we

---

[1] I.e., the human reason is right or wrong according as its conclusions conform or not to the real order of things, not vice versa.   If there is a discrepancy, the reasoning is condemned of error; the order of things is not condemned for failure to conform to human conclusions about it.   "As has been said," *sc.* by Aristotle.

[2] *Sc.*, by Aristotle.

possess in virtue of our natural participation in the divine reason the knowledge of certain universal principles, but not the specific knowledge of every truth (though this also is contained in the divine wisdom); so likewise in the sphere of practical reason man participates by nature in the natural law to the extent of certain universal principles, but not to the extent of specific rules for particular actions, although these also are contained in the eternal law. Hence it is necessary to proceed by human reasoning beyond the first principles to legal enactment of certain particular rules.

The reply to the *second* is that the human reason as such is not the rule and standard of things, but that the principles naturally implanted in it are general standards for the measuring of all human actions (natural reason is the rule and measure of human actions, though not of natural things).

The reply to the *third* is that the practical reason is concerned with that which is susceptible of alteration by action, i.e., with what is individual and contingent; not, like the theoretical reason, with what is necessary. Therefore, human laws cannot possess the infallibility which the demonstrative conclusions of the sciences possess. Nor need every standard be possessed of absolute infallibility and certitude, but only of that degree which is attainable in its kind.

The Divine Law

ART. IV. *Whether it was necessary that there should be a divine law*[1]

Concerning the fourth Article there are the following arguments.
1. It appears not to have been necessary that there should be a divine law. For, as was said in the second Article of this Question, we participate in the eternal law through the natural law in us.

---

[1] "The positive divine law which is the subject of this Article can be defined as follows: the law which proceeds immediately from God, or which God himself gives directly. It differs from the eternal law, in that the eternal law is uncreated, being identical with God himself, whereas the (positive) divine law, being laid down and promulgated in time, is an effect of God's working." (Editors' note in Marietti edition, Turin, 1932.) The divine law is promulgated by God's revelation of his will, as for example, to Moses on Sinai in the Ten Commandments.

☞But the eternal law is the divine law, as was said in the first Article of this Question. There should, therefore, be no other divine law, additional to the natural law and the human laws derived from it.

2. Further, in Ecclesiasticus xv. 14 it is said, "God left man in the hand of his own counsel." But counsel is an act of the reason, as was held above. Therefore, man is left to the governance of his own reason. But the dictate of human reason is human law, as was said in the preceding article. Therefore, there is no need that man should be governed by a divine law.

3. Further, human reason is a better equipment than irrational creatures possess. But irrational creatures have no divine law in addition to their natural instinct; much less, therefore, need a rational creature have a divine law in addition to the natural law.

But on the other hand David prays God to lay down a law for him, saying: "Teach me, O Lord, the way of thy statutes, and I shall keep it unto the end." [1]

[CONCLUSION. In addition to natural and human law a divine law was necessary, by which man might be ordered and infallibly directed towards his supernatural end, which is eternal blessedness.]

I reply that, in addition to natural law and human law, it was necessary to have a divine law for the direction of human life. And this for four reasons: (i) Because man is directed by law to the performance of the right acts for the attainment of his ultimate end. If man were destined solely for an end which did not exceed the measure of the natural faculties of man, there would be no reason why man should have an instrument for his direction by reason besides the natural law and the law laid down by man which is derived from it. But, because man is destined for the end of eternal blessedness, which exceeds the measure of the natural human faculties, as has been held earlier, it was necessary for this reason that, in addition to the natural and the human law, he should be guided towards his end also by a law given by God. (ii) Because through the uncertainty of the human judgement, especially concerning contingent and particular matters, it comes to pass that different men have different judgements concerning human actions; from which judgements different and mutually inconsistent laws

[1] PSALMS CXIX, 33.

ᴕᴕarise.   In order, therefore, that man may be able to know without
any doubt what he ought to do, and what avoid, it was necessary
that he should be directed in right actions by a law given by God;
for it is certain that this law cannot err.   (iii) Because man is able to
make law about those things about which he is able to judge.   But
man is not able to judge concerning the inward acts, which are
hidden, but only concerning the external motions, which are seen;
although inward as well as outward righteousness is needed for the
complete virtue of a man.   Hence the human law was unable sufficiently to restrain and direct the inward acts, and it was necessary
that the divine law should be added to it for this purpose.   (iv)
Because, as Augustine says, human law is not able to punish or to
prevent all bad acts; for, if it were to endeavour to remove all evils,
many good things would be destroyed together with them, and
detriment would be caused to the common good, which is necessary
for men's preservation.   In order, therefore, that no evil should
remain unforbidden and unpunished, it was necessary that a divine
law should be added, by which all sins are forbidden.   These four
reasons are touched upon in Psalms xix. 7, where it is said, "The law
of the Lord is pure," that is, it permits no defilement of sin; "con-
verting the soul," inasmuch as it directs the inward as well as the
outward acts; "the testimony of the Lord is sure," because of the
certainty of its truth and righteousness; "making wise the simple,"
inasmuch as it directs man to a divine and a supernatural end.

The reply, therefore, to the *first* argument is that the eternal law
is by the natural law imparted to man in accordance with the measure of the capacity of human nature.   But a higher means is needed
for the direction of man to his ultimate supernatural end.   And,
therefore, is added the law given by God, by which the eternal law
is imparted in a higher manner.

The reply to the *second* is that counsel is a sort of rational enquiry.   Hence it must proceed from initial principles.   But it is
not sufficient, for the reasons given in the body of this Article, that
it should proceed from those naturally implanted principles which
are the precepts of the law of nature; hence certain further principles
must be added, namely, the precepts of the divine law.

The reply to the *third* is that irrational creatures are not destined
for a higher end than that which is in accordance with their own
natural virtue.   Therefore, the cases are different.

[The following article (Article V) is devoted to a further exposition of the divine law. Aquinas divides it into two laws, the Old and the New. The Old Law is the law revealed to the Jews before the coming of Christ, and is contained in the Old Testament; the New Law is the law revealed after the coming of Christ.

These are, nevertheless, not two separate laws. They differ not as two persons differ from one another, but as a man of mature age differs from the same man in his boyhood. "As we call the boy and the man the same person, so we speak of the Old Law and the New as composing a single divine law, only distinguished as the complete from the incomplete."

The imperfection of the Old Law in comparison with the New is treated by Aquinas under three headings: (i) In respect of the end proposed by each. "It belongs to the nature of law to be ordered with a view to a common good, as an end. . . . This good may be of two kinds. It may be a sensible and terrestrial good. The Old Law directed men's actions towards a good of this kind. (Thus, in the very beginning of the law, the people is summoned to the terrestrial kingdom of the Canaanites.) Or it may be a spiritual and heavenly good; and the New Law directs to such a good. Thus Christ in the very beginning of his preaching summoned men to the kingdom of heaven, saying: 'Repent, for the kingdom of heaven is at hand.'" (ii) "It belongs to the nature of law to direct human actions according to the order of justice. In this respect also the New Law surpasses the Old, since it controls the inward acts of the mind, according to the saying in Matthew v, 20: "Except your righteousness shall exceed the righteousness of the scribes and Pharisees, you shall in no case enter into the kingdom of heaven"; and hence it is said that the Old Law restrains the hand, but the New Law the mind." (iii) "It belongs to the nature of law to induce men to observe what it commands. This the Old Law did by the fear of penalties. The New Law does it by the love which is infused in our hearts by the grace of Christ."]

The entire universe is governed by Eternal Law. Angels, men, the animal and vegetable kingdoms, material nature both in the celestial and terrestrial spheres — all these are subject to its immutable necessity.

The universe falls into the two great divisions — rational creatures on the one hand and the irrational creation, both animate and in-animate, on the other. The Eternal Law operates in a different manner upon each of these two parts. In the irrational world it takes the form of the system of the laws of Nature *in the modern sense of that term*. It is the necessary order, immutable and admitting of no exceptions, to which each natural thing conforms without understanding and without willing to conform. But rational beings are subject to the Eternal Law in a different way. It is presented to their reason, and they conform themselves to it by an act of will. The Eternal Law as it is present to the reason of a rational creature is what Aquinas calls the Natural Law.[1]

Neither the Eternal Law nor, consequently, the Natural Law, is a positive law. It is important to be clear about the meaning of this term. A positive law is a law which has been made at some time. Its making causes certain things to be obligatory which were not obligatory before. But the Eternal Law, as its name implies, has never been made. It has not been made even by God, since it is nothing but the reason of God.[2] Thus there was no time at which the Eternal Law was first imposed, either upon rational creatures, in the form of the Natural Law, or upon irrational nature, in the form of its uncon-scious laws.

Since man is not endowed by nature with a grasp of the entire system of Natural Law, but only of certain general and fundamental principles of it, he must be provided, for the regulation of his conduct, with a more detailed system of rules than the Natural Law can supply to him. These rules are supplied from two sources, (*a*) by Human Law, and (*b*) by Divine Law. Human Law is the system of rules for the regula-tion of men's conduct worked out by human reason from the principles of Natural Law. It comprises all the laws of human societies, in so far as these are truly laws and not merely the commands of a stronger will. Divine Law is the system of the commands of God's will, communi-cated to men by revelation.

---

[1] In a sense, therefore, his usage of the term "Natural Law" is the opposite of the modern. He confines it to the Eternal Law operating in the sphere of rational beings; modern usage confines it to the Eternal Law operating in the sphere of irrational na-ture. Aquinas's Natural Law is more like (though not identical with) what in later times was called the Moral Law.

[2] SUMMA THEOLOGICA, Prima Secundae, Quaest. XCI, Art. 1, quoted on pp. 250 *et seq., supra.*

Both the Human and the Divine Law are positive. This is obviously true of the former. All human laws come into existence at some time, and what they prescribe has obligatory force only from the time of their coming into existence. It is true also of the Divine Law. After God had revealed his will to the Jews on Sinai, the law which he commanded became obligatory upon them — whereas it had not been so before. Similarly with the New Law. The revelation in Christ of God's will has made modes of conduct obligatory on men, to which they need not have (indeed could not have) conformed themselves before.

All positive law is subordinate to eternal law. Human Law has to supply much that is left undetermined by the Natural Law; but Natural Law is the starting-point from which it is derived, and it is valid only so long as its prescriptions do not conflict with the principles of the Natural Law. Thus, Aquinas says in another passage: [1] "Human will by common agreement can make anything just among those things which are not in themselves repugnant to natural justice. Among such things positive law [2] has its place. Hence the Philosopher says: [3] 'the legally just is that about which it is indifferent before the law is made whether it shall be determined this way or that; but it is no longer indifferent once the law has been made.' But, if anything is repugnant in itself to the Natural Law, it cannot be made just by human will; for example, if it were decreed that it should be lawful to steal, or to commit adultery."

Divine Law cannot conflict with Eternal Law, for God cannot command by his will what is not in conformity with his reason.

The law of the state belongs to the system of human law. It is thus limited in two different ways: (1) It is subordinated, within its own sphere, to the Natural Law, which is above it. (2) It is excluded from the sphere of the Divine Law, which exists alongside it.

I. Subordination of Human to Natural Law

Of the former of these limitations not much remains to be added to what has been said in a similar connection elsewhere. Not only is the

---

[1] SUMMA THEOLOGICA, Secunda Secundae, Quaest. LVII, Art. 2.   [2] *Jus*.
[3] ARISTOTLE; in his ETHICS, Book V, chap. VII. See p. 192, *supra*.

authority of the positive law over those who are subjects conditional upon its conformity with a higher law, but every rational creature among the subjects possesses a sufficient knowledge of this higher law to enable him to judge of the conformity.   Thus, every subject of the state is to this extent in the position which Plato reserved to the Philosopher.[1]   His allegiance to the law of his society will never be unconditional.   He will own it only in so far as this law conforms to the Natural Law.   His unconditional allegiance is due to the natural law alone; i.e., to the law present to his own reason.[2]   Aquinas says, accordingly, when discussing the virtue of obedience: "Man is bound to obey the secular rulers in so far as the order of justice requires. Therefore, if they have not a just title, but an usurped one, or if they command what is unjust, their subjects are not bound to obey them; unless perhaps *per accidens* for the avoidance of scandal or of danger."[3]

[1] See p. 109, *supra*.

[2] This does not mean, of course, that every subject has the right to follow his own judgment whether to obey the positive law or not in every case.   In most matters regulated by positive law the Natural Law is indifferent, and cannot therefore be appealed to in justification of refusal.

[3] SUMMA THEOLOGICA, Secunda Secundae, Quaest. CV, Art. 6.

Here is perhaps the appropriate place for fulfilling my promise (p. 244, *supra*) of inserting a passage in which Aquinas introduces the doctrine that the ruler is the representative of his people.

SUMMA THEOLOGICA, Prima Secundae, Quaest. XC. Art. 3.
Whether the reason of every person equally is competent to make law

"Concerning the third Article there are the following arguments: 1. It appears that the reason of every person is competent to make law.   For the Apostle says (Rom. ii. 14), that, 'when the Gentiles, which have not the law, do by nature the things contained in the law, these, having not the law, are a law unto themselves.' He says this universally of all.   Therefore, everyone is able to make a law for himself.

"2. Further, as the Philosopher says (ARISTOTLE, ETHICS, II, 1), 'the purpose of the law-giver is to lead men to virtue.'   But any man can lead another to virtue.   Therefore, the reason of any man is competent to make law.

"3. Further, as the prince of a state is the director of the state, so any master of a household is the director of his household.   But the prince of the state can make law in his state.   Therefore, any master of a household can make law in his household.

"*But* on the other hand, Isidore says, and it is contained in the *Decreta*: 'Law is an enactment of the people, through which the elders together with the commons bring some rule into force.'

[CONCLUSION: Since law orders man towards the common good, not every man's reason has power to make law, but that of a multitude, or of a prince representing a multitude.]

"*I reply* that, strictly speaking, law has regard primarily and principally to an order for the end of the common good.   But to order anything to the end of the common good belongs either to the whole multitude, or to some person representing the whole multitude.   And therefore the setting up of laws belongs either to the whole multi-

II. *Exclusion of Human Law from the Sphere of Divine Law*

The authority of Human Law is limited in another way also. It is not authoritative over the whole of a man's life, but only over a

tude, or to a public person, who has care for the whole multitude; for in all matters, to order towards an end is the function of that man to whom the end belongs.

"The reply to the *first* argument is, therefore, that, as was said above, law can be present in anything not only in the sense in which it is present in the agent regulating, but also by participation as it is present in the subject regulated. In this latter way everyone is a law to himself, in so far as he participates in the order of a regulating agent. Wherefore the same passage [of St. Paul] proceeds as follows: 'which show the work of the law written in their hearts.'

"The reply to the *second* argument is, that a private person cannot effectively lead another to virtue; for he can only admonish, but, if his admonition is rejected, he has no coercive force, which the law must have if it is effectively to lead men to virtue, as the Philosopher says. But this coercive virtue [*sic*] is possessed by a multitude, or by a public person, to whom the infliction of penalties belongs, as will be shown later, and therefore the making of laws belongs to him alone.

" The reply to the *third* argument is that as the individual is part of a household, so the household is part of a state. But the state, it is said, is a complete community. And therefore as the good of an individual is not the ultimate end, but is subordinated to the common good; so the good of a single household is subordinated to the good of a single state, which is a complete community. Therefore, he who directs a household is indeed able to lay down certain precepts or rules but not laws in the strict sense of the term."

[This passage is itself not free from ambiguity. Only a public person, it is said, representing a multitude, has the right to make laws. But what is meant by "representing the multitude"? If it means no more than "consulting their good," then, indeed, there is nothing new. (The Platonic Guardians "represented the multitude" in this sense.) The ruler will still derive the rule of his conduct solely from the law of reason.

I would willingly believe that Aquinas in this passage means no more than this, for it would absolve me from the necessity of adding a qualification to the account which I have given of his political doctrine. But it is impossible to believe that he does not mean something more. In some sense or other he means that the ruler must represent his people's *will*; not, of course, a will expressed by ballot and counting of votes (such notions of popular sovereignty were alien to medieval thought), but a will, embodied in its national customs and traditions. These customs of the people, according to the practice of the Middle Ages, limited the discretion of the king. His authority was legitimate only so long as he observed them, and medieval history is full of instances in which the feudal nobles, in the name of the realm, exert their power to restrain the king from infringing them.

But, if this is what Aquinas means, the result is to place the ruler under two masters. We have already learned that the ruler is to be subject to the Natural Law, which is the eternal law of the divine reason implanted in the minds of men. We now learn that he is to be subject to the customs of his people. But what guarantee is there that the customs of his people will always coincide with the Natural Law? And if they conflict, which is he to follow? It is theoretically necessary to decide for the one or for the other of these principles. Aquinas does not make the decision, because he was not clearly aware of the conflict. But, of the two, the principle illustrated in this footnote is the more alien to the general tenor of his thought.]

certain determinate sphere of it. There is another sphere in which man is subject to another law, the Divine Law, and on this the Human Law may not encroach. How are the two spheres demarcated?

Aquinas starts from the principle that man has two ends. His natural end is preservation and temporal happiness. This end it is the function of society and, therefore, of the state, as the supreme human society, to secure; and Human Law is the instrument for securing it. So far Aquinas accepts Aristotle. But man has also a supernatural end, of which the pagan Aristotle knew nothing: namely, the salvation of his soul and the enjoyment of eternal blessedness hereafter. For the attainment of this end he needs another law, the Divine Law, and a different society, the Church.

Subordination of State to Church

But the two ends of man are not entirely independent of one another. If they were, man's life could be divided into two separate and parallel sections, in the one of which he would pursue the end of temporal happiness by the performance of his political duties, in the other the end of eternal blessedness by the performance of his religious duties. In such a case the authorities set over either sphere, namely, state and Church respectively, would be independent of one another and autonomous each in its own sphere.

In some religions, such independence might be in a large measure possible. It would be possible, for example, in so far as an attainment of eternal blessedness were held to depend solely upon the performance of certain rites and services to God, entirely unconnected with the virtues which dispose a man to be a good citizen. But it is not possible in the Christian religion, because, according to Christianity, the attainment of eternal blessedness is indissolubly connected with the attainment of moral virtue. On the Aristotelian view of the state, moral virtue is necessary in order to make a man a good citizen; on the Christian view of religion, it is necessary in order to make a man a good Christian. On this point the two ends, and therefore the two authorities, overlap. Both state and Church have a common interest in the moral virtue of their members.

The end of temporal felicity is subordinate to that of eternal blessedness, which alone is an end in itself.   Hence the temporal ruler must pursue the former end not as an end in itself, but with a view to the further end to which it is subordinate.   In doing this he must subordinate himself to the authority whose proper function is the preparation of men for their supreme end.   The state is not independent of the Church, and is subordinate to it in so far as their spheres overlap.

Aquinas expounds this relation between the state and the Church in the following passage,[1] in which the function of the temporal ruler is compared with that of the ship's carpenter, whose task it is to keep the ship in repair while on voyage.   The task of the Church is like that of the pilot, who has to steer the ship to the goal of its voyage.

To govern means to steer,[2] and the nature of government is to be understood from the analogy of steering a ship.   Government, like steering, consists in conducting its charge by the best route to its proper goal or end.   Thus, a ship is said to be steered when the labour of the helmsman succeeds in conducting it direct to its port unharmed.   If, therefore, anything is destined to an end beyond itself, as the ship is to the port, it will be part of the duty of the man in charge not only to preserve it unharmed in itself, but also to conduct it to its goal.   Now, if there were anything which had no goal or end outside itself, the care of its governor would be directed solely to the task of preserving it unharmed in its perfect condition. There is in fact nothing of such a kind, except God himself, who is the end of all things; but a thing which is destined to an end outside itself, requires a diversity of attentions from many different hands.   It may well be the task of one man to preserve it in its present state of being, and of another to conduct it to a higher perfection.   This is clearly illustrated in the example of the ship, from which the conception of government is derived.   For the carpenter has the task of repairing any damage which may occur in the ship, while the helmsman has the responsibility of conducting the ship to its port.   The case of a man is similar: it is the task of his physician to preserve his life in a condition of health, of his steward to supply him with the necessities of life, of the scholar to impart to him the knowledge of

---

[1] DE REGIMINE PRINCIPUM, I, 14.

[2] The Latin word *gubernare* (which means "to govern" and from which the word "govern" is derived) means originally to steer a ship.

🙵truth, of a moral preceptor to instruct him in the conduct of his life according to reason.

Now, if man were not destined to a good beyond himself, these ministrations would suffice for his well-being. But there is a good for man which is beyond him in this mortal life: namely, the final blessedness of the enjoyment of God which he expects after death. For, as the Apostle says in II Corinthians v. 6, "whilst we are at home in the body, we are absent from the Lord." Therefore, the Christian man, for whom that blessedness has been won by the blood of Christ and who has received the pledge of the Holy Spirit for the attainment of it, has need of another and a spiritual ministration by which he may be guided to the harbour of eternal salvation. This ministration is afforded to the faithful by the officers of the Church of Christ.

What is true concerning the end of an individual must be true also of a society of individuals. If the end of the individual were some good residing in himself, the final end of rule in a society would likewise be that the society should attain such a good and be preserved in the enjoyment of it. If such a final end, whether of individual or of society, were bodily, namely, the life and health of the body, it would be the task of the physician to secure it. If the ultimate end were abundance of wealth, the man of business would be king of the society. If the good of knowledge were such that a multitude could attain to it, the king's task would be that of a teacher. But it appears in fact that the end of a multitude gathered into society is a life according to virtue. For men associate for this purpose, that together they may live well, which each living singly could not do. But to live well is to live according to virtue. Hence a life according to virtue is the end of human association. ... But, since man is by a life according to virtue destined for the attainment of a further end, which consists, as was said above, in the enjoyment of God, human society also must have the same end as the individual man. It is not, therefore, the final end of a society to live according to virtue, but by means of a virtuous life to attain to the enjoyment of God.

If it were possible to attain this end by the virtue of human nature, it would belong to the function of the king to guide men towards this end. (For king is the title given to him who bears the highest authority in human matters; and an authority is higher in proportion as the end to which it is directed is higher. For we always find that the man whose task is the final end is in command over those whose work is about the means to the end; for example, the pilot, whose function it is to direct the sailing of the ship, gives orders to the ship-maker as to the kind of ship which he shall make, so as to be fit for sailing; and the citizen, who uses arms, instructs the smith what kind of arms to make.) But, since man attains the end of the fruition of God not by human but by divine virtue, according to the saying of the Apostle in Romans vi. 23: "The gift of God is eternal life," to conduct him to that end will be the part not of a human but of a divine governance. Such governance belongs to a king who is not man only, but God also: namely to our Lord Jesus Christ who, by making men sons of God, has introduced them into the heavenly glory.

This government, therefore, which shall be incorruptible, was entrusted to Christ, and on this account he is called in the Scriptures not only priest but king, as Jeremiah says in xxiii. 5: "He shall reign as king and deal wisely." Hence the royal priesthood is derived from him, and, what is more, all Christ's faithful followers, in so far as they are members of him, are called kings and priests. The government of this kingdom, then, in order that spiritual things might be separated from earthly, was entrusted not to secular kings, but to priests, and above all to that High Priest, the successor of Peter and Vicar of Christ, the Pope of Rome, to whom all Christian peoples ought to be subject, as to their Lord Jesus Christ himself. For those into whose charge the care of subordinate ends has been committed ought to be subject to him whose charge is the supreme end, and to be directed by his authority.

Effect of Divine Law in Limiting the Scope of Political Authority

Aquinas's doctrine of the Divine Law thus supplies to Aristotle a culmination which was lacking in Aristotle himself. Aquinas accepts Aristotle's account of the natural end of man, but crowns it with the account of a higher end. He accepts Aristotle's account of the nature of human society, but places it under the superior authority of a divine society. His system depends upon the assumption that this super-structure can be reared upon the Aristotelian foundations without the need of essential modification of the Aristotelian doctrine itself. In fact this assumption is not justified. In being subordinated to a divine society, political society must lose the character which Aristotle attributed to it. It must, in a word, take on the character of a *secular* society, which the state has retained until very modern times.

It is possible to trace the first workings of this consequence within Aquinas himself, in a passage in which he discusses the obedience owed by a Christian to the civil power.

Whether subjects are bound to obey their superiors in all things [1]

❧ [CONCLUSION. Subjects are bound to obey their superiors only in those matters in which the latter themselves obey their superiors, and in which the superiors themselves do not oppose a precept of a higher authority.]

. . . .

It may happen from two causes that a subject is not bound to obey his superior in all things. (i) Because of the precept of a higher authority. Thus when it is said in *Romans* XIII: "They that resist the power, shall receive to themselves damnation," the Commentary adds these words: "If the Curator [2] commands you, ought you to obey if it is against the command of the Proconsul? If the Proconsul issues one command and the Emperor a different one, is there any doubt that the former should be neglected and the latter obeyed? Similarly, if the Emperor bids one thing and God another, the Emperor is to be neglected and God obeyed." (ii) The inferior is not bound to obey his superior on another ground, if the latter commands him in a matter in respect of which he is not subject to him. Thus Seneca says: "It is an error if any man thinks that servitude extends to every part of a man. The better part of a man is immune from it. The bodies of slaves are bound by it and belong to

[1] SUMMA THEOLOGICA, Secunda Secundae, Quaest. CIV, Art. v, with omissions.
[2] The name of a subordinate official in the administrative hierarchy of the Roman Empire. The Proconsul held a higher position.

the slave-owners, but the mind is its own master." Similarly, in those things which pertain to the inward motion of the will, man is not bound to obey man, but God above.

Man is, however, bound to obey man in those external actions which are performed by the body; though, even among these, man is not bound to obey man, but God only, in respect of those actions which belong to the essential nature of the body (for example, in those which pertain to the sustenance of the body and the generation of children), because by nature all men are equal. Hence slaves are not bound to obey their masters, nor sons their parents in the matter of contracting marriage or in that of taking vows of celibacy, or in other things of like kind. But in those things which belong to the ordering of human actions and human affairs, the subject is bound to obey his superior within the range covered by his authority. For example, a soldier is bound to obey his general in those things which pertain to the conduct of war, a slave his master in those things which belong to the performance of his servile duty, a son his father in those which belong to the discipline of life and the maintenance of the household; and so on.

.   .   .   .

The reply to the *second* [the second argument had maintained that, as man is bound to obey God in all things, so likewise he is bound to obey in all things those set in authority over him] is that man is subject to God absolutely, in respect of all things, whether inward or external, and therefore is bound to obey him in all things. But subjects are not subjected to their superiors in all respects, but in certain determinate respects.[1] In respect of these determinate matters the superiors mediate between God and the subjects. But in respect of other things the latter are subject immediately to God, by whom they are instructed through the natural or the written [2] law.

Aquinas insists strongly on the obligation of Christian subjects (i.e., of those who possess the Divine Law) to render obedience to the secular

---

[1] I.e., in respect of external actions performed by the body, or to the ordering of human actions and affairs which fall under the authority of the superior. [Editors' note in Marietti edition.]

[2] I.e., the Divine Law, recorded in the Scriptures.

power. Thus the conclusion of the next article, in which this question is discussed, runs: "Seeing that the order of justice is rather confirmed than removed by the faith of Christ, it is necessary that the faithful of Christ be subject to the secular authorities." But the sphere in which the secular authority can claim obedience is restricted to the regulation of external actions.

This restriction is a necessary consequence of the doctrine of the Divine Law. It is for the Divine Law to regulate those actions of a man which are directly relevant to the attainment of his eternal end. These must include the interior motions of his heart and will, and to control these must therefore fall within the province of the Divine Law and be excluded from that of the state.

But the restriction makes of the state something very different from what Aristotle had conceived it to be. Aristotle pours scorn on the notion that the law of the state should be confined to the regulation of men's external actions.[1] This, he says, is to suppose that the end of the law is solely to prevent men from doing injury, not to make them good. For Aristotle the law of the state, and the ruler who is its minister, are under no such restriction. Their authority is justified for him by the fact that it is their function to make men good; not only to regulate the acts, but to mould the characters of their subjects.

FOR FURTHER READING

Translations

There are English translations of the SUMMA THEOLOGICA and of the SUMMA CONTRA GENTILES by members of Dominican Order.

There is a French series (ÉDITIONS DE LA REVUE DES JEUNES, Desclée et Cie; Paris, Tournai, Rome), in which extracts from the SUMMA THEOLOGICA upon various different topics are printed together with a French translation, commentary, and appendices. The parts of the SUMMA most important for political theory are contained in the volumes entitled LA LOI (contains SUMMA THEOLOGICA, 1^a–2^{ae}, Questions 90–97: translated by M. J. LAVERSIN, D.P.) and in the first of the three volumes entitled LA JUSTICE (contains 2^a–2^{ae}, Questions 57–62, trans-

[1] See p. 125, *supra*.

lated by R^{me} Père Gillet, D.P.). DIE STAATSLEHRE DES HEILIGEN
THOMAS VON AQUINO by J. J. BAUMANN (Leipsig, 1873) contains a selection of political passages translated into German.

Commentaries and General Works

CARLYLE, R. W. and A. J., HISTORY OF MEDIAEVAL POLITICAL THEORY IN THE
    WEST.
GILSON, ÉTIENNE, L'ESPRIT DE LA PHILOSOPHIE MÉDIÉVALE. Gifford lectures,
    1931–32. English translation by A. H. C. DOWNES: THE SPIRIT OF MEDI-
    AEVAL PHILOSOPHY. New York: Charles Scribner's Sons, 1936.
        *A brilliantly lucid account of medieval philosophy, but with no special
        reference to political theory.*
POOLE, R. L., ILLUSTRATIONS OF THE HISTORY OF MEDIAEVAL THOUGHT AND
    LEARNING. Revised edition; New York: The Macmillan Company, 1920.
        *Contains some scholarly and illuminating studies of some of the less-
        known medieval philosophers.*
TAWNEY, R. H., RELIGION AND THE RISE OF CAPITALISM, chap. I, "THE MEDIAEVAL
    BACKGROUND." New York: Harcourt, Brace & Company, 1936.

CHAPTER EIGHT
Machiavelli

THE Middle Ages were brought to a close and the modern period was begun by the two movements known as the Renaissance and the Reformation. The Renaissance was a rediscovery of pagan antiquity. It was, as its name implies, a rebirth of that ancient culture which Christianity had conquered and suppressed. Not all the ideas of antiquity required to be born again. The ideas underlying the Roman Empire and many of those expressed in Greek philosophy had been, as we have seen, already absorbed in the medieval synthesis. It was Greek art rather than Greek philosophy which came into its own at the Renaissance, and the ideas of the Roman Republic rather than those of the Roman Empire.

This resurrection of interest in pagan antiquity was something more than merely a scholarly or academic movement. It betokened also a revival of pagan sentiments in the European peoples, which had been overlaid but not dissolved by the Christian culture of the Middle Ages. Men discovered a new interest in the works of the ancients because these works were congenial to something of which they were conscious in themselves.

The Reformation, on the other hand, was a movement within Christianity itself. It was in no sense anti-Christian, but claimed to be nothing else than a purification of the Christian faith from alien elements with which it had become confused.

Renaissance and Reformation, then, are names which designate compendiously, but not misleadingly, two great sets of forces by which medieval was transformed into modern Europe.

Machiavelli represents one of these forces; he is, in political theory, the representative of the Renaissance. He was born in Italy, the original seat of the Renaissance, in 1469. Italy, during his lifetime, as for many centuries longer, was divided politically. It comprised a great number of small independent states, based, like the states of antiquity, upon the city.   Some of these, like Venice and Florence, were republics; others were governed by despots; and in many the two forms of constitution alternated rapidly.   Internally these states were the home of fierce political rivalries and personal ambitions, and of a brilliant artistic and literary culture.   In their relation with one another they were involved in constant struggles carried on by diplomacy and war, the latter waged largely by mercenary armies.   The political map of Italy was further confused by the presence in the midst of the peninsula of the territories governed directly by the Church, which had its seat in Rome.

The political disunion of Italy laid it open, further, to incursions and armed interference by the larger political units which existed in other parts of Europe, by the German Emperor, and by the national monarchies of France and Spain.   These powers were often summoned into Italy by Italian states or Italian parties to assist them against their rivals.   Spain, in particular, was the power on which the Popes continually relied for the support of their temporal dominion in Italy.

Machiavelli was born a citizen of Florence, where he entered public life in 1494 at the age of twenty-five.   In 1498 he became secretary to the Second Chancery, a body which by the constitution of Florence at that time had the general direction of the departments of war and of the interior.   He retained this post until 1512, and these years comprise the period of his active political life.   He was engaged during this time principally in conducting official correspondence, in diplomatic missions, both to other Italian states and to powers elsewhere in Europe, and in the organization of a Florentine militia.

After 1509, when France was beaten by Spain at Ravenna, the party of the Medici rose to ascendancy in Italy, and Florence, although she had taken no part in the war, a few years later, in 1512, deposed her existing government in favor of the victorious party.   Machiavelli lost his employments and was exiled from Florence.   He was involved in an unsuccessful conspiracy in the following year, was imprisoned and racked and finally released.   He retired to a farm in the country, where he devoted himself to rustic employments and to literature, and his most important works were produced in this period of his life.   The two of his works which are of principal importance for political theory are the *Discourses on the First Decade of Titus Livius* and *The Prince*.

The *Discourses* are a free commentary upon the history of the Roman Republic, in which Machiavelli draws lessons and lays down maxims for the guidance of his own time. *The Prince* is addressed to Lorenzo, the Duke of Urbino, to whom Machiavelli looked as a possible source of employment for himself and, as will appear, of deliverance for Italy from the divisions by which she was distracted. *The Prince* was finished by the end of 1513; the *Discourses* were begun before it, but completed later. The remainder of Machiavelli's life is of little importance. Lorenzo disappointed his hopes both for himself and for Italy. Machiavelli wrote other works, the chief of them being the *Art of War* and the *History of Florence*; from 1521 onward he was given some minor political employments by the Medici; he died in 1527.

POLITICAL PHILOSOPHY

It has often been said that Machiavelli is the first genuinely modern political thinker, and there is a sense in which this statement is true. He introduces a set of new ideas, which have been current in modern Europe ever since, and which were foreign to medieval thought. Nevertheless, the statement requires two important qualifications if it is not to be misleading. In the first place, the new ideas which Machiavelli represents did not banish from the European world the medieval system against which they were a reaction. The philosophy of Aquinas has remained throughout the modern period, and still remains, the accepted philosophy of the Roman Catholic Church.[1] It has thus as strong a claim as the ideas represented by Machiavelli to be recognized as an integral part of modern civilization, and neither can claim to be typically modern to the exclusion of the other.

And, secondly, Machiavelli represents only one of the two great forces which I have mentioned. If we regard him as typical of the modern spirit, we are in danger of ignoring the fact that the political ideas of Protestant Christianity played a still larger part in determining the structure of modern civilization.

---

[1] Some recent documents of Catholic political theory are given in M. G. OAKE-SHOTT'S SOCIAL AND POLITICAL DOCTRINES OF CONTEMPORARY EUROPE (Cambridge, 1939), pp. 45–77. They will convince the reader that the spirit of Aquinas is still alive.

The negative doctrines of Machiavelli are those which first strike the reader's attention. He attacks the separation of the temporal from the spiritual sphere, and he rejects the doctrine of Natural Law; thus denying the two main principles of the Catholic system. I will illustrate each in turn.

I. Machiavelli's Denial of Divine Law

Machiavelli does not believe the cardinal tenet of Christian doctrine, that man is destined to a supernatural end. This does not mean that he confines man's end to merely material well-being. But the values which he recognizes over and above material well-being are all earthly and not heavenly ones. They are the values of greatness, power, and fame. Fame which will outlast his life is the only immortality of which Machiavelli thinks the individual to be capable.

If man has, as Machiavelli thinks, no supernatural end, there is no function to be performed by a Divine Law. The view of Aquinas, as we have seen,[1] was that man had need of two laws, because he was destined to two ends; he had need of Human Law to secure his well-being in this world, and of a Divine Law to direct him to the attainment of blessedness in the next.

The medieval theory had based the separation of powers upon this distinction of the two kinds of laws. The temporal ruler was the custodian of Human Law, the custodian of Divine Law was the Church; and, as these laws were distinct from one another, each with its separate purpose, it followed that these two authorities had each its independent sphere of action. Indeed, it followed not merely that the Church should be independent of the temporal power, but (since man's supernatural end was of more importance than his natural one) that it must be in a manner superior to the latter.[2] Since Machiavelli does not recognize the distinction of these two laws, he is led to deny any claim by the Church not merely to superiority but to independence of the state.

This does not mean that Machiavelli despises religion. Those who expect him to do so will be surprised to read the title of a chapter in his

---

[1] See pp. 255 *et seq.*, *supra.*
[2] Cf. p. 263, *supra.*

Discourses: [1] "The importance of giving religion a prominent influence in a state, and how Italy was ruined because she failed in this respect through the conduct of the Church of Rome." Similarly, he says at the opening of the same chapter: "Princes and Republics who wish to maintain themselves free from corruption must above all things preserve the purity of all religious observances and treat them with proper reverence; for there is no greater indication of the ruin of a country than to see religion contemned."

Machiavelli's theory is not irreligious, but his attitude to religion is a pagan, not a Christian one. Religion, he thinks, is necessary for the health and prosperity of a state. He knows that a state will not flourish if the citizens are induced to serve it solely by fear of such punishment as the ruler can inflict. A further motive is required which will give fervor to their obedience, and which will keep them faithful even in circumstances in which they might disobey without detection. This is to attribute to religion an important place within the state; but a place *within* the state, not above it or beside it. That is the essential of the pagan view, that it regards religion as instrumental to the ends of the state, and the Church as an organ of the state.

Machiavelli's view of the place of religion in a state is brought out clearly in a passage in which he compares the benefits conferred upon Rome respectively by Romulus, the soldier and lawgiver, its founder, and by Numa Pompilius, his religious and peaceful successor: [2]

Although the founder of Rome was Romulus, to whom, like a daughter, she owed her birth and her education, yet the gods did not judge the laws of this prince sufficient for so great an empire, and therefore inspired the Roman Senate to elect Numa Pompilius as his successor, so that he might regulate all those things that had been omitted by Romulus. Numa, finding a very savage people, and wishing to reduce them to civil obedience by the arts of peace, had recourse to religion as the most necessary and assured support of any civil society; and he established it upon such foundations that for many centuries there was nowhere more fear of the gods than in that republic, which greatly facilitated all the enterprises which the Senate or its great men attempted. Whoever will examine the ac-

[1] DISCOURSES ON THE FIRST DECADE OF TITUS LIVIUS, Book I, chap. 12.
[2] DISCOURSES, I, xi.

tions of the people of Rome as a body, or of many individual Romans, will see that these citizens feared much more to break an oath than the laws; like men who esteem the power of the gods more than that of men. . . . And whoever reads Roman history attentively will see in how great a degree religion served in the command of the armies, in uniting the people and keeping them well conducted, and in covering the wicked with shame.   So that if the question were discussed whether Rome was more indebted to Romulus or to Numa, I believe that the highest merit would be conceded to Numa; for where religion exists it is easy to introduce armies and discipline, but where there are armies and no religion it is difficult to introduce the latter. . . . Considering, then, all these things, I conclude that the religion introduced by Numa into Rome was one of the chief causes of the prosperity of that city; for this religion gave rise to good laws, and good laws bring good fortune, and from good fortune results happy success in all enterprises.   And as the observance of divine institutions is the cause of the greatness of a Republic, so the disregard of them produces their ruin; for where fear of God is wanting, there the country will come to ruin.

II. *Machiavelli's Denial of Natural Law*

Machiavelli's notion of virtue is correlative to his notion of the human end.   Human virtue must comprise those qualities by which man is enabled to achieve the end for which he is destined; and since for Machiavelli this end is the attainment of success, power, and fame, it follows that for him the virtue of a man consists in the qualities which fit him to win these things.   This is what he means by the Italian word *virtu*, a term which recurs throughout his writings and stands for a notion cardinal in his philosophy.   The notion is closely akin to that which we have found already in the Greek Sophists [1]; it is something very like that "natural virtue" which Callicles [2] thought it a shame to subject to the restraints of law and conventional morality.   It has been described by J. Burckhardt as "a compound of force and intellect."   It is the sum of those qualities, whatever they may be, which tend to make a man great, powerful, and famous.

[1] See pp. 35 *et seq., supra.*   [2] *Ibid.*

The recurrence of this word *virtu* in Machiavelli's works renders the passages in which it occurs untranslatable into modern English. The literal translation is, of course, "virtue," but what Machiavelli means is something so clearly different from what we mean by that word that most modern translators substitute some word such as "valor." But to do this, however desirable it may be on stylistic grounds, is to conceal the true relation between Machiavelli's thought and our own. In the quotations which come later, I have substituted the word "virtue" for that used by the translator, but have placed it in inverted commas. It is essential to realize that Machiavelli uses, in order to designate one kind of qualities, *the same word*, "virtue," which we use in order to designate quite another kind. "Virtue," both for him and for us, means the quality whicʰ makes a good man. Where we differ from him is not in linguistic usage, but in our different notions of what the goodness of man consists in.

The difference comes from the fact that our common moral notions assume a principle which Machiavelli repudiates, namely, that man attains goodness only by being subject to law. This is the principle which, in a certain form, inspires Plato's answer to the Sophists, when he declares that restraint is an essential condition of virtue.[1] It is the principle which becomes explicit in the Stoic [2] and Christian [3] doctrines of Natural Law.

The doctrine of Natural Law implies that there are certain eternal canons of right conduct, to which the good man must conform. His virtue is judged by the measure in which his conduct conforms to these canons. But Machiavelli, as we have seen, judges conduct by another standard. He measures a man's "virtue" by his ability to attain power and fame, and just as other moralists prescribe rules for the exercise of virtue as *they* conceive it, so Machiavelli lays down rules for the exercise of "virtue" as he conceives it. As they tell man how they may conform their conduct to the laws of right and wrong he tells them how they may direct their action to the ends of greatness and power. Machiavelli's most famous book, *The Prince*, consists mainly of such rules and counsels, addressed particularly to one in a position of political power; and this is what is popularly known as "Machiavellianism."

[1] See p. 39, *supra*.
[2] See pp. 189 *et seq.*, *supra*.
[3] See pp. 251 *et seq.*, *supra*.

I quote the chapter of Machiavelli which has probably contributed more than any other to his notoriety.[1]

How Princes Should Keep Faith

Every one recognises how praiseworthy it is in a Prince to keep faith, and to act uprightly and not craftily. Nevertheless, we see from what has happened in our own days that Princes who have set little store by their word, but have known how to over-reach others by their cunning, have accomplished great things, and in the end had the better of those who trusted to honest dealing.

Be it known, then, that there are two ways of contending, one in accordance with the laws, the other by force; the first of which is proper to men, the second to beasts. But since the first method is often ineffectual, it becomes necessary to resort to the second. A Prince should, therefore, understand how to use well both the man and the beast. And this lesson has been covertly taught by the ancient writers, who relate how Achilles and many others of these old Princes were given over to be brought up and trained by Chiron the Centaur; since the only meaning of their having for teacher one who was half man and half beast is, that it is necessary for a Prince to know how to use both natures, and that the one without the other has no stability.

But, since a Prince should know how to use the beast's nature wisely, he ought of beasts to choose both the lion and the fox; for the lion cannot guard himself from the toils, nor the fox from wolves. He must therefore be a fox to discern toils, and a lion to drive off wolves.

To rely wholly on the lion is unwise; and for this reason a prudent Prince neither can nor ought to keep his word when to keep it is hurtful to him and the causes which led him to pledge it are removed. If all men were good, this would not be good advice, but since they are dishonest and do not keep faith with you, you, in return, need not keep faith with them; and no Prince was ever at a loss for plausible reasons to cloak a breach of faith. Of this numberless recent instances could be given, and it might be shown how

[1] THE PRINCE, chap. XVIII.

many solemn treaties and engagements have been rendered inoperative and idle through want of faith in Princes, and that he who has best known to play the fox has had the best success.

It is necessary, indeed, to put a good colour on this nature, and to be skilful in feigning and dissembling. But men are so simple, and governed so absolutely by their present needs, that he who wishes to deceive will never fail in finding willing dupes. One recent example I will not omit. Pope Alexander VI had no care or thought but how to deceive, and always found material to work on. No man ever had a more effective manner of asseverating, or made promises with more solemn protestations, or observed them less. And yet, because he understood this side of human nature, his frauds always succeeded.

It is not essential, then, that a Prince should have all the good qualities I have enumerated above, but it is most essential that he should seem to have them. Nay, I will venture to affirm that if he has and invariably practises them all, they are hurtful, whereas the appearance of having them is useful. Thus, it is well to seem merciful, faithful, humane, religious, and upright, and also to be so; but the mind should remain so balanced that were it needful not to be so, you should be able and know how to change to the contrary.

And you are to understand that a Prince, and most of all a new Prince, cannot observe all those rules of conduct in respect whereof men are accounted good, being often forced, in order to preserve his Princedom, to act in opposition to good faith, charity, humanity, and religion. He must therefore keep his mind ready to shift as the winds and tides of Fortune turn, and, as I have already said, ought not to quit good courses if he can help it, but should know how to follow evil if he must.

A Prince should therefore be very careful that nothing ever escapes his lips which is not replete with the five qualities above named, so that to see and hear him, one would think him the embodiment of mercy, good faith, integrity, kindliness, and religion. And there is no quality which it is more necessary for him to seem to possess than this last; because men in general judge rather by the eye than by the hand, for all can see but few can touch. Every one sees what you seem, but few know what you are, and these few dare not oppose themselves to the opinion of the many who have the majesty of the State to back them up.

Moreover, in the actions of all men, and most of all of Princes, where there is no tribunal to which we can appeal, we look to results. Wherefore if a Prince succeeds in establishing and maintaining his authority, the means will always be judged honourable and be approved by every one.

The essence of Machiavellianism is not merely that it supplies a system of technical rules for the acquisition and maintenance of power. Such a system of rules would not necessarily involve a reversal of moral standards. A handbook of carpentry provides a system of technical rules for the working of wood, and a man who has mastered them may make use of them to enable him to break into houses, or for other illicit purposes. But the handbook is not said to have an immoral tendency because it imparts a knowledge which may be used for an immoral end. Its purpose is technical only; this means that it confines itself to informing the pupil how various operations upon woodwork (including of course the breaking open of doors) may be most efficiently performed, but leaves it an open question, to be decided upon moral grounds, whether, and when, and to what purposes, this skill ought to be applied. It is conceivable that a political handbook might be merely technical in this sense; that it might merely lay down the rules by which power could be most readily acquired and maintained, leaving it to another kind of knowledge to determine on what occasions it was allowable, or in accordance with virtue, to apply these rules.

Machiavelli's *Prince* is in part just such a technical treatise: but Machiavelli's notion of "virtue" makes it something much more than this. It is not open to him to say: "These are the means by which power may be obtained: whether or not a virtuous man will employ them will depend of course upon the question whether their employment in a given set of circumstances would conform to the Natural Law (or to the rule of right and wrong)." He cannot say this because he does not hold virtue to consist in conforming to the Natural Law.[1]

---

[1] This is true in the main; but Machiavelli is not entirely consistent. There are some passages in which he seems to waver (as indeed we should expect him to waver) between his own and the Christian notion of virtue. A striking example of this conflict between the two standards of conduct is to be found in the DISCOURSES (I, 26), where Machiavelli, having laid down the rule that a prince who has newly acquired power must be ruthless in subverting old institutions, proceeds as follows: "Doubtless these means are cruel and destructive of all civilized life, and neither Christian nor even human, and should be avoided by everyone. In fact the life of a private citizen

The attainment of power is in itself a proof of "virtue," and Machiavelli recognizes no other standard by which virtue is to be judged. The counsels of the "Prince" are thus not merely technical rules: they purport to be rules for the exercise of "virtue"; and a reversal of moral values is involved in the substitution of this notion of virtue for the other.

The following passage exemplifies Machiavelli's notion of "virtue." [1]

ᑫ The other way of destroying envy is, when either violence or a natural death carries off those of your rivals who, on seeing you acquire such reputation and greatness, cannot patiently bear your being more distinguished than themselves. If men of this kind live in a corrupt city, where education has not been able to infuse any spirit of good into their minds, it is impossible that they should be restrained by any chance, but they would be willing rather to see their country ruined than not to attain their purpose, or not to satisfy their perverse natures. To overcome such envy, there is no other remedy but the death of those who harbor it. And, when fortune is so propitious to a man of "virtue" as to deliver him from such rivals by their natural death, he becomes glorious without violence, and may then display his "virtue" to its full extent without hindrance and without offence to anybody. But, when he has not such good fortune, he must strive nevertheless by all possible means to overcome this difficulty, and relieve himself of such rivals before attempting any enterprise.

"Virtue" and "Fortune"

The two great forces which govern the lives of men are Fortune and "virtue." Fortune is a capricious power, incalculable and often irresistible, influencing men's destinies from without. But men are not merely puppets on the strings of Fortune. They can wrestle with For-

would be preferable to that of a king at the expense of the ruin of so many human beings. Nevertheless whoever is unwilling to adopt the first and good course must, if he wishes to maintain his power, follow the latter evil course. But men generally decide upon a middle course, which is most hazardous; for they know neither how to be entirely good or entirely bad." "Good" and "bad" are used with reference to the Christian, not to the Machiavellian standard of virtue.

[1] DISCOURSES, III, 30.

tune, and to some extent each can control his own destiny. The power which enables him to do so is his "virtue," and, the more "virtue" a man possesses, the more he will be master of his own fate. Only a man entirely lacking in "virtue" would be quite passive in the hands of Fortune. The relation between these two forces is expressed in the following passage of *The Prince*.[1]

What Fortune can effect in human affairs, and how she may be withstood. I am not ignorant that many have been and are of the opinion that human affairs are so governed by Fortune and by God, that men cannot alter them by any prudence of theirs, and indeed have no remedy against them; and for this reason have come to think that it is not worth while to labour much about anything, but that they must leave everything to be determined by chance.

Sometimes, when I turn the matter over, I am in part inclined to agree with this opinion, which has had the readier acceptance in our own times from the great changes in things which we have seen, and every day see, happen contrary to all human expectation. Nevertheless, that our free will be not wholly set aside, I think it may be the case that Fortune is the mistress of one half our actions, and yet leaves the control of the other half, or a little less, to ourselves. And I would liken her to one of those wild torrents which, when angry, overflow the plains, sweep away trees and houses, and carry off soil from one bank to throw it down upon the other. Every one flees before them, and yields to their fury without the least power to resist. And yet, though this be their nature, it does not follow that in seasons of fair weather, men cannot, by constructing weirs and moles, make such provision as will cause them when again in flood to pass off by some artificial channel, or at least prevent their course from being so uncontrolled and destructive. And so it is with Fortune, who displays her might where there is no ordered "virtue" to resist her, and directs her onset where she knows there is neither barrier nor embankment to confine her.

And if you look at Italy, which has been at once the seat of these changes and their cause, you will perceive that it is a field without embankment or barrier. For if, like Germany, France, and Spain, it had been guarded with sufficient skill, this inundation, if it ever

[1] Chap. xxv.

came upon us, would never have wrought the violent changes we have witnessed.

"Human Affairs are as governed *by Fortune and by God....*" Machiavelli uses these two words synonymously to designate the power above man which controls man's destinies. But it needs few words to point out how widely his notion of God differs from the Christian. According to the Christian conception, the divine Providence rules human affairs by law and reason, not by caprice, and this Providence is omnipotent, so that no effort of human power can deflect it from its course. The difference is strikingly displayed in the passage with which Machiavelli concludes the chapter quoted: [1]

❧ To be brief, I say that since Fortune changes and men stand fixed in their old ways, they are prosperous so long as there is congruity between them, and unprosperous when there is not. Of this, however, I am well persuaded, that it is better to be impetuous than cautious. For Fortune is a woman who to be kept under must be beaten and roughly handled; and we see that she suffers herself to be more readily mastered by those who so treat her than by those who are more timid in their approaches. And always, like a woman, she favours the young, because they are less scrupulous, and fiercer, and command her with greater audacity.

The difference between the Machiavellian and the Christian conceptions of the power by which human affairs are controlled is the obverse side of the difference, which we have already observed, between the Machiavellian and the Christian views of human virtue. According to Machiavelli, human virtue is displayed in the power to resist the force which governs the world; according to Christianity, in willing submission to the laws and purposes of God.

Republics and Princedoms

Those who have read only *The Prince* will think Machiavelli's political theory not very different from that of Thrasymachus.[2] But *The*

[1] THE PRINCE, *loc. cit.*　　　[2] See pp. 37 *et seq., supra.*

Prince, although it is the work by which he is mainly known, by no means contains the whole of his theory. Machiavelli himself gives clear warning of this in his opening chapters, when he says: "All the States and Governments by which men are or ever have been ruled, have been and are either Republics or Princedoms.... Of Republics I shall not now speak, having elsewhere spoken of them at length. Here I shall treat exclusively of Princedoms." [1]

The work to which Machiavelli here refers is the *Discourses*. In that work, republics are distinguished from princedoms as *free* states from unfree, and are declared to be superior to the latter both in their essential nature and in many particular advantages. But the republic is a form of constitution which not every people is qualified to bear, since a high degree of "virtue" in the people is needed in order to sustain it. In proportion as they lack "virtue," peoples become "corrupt"; and a corrupt people (such as Machiavelli held the Italian peoples of his day to be) must be governed by a prince or by a tyrant, because it is not capable of governing itself.

Superiority of Free States

The following passages will illustrate Machiavelli's doctrine on this subject. In the first he compares free states with princedoms, and affirms the superiority of the former. [2]

∝ But as regards prudence and stability, I say that the people are more prudent and stable, and have better judgment than a prince; and it is not without good reason that it is said, "The voice of the people is the voice of God"; for we see popular opinion prognosticate events in such a wonderful manner that it would almost seem as if the people had some occult virtue, which enables them to forsee the good and the evil. And as to the people's capacity of judging of things, it is exceedingly rare that, when they hear two orators of equal talents advocate different measures, they do not decide in favour of the better of the two; which proves their ability to discern the truth of what they hear.

[1] THE PRINCE, chaps. I and II.
[2] DISCOURSES, I, 58.

We also see that in the election of their magistrates they make far better choice than princes; and no people will ever be persuaded to elect a man of infamous character and corrupt habits to any post of dignity, to which a prince is easily influenced in a thousand different ways ... We furthermore see cities where the people are masters make the greatest progress in the least possible time, and much greater than such as have always been governed by princes; as was the case with Rome after the expulsion of the kings, and with Athens after they rid themselves of Pisistratus; and this can be attributed to no other cause than that the governments of the people are better than those of princes ..., for if we compare the faults of a people with those of princes, as well as their respective good qualities, we shall find the people vastly superior in all that is good and glorious. And if princes show themselves superior in the making of laws, and in the forming of civil institutions and new statutes and ordinances, the people are superior in maintaining those institutions, laws and ordinances, which certainly places them on a par with those who established them.

And finally, to sum up this matter, I say that both governments of princes and of the people have lasted a long time, but both required to be regulated by laws. For a prince who knows no other control but his own will is like a madman, and a people that can do as it pleases will hardly be wise. If now we compare a prince who is controlled by laws, and a people that is untrammelled by them, we shall find more "virtue" in the people than in the prince; and if we compare them when both are freed from such control, we shall see that the people are guilty of fewer excesses than the prince, and that the errors of the people are of less importance and therefore more easily remedied.

Freedom of a State: Meaning [1]

What Machiavelli means by "liberty" or "freedom" as a quality of a state is more easily illustrated than defined. The illustration of a free state which he has constantly in mind is the ancient Roman Republic. Freedom is something which Rome possessed when she was

[1] DISCOURSES, I, 36.

a republic, but which she lost when Julius Caesar and the emperors who succeeded him abrogated the republican constitution and concentrated political power in their own hands.[1]   Thus, for a people to be free in Machiavelli's sense, it is not sufficient (although it is necessary) for it to be independent of domination by other states.   Rome under the emperors, and many Italian cities of Machiavelli's day under their tyrants, were independent states, but not free ones.

Nor does the freedom of a state consist merely in the degree of liberty of action allowed to its individual citizens; for a despotism may be liberal, in the sense that the despot may confine his interference with the lives of his subjects to a minimum.   Indeed, there have probably been few states in history in which the citizens have been freer from arbitrary interference with their private affairs than the Roman Empire after the fall of the Republic.   But a liberal despotism is not what Machiavelli means by a free state.

There is a sense in which it would be true to say that freedom for Machiavelli means self-government.   But to say it would be misleading, for it would suggest the ideas of Rousseau and of representative democracy, which were very far from Machiavelli's mind.

Machiavelli thinks of the state on the analogy of a living organic body.   A state is made a state by a certain structure of organization, as the body is made an organism by a similar structure among its parts. In the state this structure is composed of the laws and institutions by which the people is governed, and the difference between a free state and an unfree one depends upon whether the citizens conform to these laws spontaneously or by compulsion.   The unfree state is like a diseased body, of which the organs require to be compelled by the ministrations of a doctor to play their proper parts within the system.   The free state is like a healthy body in which the parts keep in order naturally, and do not need to be reduced to order by a medical régime.

"Virtue" in a People Necessary to Freedom

For a body to be independent of a doctor, a certain inherent vigor is necessary.   It is when the vital force decays that the organs cease

[1] In this Machiavelli is expressing the sentiment of the ancient Romans themselves. Brutus and Cassius were held justified in stabbing Caesar because they were avenging and hoping to restore the freedom of Rome.

to play their respective parts spontaneously. A similar vigor is necessary in a state, if it is to be independent of an absolute prince or master, and is thus to be free. Machiavelli gives the name of "virtue" to this quality of vigor in a people, and hence he holds that a people must possess "virtue" in order to be free. Where "virtue" is lacking, the people is corrupt, and a corrupt people can be reduced to order only by the drastic régime of a prince.

Thus Machiavelli says:[1] "To endeavor to make a people free that are servile in their nature is as hard a matter as to keep them in servitude who are disposed to be free." In another chapter,[2] discussing the problem of "how in a corrupt state a free Government may be maintained assuming that one exists there already, and how it could be introduced, if none had previously existed," he concludes as follows: "From these combined causes arises the difficulty or impossibility of maintaining liberty in a republic that has become corrupt, or to establish it there anew. And if it has to be introduced and maintained, then it will be necessary to reduce the state to a monarchical, rather than a republican form of government; for men whose turbulence could not be controlled by the simple force of law can be controlled in a measure only by an almost regal power."

The same doctrine is contained in a passage in which Machiavelli condemns certain feudal abuses, as follows:[3]

And to explain more clearly what is meant by the term gentleman, I say that those are called gentlemen who live idly upon the proceeds of their extensive possessions, without devoting themselves to agriculture or any other useful pursuit to gain a living. Such men are pernicious to any country or republic; but more pernicious even than these are such as have, besides their other possessions, castles which they command, and subjects who obey them. This class of men abound in the kingdom of Naples, in the Roman territory, in the Romagna, and in Lombardy; whence it is that no republic has ever been able to exist in these countries, nor have they been able to preserve any regular political existence, for that class of men are everywhere enemies of all civil government.

[1] DISCOURSES, III, 8.
[2] *Ibid.*, I, 18.
[3] *Ibid.*, I, 55.

And to attempt the establishment of a republic in a country so constituted would be impossible.   The only way to establish any kind of order there is to found a monarchical government; for where the body of the people is so thoroughly corrupt that the laws are powerless for restraint, it becomes necessary to establish some superior power which, with a royal hand, and with full and absolute powers, ma, put a curb upon the excessive ambition and corruption of the powerful.

Imperialism

That "virtue" which qualifies a people to be free shows itself in its impulse to expand its power; just as the vigor of a healthy body is shown in its power of growth.   Thus the acquisition of empire is a natural consequence of "virtue" in a people, and a normal accompaniment of freedom.   Machiavelli says,[1] "All free governments [have] two principal ends, one of which is to enlarge their dominions, and the other to preserve their liberties"; and again:[2]

It is easy to understand whence that affection for liberty arose in the people, for they had seen that cities never increased in dominion or wealth unless they were free.   And certainly it is wonderful to think of the greatness which Athens attained within the space of a hundred years after having freed herself from the tyranny of Pisistratus; and still more wonderful is it to reflect upon the greatness which Rome achieved after she was rid of her kings.   The cause of this is manifest, for it is not individual prosperity, but the general good, that makes cities great; and certainly the general good is regarded nowhere but in Republics, because whatever they do is for the common benefit, and should it happen to prove an injury to one or more individuals, those for whose benefit the thing is done are so numerous that they can always carry the measure against the few that are injured by it.   But the very reverse happens where there is a prince whose private interests are generally in opposition to those of the city, whilst the measures taken for the benefit of the city are seldom deemed personally advantageous by the prince.

[1] DISCOURSES, I, 29.   [2] Ibid., II, 2.

This state of things soon leads to a tyranny, the least evil of which is to check the advance of the city in its career of prosperity, so that it grows neither in power nor wealth, but on the contrary rather retrogrades.

The vast empire acquired by Rome in the days of the Republic, Machiavelli regards as the fruit of the Roman "virtue." No doubt, as in all human undertakings, the assistance of Fortune was needed too, but he sets out to make it "so plain and perspicuous that every one may see, how much more their virtue than their fortune contributed to their empire."[1]

Many authors, amongst them that most serious writer Plutarch, have held the opinion that the people of Rome were more indebted in the acquisition of their empire, to the favours of Fortune than to their own "virtue." And amongst other reasons adduced by Plutarch is, that by their own confession it appears that the Roman people ascribed all their victories to Fortune, because they built more temples to that goddess than to any other deity. It seems that Livius accepts that opinion, for he rarely makes a Roman speak of "virtue" without coupling Fortune with it. Now I do not share that opinion at all, and do not believe that it can be sustained; for if no other republic has ever been known to make such conquests, it is admitted that none other was so well organised for that purpose as Rome. It was the "virtue" of her armies that achieved those conquests, and it was the wisdom of her conduct and the nature of her institutions, as established by her first legislator, that enabled her to preserve these acquisitions, as we shall more fully set forth in the succeeding chapters.

Notice the striking and significant contrast between Machiavelli's doctrine of empire and Plato's. For Plato the impulse to aggrandisement was a symptom of disease;[2] the healthy state would be self-contained. For Machiavelli aggrandisement is the symptom and natural consequence of health in a state.

[1] DISCOURSES, II, I.   [2] See p. 51, *supra*.

Machiavelli's Inconsistency

It has often been felt that there is an inconsistency between the monarchical sentiments of Machiavelli's *Prince* and the republicanism of the *Discourses*. Formally, of course, this is not so. Machiavelli expressly limits his attention in *The Prince* to that form of government which he has declared to be the inferior of the two, and there is nothing necessarily inconsistent in his declaring that, although the republican form of government is the better, it cannot be established where the requisite "virtue" is not forthcoming in the people, and that he will therefore lay down maxims for the attainment of the second-best. Nevertheless, there are two different and mutually inconsistent strains confused together in Machiavelli's thought, which we may name for convenience the "monarchical" and the "republican."¹ The inconsistency shows itself in that central notion of Machiavelli's thought, the notion of "virtue." When he speaks as a monarchist, he means by "virtue" that capacity in a man which will enable him to achieve success and fame for himself as an individual. He sees, as a republican, that free states possess a "virtue" which monarchical states lack; they possess the vigor, the power of enduring, the capacity of growth which are the marks of "virtue" in Machiavelli's eyes. This "virtue" of a free state must be derived from some quality resident in the characters of its individual citizens, and Machiavelli does not hesitate to give the name of "virtue" to this quality in the individual. But what he never explicitly recognises is that this "virtue" which is presupposed in the citizen of a free state must be something very different from that "combination of intellect and force," directed to the end of individual pre-eminence, to which he gives the name of "virtue" elsewhere. A state of which all the citizens were endowed with this egoistic "virtue" would not be a free or strong or vigorous state. Indeed, it could hardly subsist as a state at all, for it would have no bond of coherence. In order that a state may be vigorous, it is necessary that its members should possess a different virtue from this. It is necessary that they should be possessed of public spirit, of a willingness to sacrifice their private advantage to the public good, of patriot-

¹ The former naturally predominates in THE PRINCE and the latter in the DIS-COURSES, but both strains are present to some degree in each work.

ism; in a word, of those qualities which were designated by the ancient Roman term *virtus*.

The *virtus* of the citizen of ancient Rome, the "virtu" of the adventurer of Renaissance Italy — these are the two incompatible conceptions of human excellence which struggle together in Machiavelli's mind. For examples of the latter he had only to observe the spectacle of the contemporary world; for examples of the former he had to delve into the records of ancient history. But it was the former rather than the latter which was to be important in the modern world which was in process of formation. Whatever its achievements in literature and art and elsewhere, the brilliant individualism of the Renaissance was barren of permanent results in the political sphere. What was of importance in this sphere was the resuscitation of the ancient principle of patriotism.

It was not resuscitated unchanged. A great and obvious difference between ancient and modern patriotism is that the former was focused upon the city, the latter upon the nation. Throughout most of his works, Machiavelli is thinking in terms of the ancient sentiment. When he speaks of free states and republics, he is thinking of city-states, such as Rome and Athens in the ancient world, or Venice and Florence in contemporary Italy. But there is a chapter, the concluding chapter of *The Prince*,[1] in which his thought takes a sudden leap, and he proclaims as the ideal to be attained no longer the independent city, but the united nation. He thus fuses the ancient tradition of public spirit with the new sentiment of national unity, and we can recognize in his words an authentic expression of the spirit of nationalism, which has been one of the moving forces of the world since his day.

Nationalism

Turning over in my mind all the matters which have above been considered, and debating with myself whether in Italy at the present hour the times are such as might serve to win honour for a new Prince, and whether fit opportunity now offers for a leader of prudence and "virtue" to bring about changes glorious for himself and advantageous for the whole Italian people, it seems to me that so

[1] Chap. XXVI.

so many conditions combine to further such an enterprise, that I know
of no time so favourable to it as now.   And if, as I have said, it was
necessary in order to display the "virtue" of Moses that the children
of Israel should be slaves in Egypt, to know the greatness and courage of Cyrus that the Persians should be oppressed by the Medes,
and to illustrate the excellence of Theseus that the Athenians should
be scattered and divided, so at this hour, to prove the worth of some
Italian hero, it was required that Italy should be brought to her
present abject condition, to be more enslaved than the Hebrews,
more oppressed than the Persians, more disunited than the Athenians, without a head, without order, beaten, spoiled, torn in pieces,
overrun and abandoned to destruction in every shape.

For although, heretofore, glimmerings may have been discerned
in this man or that, whence it might be conjectured that he was
ordained by God for her redemption, nevertheless it has afterwards
been seen at the very height of his career that Fortune has disowned
him; so that our country, left almost without life, still waits to know
who it is that is to heal her bruises, to put an end to the devastation
and plunder of Lombardy, to the exactions and imposts of Naples
and Tuscany, and to stanch those wounds of hers which long neglect
has changed into running sores.

We see how she prays God to send some one to rescue her from
these barbarous cruelties and oppressions.   We see, too, how ready
and eager she is to follow any standard were there only some one
to raise it.   But at present we see no one except in your illustrious
House (pre-eminent by its "virtue" and good fortune, and favoured
by God and by the Church whose headship it now holds), who
could assume the part of a deliverer.

But for you this will not be too hard a task, if you keep before your
eyes the lives and actions of those whom I have named above.
For although these men were singular and extraordinary, after all
they were but men, not one of whom had so great an opportunity
as now presents itself to you.   For their undertakings were not more
just than this, nor more easy, nor was God more their friend than
yours.   The justice of the cause is conspicuous; for that war is just
which is necessary, and those arms are sacred wherein lies our only
hope.   Everywhere there is the strongest disposition to engage in
this enterprise; and where the disposition is strong the difficulty

cannot be great, provided you follow the methods observed by those whom I have set before you as models.

Moreover, we see here extraordinary and unexampled proofs of Divine favour. The sea has been divided; the cloud has attended you on your way; the rock has flowed with water; the manna has rained from heaven, everything has concurred to promote your greatness. What remains to be done must be done by you; since not to deprive us of our free will and such share of glory as belongs to us, God will not do everything himself.

Nor is it to be marvelled at if none of those Italians I have spoken of has been able to effect what we hope to see effected by your illustrious House; or that amid so many revolutions and so many warlike movements it should always seem as though the military virtue of Italy were spent; for this comes from her old system being defective, and from no one being found among us who has known to strike out a new. Nothing confers such honour on a new ruler, as do the new laws and institutions he devises; for these when they stand on a solid basis and have a greatness in their scope, make him admired and venerated. And in Italy material is not wanting for improvement in every form. If the head be weak the limbs are strong, and we see daily in single combats, or where few are engaged, how superior are the vigour, dexterity, and intelligence of Italians. But when it comes to armies, they are nowhere, and this from no other reason than the defects of their leaders. For those who know are not obeyed, and every one thinks he knows, since hitherto we have had none among us so raised by "virtue" or by fortune above his fellows that they should recognize him as their superior. Whence it happens that for the long period of twenty years, during which so many wars have taken place, whenever there has been an army purely Italian it has always been beaten. To this testify, first Taro, then Alessandria, Capua, Genoa, Vaila, Bologna, Mestri.

If, then your illustrious House should seek to follow the example of those great men who have delivered their country in past ages, it is before all things necessary, as the true foundation of every such attempt, to be provided with national troops, since you can have no braver, truer, or more faithful soldiers; and although every single man of them be good, collectively they will be better, seeing themselves commanded by their own Prince, and honoured and maintained by him. That you may be able, therefore, to defend yourself against the foreigner with Italian "virtue," the first step is to provide yourself with an army such as this.

. . . .

This opportunity, then for Italy at last to look on her deliverer, ought not to be allowed to pass away. With what love he would be received in all those Provinces which have suffered from the foreign inundation, with what thirst for vengeance, with what fixed fidelity, with what devotion, and what tears, no words of mine can declare. What gates would be closed against him? What people would refuse him obedience? What jealousy would stand in his way? What Italian but would yield him homage? This barbarian tyranny stinks in all nostrils.

Let your illustrious House therefore take upon itself this charge with all the courage and all the hopes with which a just cause is undertaken; so that under your standard this our country may be ennobled, and under your auspices be fulfilled the words of Petrarch:

> 'Virtu contra furore
> Prendera l'arme, e fia il combatter' corto;
> Che l'antico valore
> Nelli Italicia cor non e ancor morto'.[1]

For Further Reading

Translations

The translation of the complete works by Nevill (1675) is pithy and vigorous, and nearer to the spirit of the original than some more modern ones. There is a translation of the complete works by C. E. Detmold (London: Trubner, 1883; 4 vols.), which I have used for the DIS-COURSES, and one of certain works by N. H. Thomson, which I have used for THE PRINCE. Thomson's translation of THE PRINCE is also published separately (third edition; Oxford: Clarendon Press, 1913).

[1] Brief will be the strife
When virtue arms against barbaric rage;
For the bold spirit of a bygone age
Still warms Italian hearts with life.

Commentary

MEINECKE, F., DIE IDEE DER STAATSRÄSON. Third edition; Munich: R. Oldenbourg, 1929.
    Contains an excellent chapter on Machiavelli.
MORLEY, J., MACHIAVELLI. Romanes Lecture. London: Macmillan, 1897.

General Background

BURCKHARDT, JAKOB, DIE RENAISSANCE IN ITALIEN. English translation by S. G. C. MIDDLEMORE: CIVILIZATION OF THE RENAISSANCE IN ITALY. New edition; New York: Oxford University Press, 1937.

Index